D1474288

(herpes simplex, tuberculosis);
F. Immunological Disturbances (lowered
resistance, auto-immune diseases);
G. Gastrointestinal Disturbances (globus
syndrome, ulcer, constipation, irritable bowel
syndrome, diarrhea, nausea and vomiting,
ulcerative colitis); H. Genitourinary
Disturbances (edema, diuresis);
I. Endocrinological Disturbances (diabetes,
hyperthyroidism, menstrual problems);
J. Dermatological Diseases (hives, eczema,
neurodermatitis, acne); K. Neurological
Diseases (epilepsy, narcolepsy, multiple
sclerosis, myasthenia gravis); L. Cancer;
M. Pain, N. Fatigue and Lethargy   **33**

4.   **Emotional Distress.** *Psychological*
disturbances and their somatic manifestations:
A. Anxiety, Fear, and Panic; B. Anger,
Hatred, and Resentment; C. Depression;
D. Feelings of Helplessness and Inadequacy;
E. Guilt   **85**

5.   **Mental Distress.** *Neuroses and psychoses*
attributable to excessive stress and tension
(manic-depressive illness, schizophrenia,
obsessive-compulsive and hysterical reactions,
decreased memory)   **91**

6.   **Self-Destructive Habits.** *Overeating,*
smoking, overuse of alcohol and drugs, lack of
exercise, poor nutrition   **94**

SECTION II.   A FUNCTIONAL MODEL OF MAN

7.   **Perception of Data or Stimuli.** *Selection*
and inhibition of data; memory and its relation
to tension (amnesia, repression)   **107**

8.   **Attitudes and Goals.** *Negative and positive*
mind-sets; conscious and unconscious
determinants of goal-oriented activity   **114**

CONTENTS

Preface   **13**

SECTION I. STRESS, TENSION, AND DISTRESS

1. **Stress.** *The sources of stress—physical,
    chemical, microbiological, psychological, and
    socio-cultural*   **17**
2. **Tension.** *The essential nature of tension;
    negative effects of excessive tension*   **28**
3. **Physical Distress.** *Bodily manifestations of
    excessive stress and tension: A. Cardiovascular
    Distress (coronary artery disease, hypertension,
    strokes, rhythm disturbances of the heart,
    migraine headache, Raynaud's phenomenon);
    B. Muscular Distress (muscle contraction
    headache, backache); C. Locomotor Distress
    (rheumatoid arthritis, related inflammatory
    diseases of connective tissue); D. Respiratory
    and Allergic Disorders (hay fever, asthma,
    hyperventilation); E. Infectious Diseases*

9

My thanks to—
Lois Biddle, Julie Di Joseph,
Jan Dow, Diane McGovern
and Katie Barber for
help in preparation of the manuscript

To my family—

My wife Joann and my
children Carol, Doug and Paul,
who encouraged me and
suppressed their own needs for
my time during the writing
and research process

Library of Congress Catalog Number 78-8308

ISBN: 0-87705-328-6

Copyright © 1978 by Human Sciences Press
72 Fifth Avenue, New York, New York 10011

Printed in the United States of America
89 987654321

Library of Congress Cataloging in Publication Data

Anderson, Robert A
    Stress power!

    Bibliography: p. 235
    Includes index.
    1. Medicine, Psychosomatic. 2. Stress (Psychology) 3. Stress (Physiology) I.
Title. [DNLM: 1. Stress, Psychological. WM172 A549s]
RC49.A419   616.08   78-8308
ISBN 0-87705-328-6

STRESS POWER!

How to Turn Tension into Energy

Robert A. Anderson, M.D.

*Clinical Instructor, Department of Family Medicine, School of
Medicine, University of Washington, Seattle, Washington*

HUMAN SCIENCES PRESS
72 Fifth Avenue   3 Henrietta Street
NEW YORK, NY 10011 ● LONDON, WC2E 8LU

STRESS POWER!

9. **Data Processing.** *The brain's response to new stimuli and incoming data as determined by past conditioning and memory*   **120**

10. **The Output System.** *Muscular behavior; the limbic system and emotions; the hypothalamus and the endocrine system; the hypothalamus and the autonomic nervous system*   **122**

11. **The Self and the Will.** *The significance of the discovery of an inner centered self affording the individual a sense of wholeness; will, generated by the self, as the agent for setting and maintaining goals*   **128**

12. **The Feedback Nature of the Message System.** *The circularity and interdependence of input and output systems; self-regulating nature of the systems*   **132**

SECTION III. DEALING WITH TENSION AND FACILITATING ADAPTABILITY

13. **The Use of Medication.** *Risks of side-effects; habituation of the patient and development of mutant strains rendering medications ineffective; medications not a "cure" for disease*   **137**

14. **Manipulation of the Environment.** *Changes in marital status, job, and residence as temporary solutions for excessive tension; necessity for internal changes*   **141**

15. **Release of Tension through Activities.** *A. Physical Exercise; B. Task-Oriented Exercise; C. Creative Pursuits; D. Vocational and Avocational Pursuits; E. Physical Expression of the Emotions; F. Self-Expression Through Writing; G. Use of Humor*   **143**

16. **Conscious Passive Relaxation.** *Autogenics, progressive relaxation, and*

biofeedback: tension-reducing exercises and techniques   **155**

17. **Meditation.** *Altered states of consciousness and reduction of tension through the practice of yoga, meditation, and related forms*   **169**

18. **Fulfilling Recognition Needs.** *Physical, verbal, and non-verbal techniques for achieving positive contact with others*   **175**

19. **Working through Emotional and Mental Blocks.** *Relief of physical distress through examination of unconsciously held negative attitudes and feelings*   **183**

20. **Cultivation of Positive Attitudes.** *The power of love, forgiveness, and empathy for others; heightened self-esteem through unconditional positive regard for others*   **189**

21. **The Setting of Goals.** *Methods and exercises for the goal-setting procedure, including repeated written exercise and daily visualization and evaluation*   **200**

22. **Creative Visualization for Goal Reinforcement and Functional Changes.** *Cybernetics and receptive visualization as aids in self-actualization and creative growth*   **206**

Notes   **218**

Selected Bibliography   **235**

Index   **239**

PREFACE

I began to discover, when I became a family physician seventeen years ago, that my patients were not staying healthy unless they did more than merely seek relief for their distress. An ulcer patient who faithfully took the medications and antacids I prescribed and adhered to a bland diet would recover from his ulcer symptoms, only to get his ulcer back later on. A patient with neurodermatitis who applied cortisone ointment as I advised got better, but her skin worsened once she stopped medication. Yet another patient prone to headaches got relief with analgesics, but continued to be plagued with frequent headaches.

I noticed especially that patients' symptoms would return with full force when their stressful life situations produced excessive levels of tension. Only as they began, with some cooperation from me, to deal with their underlying tensions were they able to regain their health.

I soon started to search for effective techniques to enhance my patients' ability to deal with stress and tension and gradually gathered experience with all of the approaches discussed in this book. Since my own practice is necessarily limited, I would like to share some of that experience with a wider circle of readers.

My intent is to present here (1) the evidence, gathered from research and from the experience of other practitioners as well as myself, bearing on the relation between tension and physical disease, emotional distress, and mental illness; (2) a workable model for understanding how human beings function; and (3) practical methods for handling tension, with accompanying exercises at the physical, emotional, and mental levels.

Tension, as the biggest single factor in the onset of disability, distress, and death, urgently needs to be understood and handled. The reader can confront life-denying patterns when he experiences increased self-awareness and discovers that he can *choose* to change. He can experience as well as understand the process of taking charge of himself to enhance his handling of tension with less distress. This growth process not only helps to handle present problems, but leads to a creative use of tension through establishing and meeting self-directed positive goals.

Studies in behavior and psychology indicate that we currently operate at only about one-tenth of our total potential capacity. It is quite apparent, then, that we have vast untapped mental, physical, emotional, and spiritual reserves. It is my hope that each reader of this book will be able to use the information herein to develop additional amounts of his own unused potential—to discover his own power to transform himself into a healthier and happier human being.

Section I

STRESS, TENSION, AND DISTRESS

Chapter 1

STRESS

Never a day passes that I am not aware of the frequent, potent, even sometimes devastating effects of stress in the daily life of my patients.

A woman is in my examining room for a routine yearly checkup. Suddenly, she bursts into tears. "I don't know why I am doing this," she says. She goes on to tell me she has been crying a lot lately. Stress is governing her emotional behavior. The routine checkup is forgotten as our conversation leads eventually to the fact that the woman's teenage daughter is in serious trouble.

My office nurse rushes a man into one of the examination rooms. His blood pressure has just been checked and found to be greatly elevated above his last reading. I recheck my patient's blood pressure and it is 180 over 105. He informs me he has been taking his medicine as I had instructed him to do at our last visit. I then ask what has been happening in the last few weeks. He tells me in angry tones that he has lost his job and that there is a financial crisis at home.

A woman whose face bears the mark of anxiety tells me she has developed an itch which has persisted for about a month. "There is nothing to see," she informs me, and indeed examination reveals no rash on the skin. I patiently explain to her that while this might be an allergic reaction, it is much more likely to be a manifestation of tension. After some conversation, she explains that she has been a "nervous-type person" all her life and that she doesn't really know why. While I am talking to her, I notice that she is sitting in a strained position, unable to relax comfortably in her chair.

Problems such as these are commonly seen by the family physician. At one time, I was of the opinion that stress was related to thirty-five to fifty percent of the problems described to me by patients. I now believe that figure is closer to eighty or ninety percent. If the influence of stress is so pervasive, it is very important for me as a physician to be aware of it and equally important for the patient affected by it to understand it and know what he can do about it.

The subject of stress currently enjoys great popularity in books, cocktail party conversations, and on TV talk shows. Wherever we turn we hear about wars, hijackings, riots, the high crime rate, the energy crisis, the breakdown of the family, the high unemployment rate, the recession, environmental pollution, the soaring incidence of cancer—yet seldom do we hear of any solutions to these stresses on individuals and society at large.

There are probably as many definitions of stress as there are persons who talk about it. My own definition of stress is any stimulus, real or imagined, which requires an individual to be or to do anything different from the way he is or the way he behaves at any given moment. Stated another way, stress is any stimulus which demands adaptation on the part of the organism involved. Indeed, adaptability may be said to be a basic aspect of life itself.

The same stress that affects one individual minimally may affect another individual with much greater intensity. It is as important to assess how the organism is perceiving and reacting to a stressful stimulus as it is to study the parameters of the stimulus, including its measurements, persistence, and intensity. It is not beneficial to look at the stimulus alone and to make assumptions as to its stressful nature without also considering the specific organism facing the stimulus.

We can trace stress to the dawn of prehistoric man. The instincts for self-preservation, sexual expression, self-assertion, herd-expression, and inquiry all required that man as a race and individually evolve into something different from what he was prior to the awareness of such instincts.

Picture prehistoric man being threatened by a predatory animal: he responds to this demand that he adapt with the instinct for self-preservation, and through his primitive brain expends the energy which causes his heartbeat to quicken, his blood sugar to rise, and the circulation to his muscles to increase. He is then ready for "fight" or "flight"—two potential forms of behavior he may adopt once his awareness has expanded to include the dangerous proximity of his enemy.

In modern times, the same instinctual drive for self-preservation exists. The young divorcee with three children arrives home from work to find her refrigerator bare and no child-support check from her ex-husband in the mail. She too is subjected to the noxious stimulus of stress.

The instinct to inquiry drives the student to study well past midnight, to sort out, organize, and understand his subject far beyond the point of being adequately prepared for the stress of a pending examination.

The narrow atmospheric layer within which life survives on the earth's crust is affected by meteorological and climatic crises which subject the mountain climber to excessive exposure to the cold and consequent hypothermia; the equatorial traveler is overcome by excessive heat and humidity and responds with heat prostration.

Humans also encounter stress from pollutants, toxins, poisons, and chemical agents. Food additives are carefully screened by the U.S. Food and Drug Administration to avoid the public's exposure to unwarranted noxious chemicals. The development of poison control centers in large cities is vivid testimony to the frequency of poisoning in contemporary life. The great increase in the death rate in persons susceptible to respiratory disease during the "London fogs" of recent years demonstrates that air pollution is a serious source of stress to which many susceptible persons fail to adapt.

Plant forms suffer as well from the effects of air pollution. Evergreens along the freeway east of Los Angeles die when they are unable to adapt to the smog-laden atmosphere. The insect and arachnid population of the world is subjected to man's deadly chemicals and adapts with resistant subspecies.

Microorganisms are frequently stressful stimuli for human beings. The importance of infectious stimuli began with the work of outstanding microbiologists in the nineteenth century, including Koch, Pasteur, and Jenner. These scientists began identifying and working with microbes to reduce their harmful effects on man. Through the work of these pioneers and their followers, the great epidemic and endemic infectious diseases which caused widespread death in the first half of this century have all but disappeared as leading causes of distress in human beings: smallpox, typhus, bacterial pneumonia, and poliomyelitis have yielded in large measure to the advances of science. Indeed, in some areas of the world medical students will finish their education without ever having seen a patient with polio or measles. Parasites, viruses, bacteria, rickettsia, and fungi are now treated by the administration of specific vaccines or antibiotics.

The mere presence of these infectious agents does not necessarily imply disease. When two or more living organisms cohabit successfully they are said to be living in a synergistic state. Synergism is commonly found in plant and animal life as well as in human existence. The human skin bears several strains of bacteria which, for the most part, exist fairly harmlessly on the surface or perform such needed functions as the processing of vitamin D in the presence of sunlight.

In the mouth, resident bacteria and yeast organisms normally maintain a healthy balance. Both forms of microorganisms also usually exist without damage to the human host in whose mouth they are found. Well known, however, is the condition known as "thrush" (moniliasis), the overgrowth of yeast elements found when potent antibiotics destroy the population of normal bacteria in the mouth.

Thus, we begin to see that the actual presence of infectious stimuli is not necessarily associated with a state of disease. In many instances, such a state implies not only the presence of a significant number of infectious stimuli but also of certain conditions present in the host, including vulnerability and lack of resistance from various causes.

Two great students of disease in the nineteenth century argued about the relative importance of the "territory"—the strength or resistance of the host—and the microbe standing ready to invade. Claude Bernard, French physiologist, maintained that the territory—the patient's resistance or susceptibility—was the most important factor in disease. Louis Pasteur, believing the microbe to be more significant, systematically set about identifying specific germs and creating vaccines to protect man against them. Pasteur, it is said, uttered on his death bed: "Bernard was right. The microbe is nothing; the terrain is everything."

While physical and microbiological stresses have, in advanced nations, become less prominent in this century, psychological and socio-cultural pressures have increased. The legacy of primitive man remains within us as we remain battle-ready for physical dangers which no longer exist—but we also remain inexperienced in ways of coping with today's stresses, unable to engage the enemy which has changed to a much subtler form. The pressures induced by working, hurrying, crime, freeway driving, mechanization, advertising, parental and peer demands, governmental regulations, status seeking, crowding, mobility and budget crises are potential tension builders in our society. All these involve external demands and expectations which others place on us and which we then accept and place upon ourselves. In experimental rats, the stress produced by overcrowding significantly reduces the body responses necessary for resistance to bacterial disease.[1]

Psychological stress may occur in the form of debilitating emotions, particularly negative ones, such as fear, anger, sadness, or a sense of loss or separation; it may also appear as mental hypo-functioning, involving excessive forgetting and excusing, minimizing, repressing, and substituting. Legacies of past hurts, unmet childhood needs, the results of parental over-indulgence, over-coercion or rejection—all may be stressful because they have not prepared us realistically for life in the adult world.[2]

Events which subject us to significant loss of objects and personal attachments are notably stressful. Even the threat of loss—severe illness of a loved one, an insecure job environment, or the possibility of radical changes in a circle of friends—may provide a stressful stimulus. Threat of injury or injury itself, whether in the physical or the psychological realm, may lead to anxiety, fear, and panic, as well as to undesirable physiological reactions within the body.

Frustration of a need (as we so perceive it), such as being cut from a Little League ball team, being denied a sexual experience by a partner, or being bumped from a reserved airplane flight, all lead typically to a feeling of anger and accompanying functional bodily changes.

Extensive work in the past two decades has been done by Dr. Thomas Holmes and his associates at the University of Washington in relating psychological and socio-cultural stresses to the onset of disease.[3] As a result of working with over 5,000 subjects, studying the quality and quantity of events in their lives empirically observed to cluster prior to the onset of disease, they have developed a social readjustment rating scale (Table 1). Two types of items can be observed: there are those indicative of occurrences involving the individual and those indicative of the life style of the individual. The Holmes study indicated a wide variation in the emotions and psychological effects experienced by their patients. All of the life events, however, on the final list had one thing in common—each event was associated with some adaptive response on the part of the adult individual. That is to say, each event proved stressful in requiring that the individual involved be or do something different in order to adapt.

Not all of the events, it will be noticed, are negative in the conventional sense. Indeed, many of the life events in the list may be considered to be socially desirable. Thus, outstanding personal achievement, marriage, marital reconciliation, retirement, vacations, and the Christmas holidays would generally be associated with pleasant and unthreatening considerations. Nevertheless, these events are found to be stressful even though pleasant. Dr. Hans Selye points out that it is immaterial whether the agent or stimulus we face is pleasant or unpleasant; all that

Table 1   Results of Social Readjustment Rating
Questionnaire

Life Event	Mean Value
1. Death of spouse	100
2. Divorce	73
3. Marital separation	65
4. Jail term	63
5. Death of close family member	63
6. Personal injury or illness	53
7. Marriage	50
8. Fired at work	47
9. Marital reconciliation	45
10. Retirement	45
11. Change in health of family member	44
12. Pregnancy	40
13. Sex difficulties	39
14. Gain of new family member	39
15. Business readjustment	39
16. Change in financial state	38
17. Death of close friend	37
18. Change to different line of work	36
19. Change in number of arguments with spouse	35
20. Mortgage over $10,000	31
21. Foreclosure of mortgage or loan	30
22. Change in responsibilities at work	29
23. Son or daughter leaving home	29
24. Trouble with in-laws	29
25. Outstanding personal achievement	28
26. Wife begins or stops work	26
27. Beginning or end of school	26
28. Change in living conditions	25
29. Revision of personal habits	24
30. Trouble with boss	23
31. Change in work hours or conditions	20
32. Change in residence	20
33. Change in schools	20
34. Change in recreation	19
35. Change in church activities	19
36. Change in social activities	18
37. Mortgage or loan less than $10,000	17
38. Change in sleeping habits	16

Table 1   Continued

Life Event	Mean Value
39. Change in number of family get-togethers	15
40. Change in eating habits	15
41. Vacation	13
42. Christmas	12
43. Minor violations of the law	11

Source: Holmes, T. H., and Rahe, R. H.: The Social Readjustment Rating Scale. *Jrnl Psychosomatic Res.*, 11 (1967): 213-218.

counts is the intensity of the demand for adaptation.[4] On Dr. Holmes' list of life events, we find that marital separation, worth 65 points, and marital reconciliation worth 45 points, are both highly stressful events.

Dr. Holmes relates the significance of his social readjustment rating scale to disease as follows: the point totals listed are in relation to the strength of the stress event and the intensity of the demand for readjustment. The scale implies that losing a spouse by death (100 points) requires twice as much readjustment as getting married (50 points) and four times as much readjustment as a change in living conditions (25 points). In addition, the more changes experienced in any given period of time, the more points are accumulated. The higher the point score, the more likely one is to suffer a decline in health. This includes serious illnesses, injuries, surgical operations, and psychiatric disorders.

Dr. Holmes also discusses the significance of his point total over a given period of time. A point total of 150 or below indicates a chance of only one in three of a serious health change in the next two years. A score between 100 and 300 points increases the chance of significant health change in the ensuing two years to about fifty percent. A score over 300 points causes a rise in health change expectancy to 90 percent.

Dr. Jonas Salk speculates that illness concerns not only genetic and immune relationships but also social and behavioral factors.[5] And another study linking psychological and social changes found a high incidence of social disorganization (threatening and disruptive stimuli) for six months prior to diseased states in children, whereas a comparison group of healthy children had significantly less threatening and disrupting stimuli in the same preceding six-month period.[6]

In my own years of practice, I have been struck by the vast differences in the stress patterns of patients. These differences are observable in the likelihood of experiencing significant distress, in the severity of a disease, and in the rate at which a patient gets well. The same stress occurring to two different patients may result in the one becoming ill and the other not. Should both become ill, one may become extremely ill and the other only slightly ill. Similarly, in a disease common to two patients, the first often recovers quickly and the other remains ill for a considerable length of time. Obviously, many factors can influence these differing reactions to stress. The late Dr. Harold G. Wolff, in his book *Stress and Disease,* points out that the stress occurring from any given situation is based in large measure on how the individual involved perceived it.[7] Man is especially vulnerable among living beings in this regard because he reacts not only to the acutal existence of stress but to its symbolic interpretations as well.

The various stressful stimuli have a cumulative effect, as implied in the Holmes-Rahe table of stressful life events. It is as if the stress of the water behind the dam is composed of the total impact of all the physical, chemical, microbiological, socio-cultural, and psychological events which happen to us: when the impact reaches a certain height, water cascades over the spillway, no matter in what portion of the watershed the downpour occurred.

Dr. Robert Rushmer has shown in experiments with dogs running on a treadmill that the heart rate and cardiac output of the animals increased in an expected, predictable way.[8] He also found, however, as the dogs became trained, that merely pointing to the treadmill switch could increase their cardiac output and pulse rate.

I observe this same phenomenon in patients who have undue anxiety about their health. Such a patient, who often has a tendency toward high blood pressure, will experience a marked increase in his pulse rate and blood pressure while a reading is being taken. If the patient is reassured and the conversation turns to different subjects, the blood pressure can frequently be checked again in as little as two or three minutes and found to be significantly decreased and the pulse rate normal. The mere taking of the blood pressure, then, is a highly stressful matter for that patient, and results in his typical response of elevated blood pressure.

Because of the great variation in individual response to the same stress, I refer to the onset of a person's response as tension. Tension is distinctly different from stress. (It will be fully discussed in the next chapter.) To clarify terminology at this point, I need to make clear that Drs. Wolff and Selye refer to "stress" as the response occurring within an organism as the result of a life event. For this I use the word "tension" instead. Dr. Selye refers to the life event or stimulus as a "stressor", while Dr. Wolff refers to it as a demand for adaptation. For these latter meanings I prefer to use the word "stress".

Many readers may by now feel that stress is something to be avoided. It is apparent, however, from the above discussion that stress cannot be avoided and is indeed essential for survival, learning, and individual growth, and probably for progress in society as well. Complete freedom from tension, Dr. Selye notes, is attained only with death.

We live in a world of constantly incoming information. If a normal person is deprived of this contact, he tolerates the isolation poorly and may hallucinate as a compensatory mechanism.[9] An infant human or primate will not develop normally when only fed and kept clean. If other stimulation is lacking, normal physical, mental, and emotional development will fail to occur and the infant may die of a condition known as marasmus. Thus, stimulation or challenge—some form of stress—is necessary for our very survival.

One of the basic stresses upon which we depend for survival from week to week is hunger. If for some reason we do not experience hunger, most of us would no longer eat and would eventually die. It is therefore obvious that many of the adaptations we make to stress are normal and quite healthy. Problems arise when stress becomes excessive, for excessive stress tends to bring on excessive tension, which in turn leads to some mal-adaptive response, or, in Dr. Selye's terminology, to a "distress" of some sort.

In examining the categories of stress—physical, chemical, microbiological, socio-cultural, and psychological—it is inter-esting to trace the effects of the most commonly experienced types of stress on man's development. Primitive man faced stresses at the level of exposure, injury, starvation, and the un-predictable elements on the earth's crust. As civilization devel-oped over thousands of years, these problems gradually became less important. As mentioned previously, in the last one hun-dred years infectious stimuli have largely come under control. As industrialized society has coped with physical and infectious elements, and as better life survival has consequently increased the population, other causes of stress have become more impor-tant. Pollution of the environment, overcrowding, the increased pace of living, the mobility of families, and the sheer increase in the number of stimuli to which we are subjected are now the major causes of stress in man.[10]

Chapter 2

TENSION

Tension is the onset of an organism's response to stress. It constitutes the beginning of adaptation after the encountering of a stressful stimulus. Tension may also be defined as the difference between the perceived level of a stressful stimulus and the comfortable ability of the individual to meet it.

The tension arising from a situation is based largely on the way the individual perceives that situation, as Wolff notes. The perception depends upon a multiplicity of factors, the most important of which are genetic make-up, basic needs and longings, the influences of early conditioning and life experiences, cultural pressures, present attitudes, future goals, and present awareness.

Different persons experience different degrees of tension in response to precisely the same stress. The likelihood of experiencing physical, emotional, or mental distress increases as tension increases. The human system attempts constantly to adapt in various ways so as to bring tension within manageable limits.

The following example demonstrates the great differences in tension response. One man, on being fired from work, may experience excessive tension, aggravated by his cultural upbringing which has taught him that to be unemployed is to be worthless. Another man may experience considerably less tension at the loss of his job, partly because his cultural influences have taught him that unemployment is a recognized factor in modern American life and that one copes with it in many different ways. Both men begin their adaptive response to the same stress with tension, but because the man who feels worthless experiences excessive tension he may become immobilized and thus unable to make a satisfactory adaptive response to his plight.

Much work in scientific research in the past thirty years has concentrated on the question of specificity in response. Wolff points out that there has been in recent years a growing awareness that grossly different agents and stresses may cause indistinguishable reactions in the individuals subjected to them.[1] In addition, stresses which would ordinarily be considered quite benign, because of their unique significance to any given individual, may be perceived as highly stressful, inducing a high level of excess tension leading to a prolonged and stormy period of adaptation.

One patient I recall was faced with considerable stress when he was informed he was to be moved to a division of his employer's company where the demands were much greater than those of his previous position. It was impossible for him to go home with a clear desk, and at the end of each day he was forced to leave many matters unattended. Because this particular patient was highly perfectionistic, the new situation into which he was forced led to a very high level of tension. Since he could not meet the demands which he placed upon himself out of past experience (to go home with a clean desk every night), the patient manifested great anxiety which began to interfere with his work performance. Daily medication was required to allay his anxiety for many months before he was able to adapt to his situation.

Tension may be thought of as the result of maintaining conflicting bits of information on the same subject within the mind, whether consciously or unconsciously. The total tension experienced results from the sum of all the situations in which conflicting bits of information are present within the mind.

When the areas of the brain containing those bits of information continue to be activated, tension builds up as a form of energy.

The energy buildup in the form of tension finds its way to whatever areas in the system are determined by a particular individual's unique pattern of neurochemical responses. Our perfectionistic executive who had difficulty adapting to his stressful job because he had to leave work incomplete much of the time was energizing areas of his brain which were telling him that to leave work incomplete was unacceptable. This was in conflict with his conscious awareness of the demands of his job. The energy arising from that tension was then transmitted through his brain and nervous system to generate excessive anxiety.

James Vargiu draws the analogy of the buildup of energy to that of iron filings placed upon a surface to which a magnet is gradually approached.[2] Energy begins to be transmitted to the iron filings with the approach of the magnet. The filings shift slightly, changing position as the force from the magnet approaches. The force of the magnet is comparable to stress as we have previously defined it. There is, in other words, a demand that the iron filings adapt to the presence of the stress or force. As the magnet is brought closer, the particles begin to move. If they are close to one another, they absorb the magnetic energy and become magnets themselves. They may attract each other as the energy level becomes greater. Finally, they will be seen to move toward each other and align themselves with other particles, thus reducing the tension within the field. This is analogous to the process of adaptation, tension being reduced as adaptation takes place.

Usually, as the magnet approaches the iron filings, the adaptations are almost imperceptible and take place in minute steps. Occasionally, however, large steps in realignment occur rather suddenly. A slight movement of the surface on which the iron filings rest may cause great shifts in alignment, even though the magnet may at that time be stationary.

In learning processes, Vargiu reports, this sudden quantum leap sometimes takes place as an "ah-ha" experience, in which there is a sudden change in the state of awareness, leading to resolution of the state of tension. In psychological experiences, as in physics, the tension buildup is greatest just before an event leading to the "ah-ha" experience.

Adaptability, as Selye observed, is probably the most distinctive characteristic of life. Part of this adaptability is the unrelenting quest of the system to so arrange itself that tension is brought within manageable limits, permitting us to experience less distress and more comfort.[3] We all have a very strong distaste for conflict—the active presence of which is tension—and a very strong drive to eliminate or release the tension. The tension energy is generated by the presence in the mind of conflicting bits of information on a subject. The mind is then predisposed to work at dissolving that tension by some form of adaptation to the conflicts either through the mind, body, or emotions.

Dr. Selye points out that occasionally, though rarely, an individual suffers from a lack of sufficient tension. Such an individual vegetates and seems to be satisfied with a minimal existence. Indifference to stimuli or inputs leads to an extremely low tension level, which may be perceived as boredom or ennui and which in itself may then be experienced as distress. Distress may result from not having enough anxiety or fear. My patients who fall into this category do not experience enough fear in threatening situations, tend to be accident-prone, and suffer from the consequences of unwise ventures. The vast majority of adaptation problems, however, involve learning, growth, and development—all of which require tension in order to occur. Both extremes—excessive tension or inadequate tension—lead to distress. Between the two is an ideal range, the striving for which is a chief function of the mind.

It will, I think, be helpful at this point to distinguish some of the things which tension is not.

First, tension is not anxiety. Anxiety, as used in this book, is an extremely common emotion akin to fear and, like all emotions, is an integral part of our being. It is distressing when experienced in excessive amounts.

Second, tension is not mere muscle contraction, though it is altogether true that tension can lead to the distresses caused by excessive muscular contraction, including backaches and muscle contraction headaches (commonly called tension headaches). Excessive muscular tension is best referred to as "muscle contraction" or "muscle action".

Third, tension is not "bad". I have indicated in the previous chapter on stress that certain amounts of stress are essential for survival. Likewise, certain optimum levels of tension are essential for growth and for healthy functioning of the human organism. However, both insufficient and excessive tension tend to lead to maladaptive reactions and to physical, mental, or emotional distresses. Tension exists as a dynamic state within the system with an energy that eventually manifests itself in muscular or glandular disturbances.

Excessive tension may build up as water behind a dam. When heavy rainfall occurs in the lands drained by the river whose flow is stopped by the dam, pressure builds up in the system as the water level rises. The flow through the penstocks continues to energize the turbines and electricity is consistently produced and the dam reliably functions in the manner for which it was designed. When the state of tension remains manageable, energy continues to flow and supplies power to the users.

If the water level builds up higher than the intake of the penstocks, the excess flows over the top of the dam and down the spillways. The flow of this water is lost to productive activity. Indeed, if the flow over the spillways becomes too great, there is the danger of flooding below the dam. Thus does distress occur in the human system when the tension level becomes significantly excessive.

Should the rainfall behind the dam be insufficient to keep up the level of tension behind the dam to the height at which water is taken into the penstocks, the turbine ceases to turn because of insufficient water flow, and the production of electricity, the purpose for which the dam was designed, ceases. This is the state of boredom which occurs when an individual does not experience sufficient tension.

The principle of homeostasis (equilibrium) governs a system which, if it is to maintain itself within tolerable limits, must act to reestablish itself to the state of existence before the input of new information.[4] The homeostatic expression of the life force is directed by the state of tension within the organism.

Chapter 3

PHYSICAL DISTRESS

A. Cardiovascular Distress

Coronary Artery Disease

The incidence of coronary artery disease (CAD) in most Western countries has increased at an alarming rate in the past sixty years. CAD may take the form of angina pectoris, a condition in which chest pain results from borderline circulation to the heart muscle because of narrowing of the lumen or passageway of the coronary arteries; or it may take the form of heart attack (myocardial infarction), in which complete blockage of a coronary artery occurs, a segment of heart muscle is totally deprived of its blood supply, undergoes death, and, if the patient survives, heals with formation of a scar.

The medical and scientific community became fairly well convinced in the 1950s and 1960s that dietary cholesterol was the cause of CAD. (Cholesterol, a complex molecule having a greasy, waxy appearance in its isolated form, is normally found in many body cells. It participates in the synthesis or manufacture of several body hormones and bile acids, and acts as an insulator around nerve cells. It is manufactured by many different body cells, especially in the intestine and liver. It is also accepted into the body from digestion of cholesterol-containing foods.) Body-manufactured cholesterol is transported in very soluble forms in the bloodstream. If any of it escapes from the bloodstream to lodge in corners or crevices in the lining of arteries, it will usually not stay because it is so soluble. Dietary cholesterol, on the other hand, travels to a great extent in a much less soluble form and when precipitated from the bloodstream onto the surface of the arterial lining will tend to lodge there permanently. Elevated levels of cholesterol, especially in less soluble forms, are found in many victims of CAD.

The buildup of placques of cholesterol inside arteries and arterioles is called arteriosclerosis, or hardening of the arteries. When the deposition of cholesterol reaches a certain point, the lumen or hollow in the blood vessel is significantly narrowed and may eventually be blocked off completely. If the artery so obstructed is in the heart, a heart attack occurs. If the obstruction is as yet incomplete, the patient may experience the pain of angina pectoris due to the inability of the artery to supply sufficient oxygen to meet the demands of the heart muscle.

In the 1950s, certain families were discovered to have exceedingly high cholesterols of 300 to 1200 mgm % (normal, 150 to 250 mgm %), due to a hereditary defect in the ability to handle cholesterol. Members of these families experienced a very high rate of CAD, including some with heart attacks before the age of twenty-five. Animal studies, too, confirmed the correlation between a diet high in cholesterol and the predisposition to heart attacks.

The only problem with this "cholesterol-is-the-culprit" theory is that many reports were also made public which indicated that certain groups or populations with a heavy cholesterol intake had few or no coronary attacks. I myself have had personal experience of this with the Plains Indians while working with the U.S. Division of Indian Health. During two years of service to a population of 6,000, I had only four patients who suffered heart attacks, in spite of a high incidence of diabetes and a cultural diet that was high in carbohydrates and cholesterol.

Medical authorities agree that the cause of CAD is multifaceted. There is general agreement that diabetes, sustained hypertension (high blood pressure), hereditary forms of elevated cholesterol, and hypothyroidism (low or deficient thyroid) are definite causes. Other factors that are still debated include the dietary intake of cholesterol and simple sugars, smoking, physical inactivity, and obesity.

Drs. Meyer Friedman and Ray H. Rosenman, cardiologists in San Francisco, had been frustrated in trying to relate such causal factors as high cholesterol, poor diet, insufficient exercise, and smoking to the incidence of CAD, since no one factor or combination seemed to accurately predict the fate of their patients. Two incidents finally influenced them toward their hypothesis of the last two decades, outlined in *Type A Behavior and Your Heart.* An upholsterer was engaged to reupholster chairs in their waiting room. He commented on the peculiar fact that only the front edges of the seats were worn. In retrospect, this revealed to the doctors the state of tension of their patients, who usually were not relaxed enough to sit all the way back in a chair and be comfortable.

Drs. Rosenman and Friedman were also at that time engaged in a study of heart attacks in women versus men. Their study showed that women were much less susceptible to heart attack in spite of equally high levels of cholesterol intake. They were informed by the president of the San Francisco Junior League, through whom volunteers for the study were obtained, that the real cause of heart attacks in men was stress, "the stress they receive in their work, that's what's doing it."

The cardiologists then began to study the relation of stress to coronary heart attacks. Their pioneering contribution to the understanding of myocardial infarctions came in a study of 2,750 men, aged thirty-nine to fifty-nine, who were followed for eight and a half years.[1]

Initially, these men completed the Jenkins Activity Survey and on entering the study were free from coronary disease on the basis of history, physical examination, and testing. The Jenkins Activity Survey is a 61-item multiple-choice questionnaire. Subjects were classified on the basis of test results as Type A personalities or Type B personalities. The Type A's included approximately fifty percent of the subjects, the Type B's, forty percent. Approximately ten percent showed a significant mixture of A and B characteristics.

The followup after eight and a half years showed that the men having Type A personalities experienced three times the incidence of new coronary heart disease as compared to their Type B control counterparts.[2] Of the Type B patients, excluding those who had hypertension and diabetes, not one had yet died of a heart attack as of 1974.

The Friedman-Rosenman study is especially valuable because it is based on a prospective (i.e., predictive) rather than retrospective approach. Previous studies had indicated similar results but were based on interviews and psychological tests on subjects *after* the development of CAD and heart attacks. The study is also doubly valid because results were handled on a double-blind basis—that is, the medical group dealing with the patients did not know what their previous personality-type scores had been on the Jenkins Activity Survey.

What, then, are the Type A characteristics as brought out in the Jenkins Activity Survey?

Type A men typically involve themselves in an aggressive, chronic struggle to achieve more and more in less and less time. If challenged by another situation or person, the struggle would turn in opposition to that challenge. They are quite prone to a free-floating but well-rationalized attitude of hostility. It must be emphasized that this trait becomes particularly obvious when Type A persons meet an environmental challenge. At other times, their hard-driving style is subtle, although still present. A Type B counterpart may have the same amount of ambition and drive, yet somehow the environmental challenge or stress induces less tension and greater equanimity in him, with less consequent irritability and anger.

Type A persons, by contrast, feel impatient with the rate at which most events take place; they fret when the auto in front of them is moving below the speed limit or hesitates after the light turns green; they finish the sentences of other people; they do not tolerate waiting in line to be served; they *always* move, walk, and eat rapidly. They think polyphasically, say Friedman and Rosenman, considering several things at once. The doctors have had subjects who ate breakfast, shaved, and read a business journal all at the same time. The Type A man is vaguely guilty when he relaxes and does nothing. He has no time to observe the beautiful and varied happenings in his existence.

Another major characteristic is his slavish commitment to the "numbers game"—the number of houses his firm built, the number of sales his company made, the number of people attending his performance. This represents a certain insecurity in facing the world, since his self-esteem is based on the sheer numbers of his accomplishments and on getting things considered by others to be worth having rather than on the degree of satisfaction they offer.

Other clues to spotting the Type A person are explosive staccato speech with a rapidly uttered closing phrase in a sentence; nervous tics and gestures around the eyes or mouth; the tendency to continually turn conversations to subjects which interest him; and the frequent habit of openly challenging another Type A person with hostility.

The Type B subject is free of much of this sense of urgency and free-floating hostility. He feels no compulsion to bring his own achievements into a conversation; he is content to experience periods of relaxation and non-accomplishment without guilt; he plays without working against a stopwatch or a competitive score. He derives more pleasure from being than from having.

Hypertension

The current heightened interest in high blood pressure has made most thoughtful persons aware of the relationship between it and a shorter life span. In my experience, hypertension is one of the subjects most frequently brought into question by a patient with some anxiety about his health. Many patients, upon having their blood pressure taken, will want to know the exact readings as well as the interpretation of the pressure recording on that particular day.

It is known that the ability of the organism to increase blood pressure is a response to a threat of injury or stress of some sort. In terms of the primitive physiological responses of fight or flight, the blood pressure seems to increase in either situation. This is not difficult to understand, since both fighting and fleeing require greater muscular activity than normal and hence an increased supply of blood to bring the nutrients necessary for the use of increased energy within the muscles as well as carrying off the metabolic breakdown products more rapidly.

The mechanism which seems to occur predominantly when muscular activity is happening or is anticipated is that of an increase in the heart rate and in the amount of blood ejected per stroke from the heart. If the heart is visualized as a pump, it can be appreciated that a certain amount of blood may be pumped from the valves of the heart with each stroke. It is this stroke-volume which increases, along with the heart rate, when muscular effort is required.

A second pattern of elevation of blood pressure is characterized by an increase in peripheral resistance within the arterial tree. This can be visualized by picturing the reduction of the caliber of a waterpipe entering a building from two inches to one inch. With the reduction in the size of the waterpipe, the same amount of water can be delivered to the building only if the rate of delivery or flow is increased. This then requires the pressure to be increased to deliver the water faster to make up for the reduction in the size of the pipe. The arterial control systems within the human body include a muscular apparatus surrounding a point along each small artery (arteriole). Each of these muscular controls responds to stimuli via its nerve supply from the autonomic centers in the hypothalamus of the brain. In experiments in which the organism is faced with injury or hemorrhage, a typical elevation in blood pressure occurs because of increase in peripheral arterial resistance without a concomitant increase in stroke volume from the heart.

These two somewhat different patterns were observed during interviews while subjects were being monitored as follows: the first or "exercise" pattern occurred when emotional disturbance was relatively visible and overt, while the second or "high resistance" pattern was encountered more often when there was suppression or repression of emotions by a calm exterior appearance.[3]

It is important to note that these adaptations in blood pressure may also occur in anticipation of some strenuous effort, as with an athlete preparing to run a race. It has been shown too that there may be an increase in blood flow as a result of emotionally charged situations in which there is no conscious contemplation of muscular activity. In such cases it is as if the regulatory mechanism of blood pressure which would have been appropriate to an earlier period of man's evolutionary development, with its highly visible threats from the environment, is now somewhat inappropriately triggered by the rise of emotion in situations symbolically interpreted as threatening.

The importance of hereditary influences over and against environmental influences in the genesis of disease in the integrated behavior pattern of adults is widely debated. Environmental factors include basic needs and longings resulting from early training, conditioning influences, and a whole host of life experiences and cultural pressures. In an excellent study on the subject of hypertension by Flynn, Kennedy and Wolf, twin girls, age twenty, were described as identical as far as could be ascertained from birth history, early photographs, dominant handedness, fingerprints, palmprints, blood groups, somatotypes, hair structure, and skeletal structure.[4] Nevertheless, they exhibited important differences. One had had elevated blood pressure for eight years, and the other had normal blood pressure. One of the twins had been an "also-ran," being compared unfavorably to her sister during her entire infancy and childhood. She was slightly slower in growth, less well developed, less capable of evoking love, less imaginative in work, and burdened with more frequent and severe infections. It was this twin who developed high blood pressure. She felt obliged to strive almost continually from birth, and the physicians concluded that she exhibited in the behavior of her cardiovascular system the effects of sustained attempts to compensate for what she considered her inadequacies. While this example does not detract from the possibility of inherent genetic differences exerting significant influences on the twins' behavior patterns as adults, it does emphasize the strong contribution of conditioning and environmental influences to disease.

Psychiatrists have for years noted that patients with high blood pressure are frequently psychologically battle-ready, but that aggressive behavior to carry out this readiness is unconsciously restrained.[5] After all the heredity-versus-environment theories are thoroughly examined, the fact remains that mechanisms in man controlling blood pressure are connected with and capable of reacting to nervous system connections in the interpretive sections of the brain. Stressful life experiences are sufficiently prominent among stimuli causing elevated blood pressure to be seriously considered in every patient who suffers from this disease. Hypertension, as well as some other stress-related disorders, including peptic ulcer and endocrine (hormone) disruptions, may frequently be found to be the most serious medical problems associated with stressful situations such as wars, civilian catastrophes, fires, or earthquakes. It is reported that during the three-year siege of Leningrad in World War II, the incidence of high blood pressure increased from four to sixty-four percent. In most of the persons affected, the elevated blood pressure persisted even after the end of the war, and the majority suffered premature death from causes related to high blood pressure.[6]

A calm exterior and a picture of nonchalance is commonly observed in the examination room with patients having high blood pressure. Studies have shown that hypertensive subjects frequently grow up feeling that they must excel, but at the same time avoid competing for vigorous self-assertion. It is easy to see how these conflicting images can pose a dilemma for the person harboring them—an example of the way conflicting bits of information lead to tension. Grace and Graham, in a study published in 1952, using a technique in which they ask the patient to make a statement of what he felt was happening to him at the time of the occurrence of a symptom, concluded that patients with elevated blood pressure felt they must constantly be prepared to meet all possible threats.[7] Typical statements included "I had to be ready for anything" and "Nobody is ever going to beat me —I'm ready for anything." The striving to excel, matched with the conflicting signal to avoid vigorous self-assertion, frequently resulted in wary, tentative attitudes with respect to major life events and relationships with other persons.

Many people think of the blood pressure level as static. On the contrary, it is quite variable and in a constantly changing dynamic state. Early in my practice I became impressed with the variability of blood pressure under different circumstances. It was very common to find the blood pressure initially elevated and subsequently, after the patient rested or engaged in a pleasant conversation with me, to find the reading significantly decreased, oftentimes to normal. Similarly, Dr. Flanders Dunbar, doing extensive studies in the 1930s in high blood pressure, described a patient whose blood pressure went up promptly when stressful topics were introduced into the conversation and went down promptly when the patient began expressing his deeper feelings about the stressful subjects.[8]

It is important at this point to note that elevated blood pressure is of itself not significant, but that its continuance over long periods causes damage to the circulatory structures of the heart, brain and kidney, leading to a higher incidence of premature heart attacks, strokes, and kidney damage.

In a 1973 study of high blood pressure in air-traffic controllers as compared to second-class airmen, the rate of high blood pressure was found to be four times as high in the air-traffic controllers. In addition, it was found that the age of onset of high blood pressure was seven years earlier for the air-traffic controllers. New cases of high blood pressure were about one-sixth as high in the second-class airmen in any given year. The authors concluded that it is probable that air-traffic controllers are at a higher risk of developing high blood pressure than second-class airmen, this added risk being related to centers with high traffic density and to the stress associated with working in such a pressured environment.[9]

Threats or noxious stimuli call forth certain biological response patterns whose purpose is to adapt to the potentially injurious stimuli and master the challenge they pose. Response systems are already developed at birth to some degree. Through systematic experimental research it seems clear that, as the human being develops, the response systems are functionally differentiated depending on experience and learning, endocrinological (hormonal) influences, and programming of the neural circuitry. This leads to distinct and rather stereotyped stable patterns of psychophysiological response in behavior and hormone systems.[10]

Strokes

The Continuing Health Hazard Appraisal Study at Methodist Hospital in Indianapolis has identified strokes as the fifth leading cause of death in most groups in the United States.[11] This study has also indicated a statistical relationship with four known variables—level of blood pressure, level of cholesterol, presence of diabetes, and the smoking habit. Furthermore, it indicates a rather linear relationship between sustained high blood pressure and a gradually increased incidence of death and disability as a result of strokes.

It is generally agreed by authorities that the process eventually leading to the pathology of stroke begins with the gradual narrowing of the arteries supplying blood to the brain by the deposit of fatty materials along the inner lining of the blood vessels. This process is especially well described in Rosenman and Friedman's *Type A Behavior and Your Heart.* There is strong evidence from many sources that the rate at which this process of narrowing of the inside of the blood vessels occurs is related to the level of cholesterol and other lipids in the blood. In other words, the higher the level of cholesterol found in the blood, the more likely it is that the arteriosclerotic process will be hastened.

Cholesterol is a substance normally found in the healthy body. It arrives in the bloodstream as a result of the breakdown of certain cholesterol-containing tissues in the body in the normal regenerative cycle of those cells. It is manufactured by the liver cells, and it is also absorbed from food sources through the intestine.

While the cholesterol is chemically similar whether it comes from any of these sources, we must note that it travels in the bloodstream in a container or vehicle of protein, the resulting chemical complex being called a lipoprotein. The lipoprotein vehicle is significantly different depending on whether the cholesterol source is absorption from food sources through the intestine or manufacture from the liver. The nature of the lipoprotein packaging for cholesterol absorbed from the intestine is such that when the entire chemical complex affixes itself to the inner lining of an artery, it is very difficult for the cholesterol to escape back into the blood. By contrast, the lipoprotein packaging for cholesterol manufactured from the liver is such that escape from the inner lining of the arteries to which the complex has been affixed is rather easy.

The question then arises, what means are used by the system to control the amount of cholesterol manufactured and absorbed from food stuffs, and why do those levels vary within an individual and between individuals? The best evidence is that the endocrine or hormone systems within the body are the means by which cholesterol levels are controlled. It has been known for decades, for example, that the level of thyroid hormone or thyroxin in the blood stream has a profound influence on levels of cholesterol. A person deficient in thyroxin tends to have very high levels of cholesterol in the blood. Other hormones, including growth hormone (manufactured by the anterior pituitary) and glucagon (a pancreatic hormone), are also known to play a role in the control of cholesterol levels.[12] Drs. Friedman and Rosenman advanced the idea that the ultimate center for cholesterol control may, however, lie within the brain. There is some evidence that this may be true in animals, since destruction of certain portions of the emotional centers of a rat's brain promptly results in a two- to five-fold rise in the rat's serum cholesterol level. The centers of the hypothalamus of the brain may be the correlating centers for the control of the hormonal factors leading to regulation of serum cholesterol levels.

What evidence is there, then, that stress may be related to these phenomena? Numerous studies have shown that stressful life experiences are capable of causing cholesterol levels to become elevated.[13] Students have been studied before, during, and after examinations; higher cholesterol levels were consistently found during the stressful periods. In controlled interviews covering neutral topics, in one study, no elevations of cholesterol were found. After an hour's stressful discussion, however, increases in serum cholesterol were consistently found.[14]

Studies have also been done with groups subjected to periodic stresses—accountants, for example. One such group, facing the stress of tax deadlines, was noted to have sharply increased levels of cholesterol in April. In May and June, their serum cholesterol fell to considerably lower levels.[15] Similarly, blood tests done on a small number of workers on Mondays as compared to Wednesdays would seem to indicate that the chemical changes in the body by the middle of a stressful work week are consistently higher than those found earlier on.[16]

The relationship of exercise to health will be fully discussed in Chapter 16, but I mention here the fact that a Stanford research project involving long-distance runners has shown significantly decreased patterns of blood fats, including cholesterol, compared with sedentary controls.[17]

One final factor deserves mention. It relates to the clotting factors within the blood of subjects under stress. Dreyfus measured the clotting time in medical students subjected to the stress of final examinations and found it to be decreased or shortened, predisposing them to the faster formation of clots.[18] Plasma fibrinogen, a factor in the clotting sequence, was found to be far more variable in subjects with known coronary artery disease when compared with normal subjects.[19]

Rhythm Disturbances of the Heart

Consider for a moment the extreme importance to the human being of the heartbeat. For the duration of a lifetime, the human heart beats between fifty and one hundred times per minute in sleep and relatively quiet activity, each beat delivering into the arterial system of the body approximately one teaspoonful of oxygen-enriched blood that has been returned from the lungs for distribution to the body. Except in advanced stages of physical disease or marked states of excessive tension, a very reliable system controls the beating of this organ which rarely fails to deliver the required amount of oxygen to the body tissues.

The basic rhythm of the heart is controlled by the hypothalamus and the autonomic nervous system (ANS). The cardiac nerves transmit the electrical impulses from the ANS centers to a control center of nerve fibers located on top of the heart. From this center, a special system of fibers conducts electrical impulses to the remainder of the heart muscle, causing its contractions, opening and closing of valves, and the discharge of

blood into the arterial tree in a rhythmical fashion, with pulsa-
tions in the arteries which can be felt in the superficial vessels
of the neck and wrists. As with other parts of the ANS, the fibers
leading to the heart are composed of sympathetic and parasympathetic branches. These two parts of the ANS have somewhat
opposite effects; in the case of the heart, stimulation of the
sympathetic fibers increases the heart rate, whereas stimulation
of the parasympathetic fibers slows the rate.

The generally "failsafe" system of regulation of heart
rhythm has a backup system: if all the nerve fibers to the heart
are severed by surgery or injury, the heart continues to beat in
its own intrinsic rhythm. That is to say, the heart, without outside regulation from the brain, will continue to beat in a somewhat regular rhythm in order to maintain life. Indeed, in
mammalian experiments, when segments of the heart are removed and preserved in nutrient media, the fibers will continue
to contract for many hours.

Thus, electrical energy from the brain, hypothalamus, and
ANS centers is regularly transmitted to the heart and is faithfully
transmuted into muscle contractions of the heart. In young persons and athletic types, the rhythm is slightly irregular, each
inhalation being followed by a slight increase in the heart rate
and each exhalation from the lungs being followed by a slight
decrease. Other than these exceptions, and in certain cases of
functional or organic cardiac disease, the heart rhythm is generally exceedingly regular.

Organic difficulties are associated largely with heart disease
in which coronary artery atherosclerosis (hardening of the arteries) has gradually decreased the oxygen supply to the heart
muscle itself. When the special fibers within the heart compris-
ing the electrical conducting system are affected by this loss of
blood supply, the heart rhythm may falter.

Research has uncovered evidence that most of the deaths
occurring within the first few moments after a heart attack are
due to failure of the heart rhythm to maintain adequate oxygenation of the body. This is due to lack of oxygenation of the
special nerve fibers within the heart conducting the electrical
impulses, resulting in wild and unstable rhythms insufficient to
maintain the heart's pumping action.

In heart disease where the damage is not so abrupt or profound as that which occurs in a heart attack, mild lack of oxygenation can likewise cause somewhat unstable rhythms, including extra beats, speedup of the contraction rate, and lack of good coordination between the two atrial (upper) chambers of the heart and the two ventricular (lower) chambers. When these rhythm disturbances can be diagnosed, they can be stabilized many times by giving appropriate medications.

In addition to structural causes of unstable heart rhythms, many irregularities have a functional basis. That is to say, a great percentage of rhythm disturbances, which can be documented by electrocardiograms, occur in persons in whom there is no organic or structural damage to the heart and in which the oxygen supply of the heart to itself is wholly adequate. There is now a solid core of scientific evidence indicating that many body structures—including the hypothalamus and parts of the brain, the thyroid, pituitary, and adrenal glands, the kidneys, and possibly other organs including the blood vessels, heart structures, and liver—may participate in the responses to the excitation of the nervous system in the interpretive areas of the brain, thereby becoming capable of producing significant disturbances in heart rhythms. This evidence also indicates that many alterations occur in stressful life experiences from day to day in which there are no particular symptoms of which the patient may be aware.[20] When the degree of awareness increases, symptoms may be apparent, especially when the variations in rhythm become marked.

It is exceedingly common for a patient to complain to me of palpitations or some kind of irregularity in the heartbeat. Excessively fast or slow regular rhythms, irregular extra beats, and irregular fast rhythms are all fairly common functional difficulties. Occasionally, severe types of functional rhythm disturbances may be life-threatening.[21] Many such disorders, in which there is no apparent structural disease of the heart muscle or blood vessels, may be precipitated by and seem to be fundamentally related to stresses arising out of life situations.

The most common functional heart rhythm disturbance which I find in patients is called extrasystole. I, myself, experienced this during a year in my practice in which I had the responsibility for organizing the medical staff at a new hospital built in my community. The stresses of the year involved not only the routine ones associated with organizing such a community of physicians, but also involved the firing of the hospital administrator and the enforced resignations of two hospital commissioners. During the year in which those stresses resulted in considerable tension within me, I experienced the extrasystoles several times weekly. This stress disappeared in the following years; the extrasystoles have since occurred only rarely. Extrasystoles are irregular, extra beats in the heart's rhythm, due apparently to an overabundance of electrical impulses passing down the cardiac nerves to the heart. The conducting mechanism is overwhelmed with this excess energy and discharges it prior to its appointed time, resulting in an extra contraction occurring soon after the previous regular contraction. The compensatory ability of the heart then causes a slightly longer pause to allow the heart to return to its regular rhythm. It is this extra pause which is usually perceived by the patient, giving him the sensation that his heart has skipped a beat.

Profound slowing of the heart in physical situations in which deprivation of oxygen is encountered, such as submersion underwater, can likewise be duplicated in a variety of stressful situations even to the point of apparent cardiac arrest.[22] McClure has reported a patient who was able to produce temporary cardiac arrest at will.[23] Dr. Elmer Green, of the Menninger Clinic, has also reported on a number of highly trained individuals, observed during periods of meditation or deep introspection, in which cardiac rhythms had been greatly altered or completely disrupted, returning to normal within a few seconds or minutes.[24] Such observations would seem to bear out the conclusion that while the activity of the highest neural centers governing the heart rhythm apparatus is usually part of unconscious processes, those processes are subject to adaptation and training, at least in certain individuals.

It is also apparent in my own observation that the times heart irregularities are most commonly observed by an individual are when his total system is the quietest. This frequently means awareness of extrasystoles during the few minutes before sleep or in some quiet activity—reading or sitting and "doing nothing." Indeed, one of the most helpful diagnostic points to me has been the fact that most persons experiencing functional heart irregularities and rhythms say the irregularity frequently disappears when increased activity is undertaken.

In addition to electrocardiographic observations of irregularities in rhythm, Stevenson and Duncan have reported significant electrocardiographic changes indicating decreased oxygen supply to the myocardium or heart muscle, occurring when exercise was performed during a period of stress.[25] The same exercise performed on a day of relative security and relaxation showed far less change or none at all in the electrocardiogram. In nearly all of Stevenson's patients, it was also possible to produce electrocardiographic changes indicating decreased oxygen supply during a stressful interview regarding pertinent personal problems, without exercise or anticipation of exercise. The precise mechanisms for the production of these electrocardiographic changes cannot, however, be firmly defined on the basis of present knowledge.

Hellerstein has shown that the workload of the heart in surgeons standing at an operating table is equal to that of men engaged in heavy physical labor moving heavy objects in a steel plant.[26] Experiments also show unsuspected demands on the heart apparatus of inactive persons during periods of responsibility.[27] A group of foremen were found to have significantly higher heart rates than those men whom they directed; the latter engaged in greater bodily activity, but had less job responsibility. Wolff has also shown that the variations in the heart's work correspond to changes in life situations and emotional state.[28]

Migraine Headache

Headache is one of the most frequent complaints of patients in my practice. Probably the commonest variety is that called muscle contraction headache or "tension" headache. A less frequently encountered variety, although often of greater severity, is migraine (vascular) headache. A typical migraine headache is unilateral, involving only one side of the head, and is preceded by neurological and ocular (eye) symptoms, including transient weakness, electric-like feelings (parasthesias) on the affected side, and such visual phenomena as bright lights and spots or even partial blindness. These warning signs occur during the initial phase of arterial constriction reducing the arterial caliber, in turn reducing the oxygen supply to parts of the nervous system, including peripheral and ocular nerves. The later headache stage appears to be caused by a painful dilation or relaxation of the arteries on the affected side in which the caliber of the arteries is increased. The chemical involved in this painful dilation is neurokinin, which forms part of the kallikrein system, a series of inflammatory bodily responses following injury or other noxious stimulation. Other predisposing stimuli appear to be an unstable condition in the nervous controls of the arteries, occurring in migraine headache-prone individuals primarily in the days preceding a migraine attack, but occurring to some extent in headache-free periods as well. This instability renders the arteries of the temporal portion of the scalp—those chiefly involved in the migraine syndrome—overly susceptible to the normal effects of body chemicals causing constriction or dilation of the arteries. Typical statistics collected on migraine-susceptible persons indicate that the majority are women. A variety of migraine headaches, called "cluster headaches," in which the headaches follow one another in quick sequence for a period of days or weeks, appear to occur more frequently in men.

The most extensive studies on migraine have been done by the late Harold G. Wolff. He found that the migraine headache typically has its onset after a long period of alertness with excessive striving to continue difficult tasks and maintain schedules with extraordinary effort and high energy output, and frequently is accompanied by feelings of anger and resentment.[29] Personality profiles of migraine subjects commonly reveal feelings of insecurity, with tension manifested as conscientiousness, meticulousness, perfectionism, resentment, and often inflexibility. The migraine-prone individual aims to gain approval and a sense of security by performing better than his colleagues through hard work. The consequent reward or period of leisure enjoyed by most other persons after accomplishing a difficult task is very difficult for the migraine patient to handle.

The question of how often tension is involved in the production of migraine headache and how important any possible hereditary predisposition may be has not yet been settled. Goodell, Lewontin, and Wolff studied hereditary patterns of migraine in families, concluding that certain persons may have a predisposition in their biological equipment, making them prone to sustained and pernicious emotional states and to unstable regulatory mechanisms in the cranial arteries.[30] This hereditary aspect is very difficult to prove or disprove. In this connection it is important to observe that parents not only supply their children with their biological inheritance but with their environmental inheritance as well. Regardless of the degree of hereditary predisposition which may be present in migraine, nearly all investigators agree that the pattern of migraine attacks and its precipitating factors clearly involve the tensions generated by the demands upon the biological system of the individual.

Raynaud's Phenomenon

Raynaud's disease is the name given to the onset of cold, pale, moist, and frequently numb or painful extremities. It may be limited to one, two, or more fingers or toes, or involve hands or feet. Typically, it may be set off by exposure to cold climate or immersion in cold water. The coldness of the skin in these circumstances is the result of marked vasoconstriction or decreased caliber of the arteries to the skin and consequent greatly decreased skin circulation. Individuals with Raynaud's disease typically harbor hostile feelings when faced with stressful situations.[31] The cooling of the extremities may possibly be a physiological overreaction to the raising of body temperature in anticipation of action.

B. MUSCULAR DISTRESS

Behavior is largely, if not totally, the result of muscular activity. The skeletal muscles, which give rise to facial expressions, blinking of the eyes, moving of the extremities, walking, running, swallowing, and athletic activity, have been called the voluntary muscles. They are voluntary in the sense that the brain energy can at will initiate movements of all these body parts. In a sense, however, they are also involuntary: the arm which is violently jerked away from the stove by contraction of the biceps muscle when the brain receives the impact of the searing heat of a finger touching a burner is a conditioned reflex. The sequence of electrical and chemical events culminating in the movement of a group of muscles originates in the nervous system.

The simplest illustration is that of the three-neuron-arc. Tapping on the patellar (knee) tendon with a reflex hammer sends to the spinal cord an incoming message which is transferred through two connections in the spinal cord to the outgoing motor nerve leading to the quadriceps (thigh) muscle. A fraction of a second later, after the tapping of the patellar tendon, the quadriceps muscle contracts and the lower portion of the leg jerks. Thus the knee-jerk reflex arc is completed. More complicated phenomena involve the stimulation of the motor cortex in the frontal portions of the brain. Electrical stimulation of the appropriate portion of the brain during surgery results in the contraction of a corresponding set of muscles in the peripheral part of the body.

Muscular activity also tends to accompany certain emotions. The emotion of joy or happiness is usually expressed by a smiling face and frequently by exuberant activity, sadness by crying, a downcast face, and drooping shoulders. Anger may be manifested by a set jaw, clenched fists, and explosive speech or punctuated muscular activity, while fear or anxiety are accompanied by widened eyes, raised brows, speaking at the height of inspiration, and poor exhalation.

Studies have shown that the normal person uses only a portion of the muscle fibers to perform a particular activity, as if a reserve were held for emergencies. In addition, muscle fibers work in relays to allow rest of a particular group of fibers after a state of contraction. In normal activity of the back muscles, for instance, only about thirty percent of the fibers contract at a given time with normal quiet activity. A moment later, thirty percent are still being used, but a different thirty percent. Even in violent muscle activity of the back, only sixty to seventy percent of the muscle fibers contract at one time.

This rotation of the contracting portions of a muscle from one fiber to the next in quick sequence can be imagined by drawing an analogy to an old-style theater marquee with hundreds of individual bulbs blinking off and on. Each bulb goes on and off every few seconds, but since the same off-on phenomenon is going on with all the other hundreds of lights, the amount of light produced by the sign remains constant and a twinkling effect is observed.

Likewise, with the muscles of the back, a more or less constant state of contraction is obtained, although different sets of fibers are continually phasing in and out of contraction and relaxation. The apparent purpose which this phenomenon serves is that of permitting a continual amount of oxygen to be supplied to the muscles and a continual flow of lactic acid—produced by the metabolism of the muscles—to be returned toward the heart via the veins. An excess of lactic acid accumulating in a portion of the body produces pain, and may also be associated with anxiety.[32]

If muscle fiber rotation did not exist, the supply of oxygen through the arteries and the return of lactic acid through the veins would stop because the press of the contracted muscles would squeeze the blood flow in the arteries and veins to a standstill. An approximation of this phenomenon can be obtained by anyone who is willing to contract all of the muscles of his forearm and fist continually for two minutes. When the forearm and hand-fist muscle contraction has been sustained for forty to fifty seconds, the forearm begins to become uncomfortable and by two minutes it is for most people downright painful. The pain is caused by the accumulation of lactic acid in the tissues as the muscles prevent its exit into the veins on the way to returning to the heart.

I frequently give to participants in my classes on stress and tension the assignment of observing the state of contraction of their shoulder and neck muscles as they drive an automobile. A majority report excessive contraction of those muscles. They also find that they can voluntarily induce relaxation in those muscles.

Muscle contraction headache, less precisely called tension headache, is a type of head pain resulting from excessive contraction of neck and scalp muscles. The brain and skull have practically no pain endings (for this reason brain surgery, including removal of an overlying portion of the skull, can be done under local anesthesia for the scalp). The sources of pain in migraine headache are the pain endings in the blood vessels of the scalp and the base of the brain, and in muscle contraction headache the sources of pain are the pain endings in the neck and scalp muscles. Many patients experiencing muscle contraction headache have excessively contracted and spastic neck muscles. The excessively contracted muscle which produces the typical "charlie-horse" in a calf or thigh is similar to the tight neck muscles of a person with muscle contraction headache.

Once the discomfort of excessive muscular contraction is perceived in an area, the body's natural protective reflexes tend to worsen it by sending the area into a state of contraction to prevent painful movement. An appendicitis patient with pain in the right lower quadrant of the abdomen faces the examiner with a so-called "board-like" muscular contraction in the right side of the abdomen as a defense against experiencing the pain of further movement, including examination by the physician. This is called the "pain-spasm cycle." Initial excess muscle contraction, regardless of cause, thus leads to more pain and muscle contraction in order to prevent movement and alleviate pain.

Drs. Holmes and Wolff have demonstrated that, compared to control subjects without backache, persons subject to low backache exhibited sustained intense contractions of an excessive portion of the skeletal musculature when responding to threatening situations engendering apprehension, frustration, anxiety, humiliation, guilt, and resentment.[33] Backache subjects asked to perform a particular muscular task such as making a fist not only mobilized the necessary muscles but also surrounding and distant muscle groups, and often clenched the jaw. The non-backache subjects generally mobilized the necessary muscle groups only. The backache subjects related to the research examiners with insecurity, wariness, and apprehension.

Excessive contractions in muscles lead to ischemia (oxygen depletion) and to the accumulation of high amounts of lactic acid which then causes discomfort. Tension is not the only cause of the excessive muscle contraction state; it can also occur if a person is anticipating an action requiring muscular activity. This attitude of readiness induces the rather constant state of muscle contraction, especially if the action anticipated is never carried out. Grace and Graham, in their 1952 study, found that their patients with low back pain wanted to flee from overburdening situations. Many actually complained of having too much expected of them and of having been given too much to do. It is as if the anger and resentment for these kinds of expectations are not expressible in any other way except through preparing to take some muscular action. When no action is taken, the continuing state of preparation leads to muscular pain.

Backache and headache may be present on awakening, much to the surprise of the persons who experience it, due to the excessive contraction of the neck and back muscles even during the supposed period of relaxation called sleep. Grinding of the teeth often becomes a dental problem due to clenching of the jaw during sleep. Uncomfortable phenomena in other connective tissues, commonly called fibrositis and myositis, can also be caused and aggravated by excessive muscle contraction. This will be explored in the next subchapter.

C. Locomotor Distress

The distresses which affect the locomotor system include inflammatory processes in connective tissues such as joints (arthritis), muscles (myositis), joint linings (synovitis), and fibrous tissues (fibrositis).

As with most body systems, the mechanisms leading to distress in the locomotor system are not completely understood. It is helpful, however, to learn about those parts of the inflammatory system which are better understood, including those relating to stressful experiences.

In the last two decades, a category of body chemicals called kallikreins has been discovered. These polypeptides (intermediate-length protein chains) called bradykinin and neurokinin were isolated in specimens of tissue fluid taken from areas where pain was concentrated in migraine headache subjects.[34] The significance of these inflammatory chemicals quickly became apparent when concentrations found in persons suffering headaches at the time the specimen was taken were between eight and thirty-five times greater than when no headache was present. The quantity of the neurokinin activity was also closely correlated with the intensity of the headache. In addition, neurokinin was found to be released in tissues of body structures other than the head during excitation of nerves by electrical stimulation of nerve roots near the spine.

When these kallikrein chemicals are injected into the skin, pain, reddening (inflammation), and swelling result. These inflammation-inducing chemicals appear to be stimulated into production and activity as a result of injury to a body part or certain other stimuli presented to the neurological system. The inflammatory reaction apparently exists in the human system for the purpose of localizing irritants or foreign invaders by putting a barricade of inflammatory tissue around them. It may also be important in carrying off blood or injured cells from the site of an injury and in helping to erect a barrier to bridge a gap where the body's defensive shell (skin) has been breached.

A second body of knowledge regarding the system's inflammatory reaction exists in its relationship to the pro-inflammatory mineralocorticoids secreted by the adrenal cortex gland. The pro-inflammatory adrenal hormones thus far identified in man appear to be weak chemical substances. Synthetically produced similar compounds (pregnenolone-16-alpha-carbonitrile) are very potent and exhibit a non-specific destructive ability against a large number of toxins. The pro-inflammatory compounds are an example of what Dr. Hans Selye terms catatoxic hormones.[35] That is to say, they represent the body's inclination to fight a foreign invader. (This will be further explored in the subchapter on the surveillance system.)

An additional aid in localizing and destroying foreign invaders is the system of immune defense reactions. These cellular and chemical agents are produced by the thymico-lymphatic apparatus. The thymus is a large lymphatic organ located in the chest, in front of the windpipe. It and the lymph glands form a single organ system, among whose functions are the production of white blood corpuscles of various types (these immobilize or destroy invading viruses and bacteria) and of immune chemicals called antibodies.

The third aspect of the inflammatory reaction involves the anti-inflammatory activity of glucocorticoids. Produced in the adrenal cortex, these compounds (prototype: cortisone) have an anti-inflammatory potency that was noted shortly after the discovery of the chemicals themselves. The treatment benefits in certain inflammatory and allergic diseases are now well known. Control of the secretion of these hormones from the adrenal cortex rests in the production of ACTH (adrenocorticotropic hormone) in the anterior pituitary gland, in turn controlled by the hypothalamus of the brain. The cortisone-like compounds produced by the adrenal cortex are an example of what Selye calls syntoxic hormones. These compounds act as tissue tranquilizers, as it were, creating a state of passive tolerance for and peaceful co-existence with foreign invaders, without trying to attack them.

The interrelationships of the two parts of the inflammatory and anti-inflammatory systems within the body are not completely understood. That they are indeed closely interrelated was shown in experiments by Dr. Selye in 1936 in which toxic preparations were injected into laboratory rats, resulting in a set of simultaneously occurring changes in organ systems, including great enlargement and increased activity of the adrenal cortex, shrinkage of the thymus gland and lymph nodes, as well as appearance of gastric ulcers. This alarm-rat reaction is mediated through stimulation of the hypothalamus, pituitary gland, and adrenal cortex. As the adrenal cortex increased its activity, the thymico-lymphatic system appeared to decrease its activity.

Of the various inflammatory conditions in the locomotor system, rheumatoid arthritis is both widespread and commonly mentioned as having some relationship to stress.[36] It is a more or less continuous inflammatory process involving joint surfaces and linings around joints. For some years, it has been known that the presence of a chemical called rheumatoid factor accompanied most cases of rheumatoid arthritis. In advanced cases, the joint inflammation and injury process eventually leads to swelling, destruction of surface cartilages, bone changes, pain, and immobilization.

The rheumatoid factor has been identified chemically as an auto-antibody (literally, antibody against oneself).[37] Such an antibody arises in response to the presence in the system of an antigen-antibody complex.[38] The antigen-antibody complexes appear to be produced when the initial antigen appears in great excess in the presence of a relatively insufficient or incompetent antibody.[39] The antigen-antibody complexes inactivate complement (a protein chemical substance) to release inflammatory chemicals from certain white blood cells (mast cells) which may produce widespread inflammatory lesions, while they activate the proteolytic (protein-digesting) enzyme, plasmin. In other experiments, plasmin has been noted to be elevated in conditions of emotional stress.

Rheumatoid arthritis is such an auto-immune disease. The auto-immune process also appears to participate in the production of other disease states such as lupus erythematosus, myasthenia gravis, and acquired hemolytic anemia.[40] Related connective tissue diseases, including scleroderma and dermatomyositis, may involve similar types of tissue damage, inflammatory reaction, and antigen-antibody response mechanisms. Rheumatic fever involves an immune reactive process with reproduction of destructive inflammatory elements in joints, subcutaneous tissues, and heart valves. Rheumatic heart disease has been studied in relation to evidence of socio-cultural as well as genetic, dietary, climatic, and meteorological influences.[41]

In one study, women with definite or classical rheumatoid arthritis scored higher than other female family members on MMPI (Minnesota Multiphasic Personality Inventory) scales with regard to denial and inhibition of anger toward parents, anxiety, depression, compliance, subservience, conservatism, security-seeking, shyness, and introversion.[42] In many instances, both the rheumatoid arthritis patients and their healthy sisters carried the rheumatoid factor in their bloodstream.[43]

Research has also suggested that the antigen which stimulates the production of the rheumatoid factor antibody may be the cellular constituents of the joint areas which have been altered by the enzymatic activity of lysosomes (intracellular structures visible in many body cells, particularly white blood corpuscles). Their digestive activity clearly leads, among other things, to kinin chemical generation, and may be related to the body's kallikrein response system as indicated previously.

Bursitis (inflammation in the bursae, which are fluid-filled sacs the body manufactures around moving joints and tendons to prevent friction) and tendonitis are recognized as stress-related inflammatory responses triggered by excessive activity. As a physician, I see acute bursitis to some extent seasonally, especially during the spring as patients undertake some strenuous and repetitive activity such as gardening, lawn clipping, and athletic pursuits which accompany the arrival of good weather.

Fibrositis and myositis, inflammatory reactions in fibrous tissues and muscles, are diseases whose characteristics are less clear and whose causes are likewise less clear. Some authorities attribute the pain of these reactions to excessive inflammatory response triggered by chronic or recurrent excessive contraction of the muscular or fibrous connective tissue involved.

D. RESPIRATORY AND ALLERGIC DISORDERS

An extensive study conducted in 1950 by Holmes, Goodell, Wolf, and Wolff demonstrated inflammation and subsequent swelling in nasal membranes, typical of a hay fever attack, not only when subjects were exposed to an allergen such as pollen, but also when exposed to other painful stimuli.[44] The subjects also exhibited the same nasal changes when participating in a stressful interview recalling threatening psychological bits of data, even when no pollen was present. In other studies, subjects susceptible to hay fever experienced marked nasal symptoms when inhaling pollen, but experienced termination of the symptoms when reassurance was offered them even though the pollen was still being inhaled.[45]

The typical attitude expressed by individuals studied during attacks of hay fever (vasomotor rhinitis) was that they were facing a situation with the wish that they would not have to do anything about it, that it would go away, or that somebody else would take over responsibility.[46] There was a desire to have nothing to do with the situation and to deal with it by excluding it. The typical two-stage nasal changes of inflammation and subsequent swelling were common in these patients. A second type of reaction was also observed, associated with extreme terror, in which dryness, paleness, and shrinkage of the nasal passage occurred.

Similar reactions are typical of patients susceptible to asthma, particularly during the buildup to an attack. In such susceptible persons it is well recognized that the introduction of an allergen to which the patient reacts can trigger an asthma attack. It is also apparent that psychogenic stress can trigger an attack. One of my patients, for example, responds to my introduction of stressful stimuli in the conversation with a relatively full-blown asthma attack within a very few minutes, to be relieved a short time later as I turn the topic of conversation to less tension-producing subjects.

I have also observed childhood asthma related to stress. Two brothers, four and six, exhibiting intermittent to continuous asthma requiring daily medication for control, lived in a household where there was great marital turmoil between the parents. On one occasion, talking with the mother in my office, I remarked that I had not seen the boys for several months. She revealed that separation and divorce had taken place, and that her husband was seldom in the house. The boys had been asthma-free for almost a complete year and continued with no significant asthma for two more years until I lost track of them.

Allergic reactions clearly have a strong relation to stress and tension, and seem to be the result of the presence of excessive antibodies (immune chemicals) and inflammatory elements carried to the site of invasion of foreign protein (antigen).[47] If the site of reaction is the nose, hay fever is the symptom; if the lung is the site of the encounter, asthma results; and if the skin is the site, eczema is the result. It has been shown that the quantity of mucus produced in the bronchial tree varies with the subject's prevailing emotional state, increasing markedly during a stressful experience.[48] This increase in mucus secretion and interference with bronchial drainage undoubtedly increases the hazard of lung infection.

Hyperventilation is a phenomenon in which the patient feels great shortness of breath but is breathing and exchanging air at a greater than average rate. This has long been recognized as psychologically induced, and usually responds quickly to reassurance and the use of tranquilizers. It is due to an imbalance in the respiratory centers of the brain stem which control the rate of respiration. These centers regularly respond to the buildup of carbon dioxide and the fall in oxygen in the bloodstream which occurs every few seconds at the end of exhalation. When excessive emotional reactions are present, the respiratory center is inhibited and the drawing of deep breaths does not satisfy the feeling of air hunger in the usual fashion. G. A. Wolf and Harold Wolff have studied a patient complaining of attacks of shortness of breath at night. This patient demonstrated a doubling of her respiratory rate during a discussion of her extremely difficult marriage and home situation, causing the same shortness of breath she had been experiencing at night.

E. INFECTIOUS DISEASES

A study of upper-respiratory viral disease completed in 1963 revealed that the patients involved exhibited periods of illness which correlated strikingly with periods of intense emotional turmoil and tended to occur frequently in those whose life adjustment was most precarious.[49]

The presence of latent viruses in human beings provides a source of study in predisposing factors.[50] Herpes simplex, for example, causes lesions on the skin which, when present about the lips or face, are called fever blisters or cold sores. Many authorities believe that this virus is dormant in the majority of human beings. Some form of natural resistance keeps most of us from having an actual outbreak of the viral infection, however, except where certain stress factors (fever, infection, colds, menstruation, exposure to sun, tension, emotional upsets) are present to trigger actual infection. The chief psychological factors in patients having recurrent attacks of herpes simplex without other apparent triggering circumstances are anxiety, frustration, shame, and guilt. There is also evidence that hypnotic suggestion can reactivate herpes simplex infection.

Extensive studies of tuberculosis have indicated that the stress of dislocation appears to be a significant factor in the attack and death rate from this disease. A sizable block of Ireland's population emigrated to America in the late 1800s and early 1900s. As naturalized U.S. citizens, they were better fed and had more promising futures than their brethren in Ireland.

Yet, the death rate from tuberculosis was one hundred percent greater than that for a comparable group in Ireland at the same time.[51] Likewise, studies of American Indians relocated from the plains to reservations not far away, where sanitation was actually better, have revealed that the death rate was far greater among those moved to the reservations.[52]

William Osler is alleged to have commented on the importance of knowing what is going on in a man's head in order to predict the course of his tuberculosis. Day has written that to acquire active tuberculosis required tuberculi bacilli, inflammable lungs, and an internal or external factor (I would call this stress) which lowers resistance. He believes that unhappiness is one such factor.[53]

Prolonged recovery from influenza and tuberculosis has been correlated with depression.[54] Length of recovery from infectious mononucleosis has been linked to self-image, higher self-esteem being correlated with a shorter period of convalescence.[55]

The immune reaction of body chemicals secreted by the thymico-lymphatic system is a significant element in determining the result within the body when microorganisms attempt to invade. Clearly, susceptibility and resistance to infectious diseases seem distinctly linked to stress, tension, and emotional states.[56]

The well-known microbiologist, Rene Dubos, concluded, "Thus, there are many circumstances, some of which are of common occurrence in human medicine, where the physical, chemical, physiological and, probably, psychological factors which affect the host play far more decisive parts in the causation of disease than does the presence of this or that microorganism."[57]

F. IMMUNOLOGICAL DISTURBANCES

Immunological responses are cellular (involving white blood corpuscles) and chemical. These protective responses are made through the thymico-lymphatic system, comprised of the thymus gland in the center of the chest and the variety of lymph glands throughout the body. Cellular immunity is largely responsible for resistance to neoplastic (cancerous) cells, while chemical immunity is largely responsible for resistance to infection by microorganisms.

As previously mentioned, certain events may reduce the competence and resistance of the immunologic system at a critical time, allowing a mutant cancerous cell to develop and multiply. Stress and emotions may influence the function of the immunologic system via the central nervous system and production of hormones.[58] There is considerable data linking personality factors, stress, and failure of psychological adaptations to the onset of cancer, infectious disease, and auto-immune diseases (rheumatoid arthritis, systemic lupus erythematosus, acquired hemolytic anemia, and pernicious anemia).[59]

Possible links between stressful experiences and these diseases are the production of stress-responsive adrenal cortical steroid hormones (hydrocortisone), which decrease or suppress immunologic responses, and hypothalamic regulation of the immune response in the thymus and lymph glands.

Russian research has indicated that the electrical stimulation of a specific region of the hypothalamus enhances antibody response in animals.[60] Destruction of this region in animals leads to complete suppression of primary antibody response and prolonged recovery from illnesses requiring immune mechanisms.[61] In experimental animals, removal of the thymus at the time cancer-causing viruses are injected into their bodies increases the death rate and the rate of growth of tumors.[62] These studies and others imply the existence of a hormone, probably produced by the pituitary gland, controlled by the hypothalamus. Such a hormone may be related to or the same as human growth hormone, produced by the anterior pituitary gland.

Mice subjected to persistent forms of stress in experiments showed enlargement of the adrenal glands, decreased white blood corpuscle counts, decrease in the spleen, thymus, and lymph glands, and increased susceptibility to a variety of infectious diseases.[63]

In the auto-immune diseases, antigen-antibody complexes form when the system responds to antigens (foreign or abnormal proteins) with insufficient antibodies.[64] This is perhaps due to insufficient stimulation from the hypothalamus and from the anterior pituitary gland. The antigen-antibody complexes produce widespread inflammatory responses, activating inflammatory enzymes, and act as new antigens themselves for formation of new autoantibodies, including rheumatoid factor present in patients with rheumatoid arthritis.[65]

G. GASTROINTESTINAL DISTURBANCES

The nerve supply for the entire alimentary tract—from the lips through the intestines and colon to the anus—is largely provided through the autonomic nervous system (ANS). (Functions of this part of the nervous system and the implications of relationships to tension will be further discussed in Chapter 11.) Extensive research has been reported over the years which gives adequate testimony to the close relationship between the state of tension within the organism and the function of the alimentary tract.

One ANS function of the mouth, the secretion of saliva, has been studied by classifying randomly chosen subjects into two groups, one assessed as predominantly assertive and the other passive. During the stress of a dentist's tooth-drilling procedure, the assertive subjects secreted greatly increased amounts of saliva, while the salivary flow of the passive subjects decreased sharply.[66]

The lack of salivary secretions in persons under stress has long been recognized: the custom of providing a glass of water for speakers on the rostrum bears witness to this knowledge. In ancient China, the deficiency of saliva thought to occur when fear was present became the basis for a procedure in which suspected criminals were required to chew rice to show how much saliva they could produce.

Cold sores and canker sores of the lips and mouth, known to be caused by viral agents, have frequently been noted to occur during adverse life adjustments and stressful circumstances.

Globus syndrome is a condition in which a patient has a constant feeling that a foreign body is lodged in the mid-portion of the throat, making him continually swallow in order to get rid of the uncomfortable feeling. This condition has been explained by the continuing excessive contraction of the middle pharyngeal constrictor muscle, one of the muscles in the lower throat which initiates the act of swallowing. It is another manifestation of excessive tension and distress, much the same as that experienced in muscle contraction headaches and backaches. It is also widely known that the syndrome responds readily to reassurance, positive suggestion, or the use of mild tranquilizers.

Knowledge concerning the functions of the digestive tract was greatly enhanced when a patient suffering from closure of the esophagus came under treatment by the late Dr. Harold Wolff. Tom had extensive burns and scarring of the esophagus —the result of accidentally swallowing scalding hot chowder as a young person. Efforts to keep Tom's esophagus open were unsuccessful, and in order to provide nourishment, a surgical opening into the stomach was made through the abdominal wall. Soft foods could then be introduced through the opening, and the digestive and mechanical action of the stomach would carry the contents into the small intestine for further digestion and absorption. From 1941 until his death in 1958, Tom was employed in a medical center and was studied extensively by Dr. Wolff and his associates.[67]

Two distinct patterns of gastric reactions were recognized. One pattern was characterized by inflammation and engorgement of the inner (mucosal) lining of the stomach, as observed through the opening from the outside. At the same time, increased secretion of stomach acid and enzymes (digestive juices) and rapid emptying of the stomach cavity were observed to occur. A second type of stomach reaction was characterized by paleness and greatly decreased activity of the stomach muscular linings, and greatly decreased acid and enzyme secretions.

Through extensive studies, Dr. Wolff established that the first pattern of activity was associated with mealtimes, but could also be reliably stimulated by inducing anxiety, resentment, and hostility. This first (hyperactive) pattern of reaction of the stomach was found to be associated with a lowering of the pain threshold, so that stimuli which ordinarily were not perceived as painful became noticeably uncomfortable. In addition, during periods of hyperactivity, the inner lining of the stomach became so fragile that relatively minor traumas stimulated bleeding and a tendency to ulceration.

The basis for the formation of ulcers, of which ninety-five percent occur in the duodenum (the first portion of the intestine beyond the stomach), is the continuing insult to the duodenal lining by excessive amounts of acid and digestive enzymes (pepsin) produced by the stomach lining. The harmful enzymes and stomach acids are more than the duodenum can handle, since its lining is designed to protect itself from alkaline secretions from the pancreas and from the duodenum itself, and not from the excessively acid secretions of the stomach. In the presence of enough acid, the pepsin secreted by the stomach lining digests foodstuffs until that process is relatively complete. When an excess of pepsin is produced, it continues its digestion on the mucosal lining of the duodenum, resulting in ulceration.

Peptic ulcer patients are known to secrete two to ten times as much acid as the average non-peptic ulcer patient. The control of enzyme and acid secretion in the stomach is based upon at least two known mechanisms. The first is the stimulation of the secreting cells of the stomach by the vagus nerve, part of the autonomic nervous system. The second is a response of the production of gastrin, a hormone, by certain specialized cells in the lower third of the stomach lining, in response to the presence of food and other stimuli.

The autonomic nervous system, then, controlled by the hypothalamus, is once again shown to be greatly influenced by nervous stimulation of surrounding portions of the primitive brain. These portions of the brain respond to excessive tension, producing the anxiety, resentment, and hostility induced in Tom during Dr. Wolff's studies. In Tom's case, the ulcerative-type changes in the stomach lining could be observed through the unusual surgical opening in his abdomen.

Studies of patients with duodenal ulcers have commonly revealed them to be persons craving support and recognition, feeling deprived of what is due them and consequently wanting revenge, feeling vulnerable to threats to their assertive independence, and generally experiencing frustration in expressing these feelings.

The studies of Tom's gastric opening revealed a pattern of decreased motility, pale coloring of the mucosal lining, and decreased secretion of acid and enzyme, accompanied by lack of appetite (anorexia) and nausea, with a tendency toward vomiting. The vomiting may be looked upon as a protective reaction tending to limit absorption of foodstuffs. This low-functioning pattern was typically encountered in patients overwhelmed with feelings of terror, dejection, and despair.[68] Depression has similarly been observed to be accompanied by nausea, lack of appetite, and vomiting.

The studies of Grace and Graham confirmed the presence of nausea and vomiting in individuals confronted by facts concerning events they wish had never happened.[69] A typical statement by the subjects in their study was, "I wish things were the way they were before." The vomiting appears to correspond to the patient's efforts to restore equilibrium in the face of psychologically painful material.

The problems of diarrhea, especially of a recurring and explosive nature, are closely related to stress. It is not unusual for persons to experience nausea, vomiting or an urgent need to defecate in anticipation of some stressful event. "Butterflies" in the stomach are typical signs of nervous tension.

The colon ordinarily propels fecal contents forward by rhythmic peristaltic (contractile) waves through the right side of the colon and the transverse colon. A sequence of neural events takes place to propel the contents through the descending (left) colon, sigmoid colon, and rectum to the point of evacuation of feces. This sequence of events, called the gastrocolic reflex, is initiated by the presentation of food to the stomach, the transmission of a neural message back to the lower centers of the brain, and the subsequent transmission of a neural message to the efferent (leading away from the brain) autonomic nerves, causing contractions of the colon musculature. This is a somewhat conditioned reflex which can be learned in order to produce defecation at a designated time of day.

Diarrhea occurs when the gastrocolic reflex is too vigorous or occurs too often. The gastrocolic reflex has been shown by Grace and Graham to be likewise excessively provoked by symbolic stimuli in which a reaction of hostility is prominent. Use of the stress interview technique made it possible for the doctors to manipulate colon function and induce the characteristic pattern of the gastrocolic reflex. Patients who experienced recurring and inappropriate diarrhea typically expressed their desire to have things over with. "I wanted to get finished with it" and "I wanted to get done with it" were statements typical of these subjects.

"H. R." is a fifty-six-year-old woman with a history of diarrhea for twelve years. She initially had minor periods of diarrhea, which became persistent at the time her husband retired. She began to feel more and more restricted in her home situation and stifled by her relationship with her husband, whom she perceived as authoritarian, rigid, and demanding. She has been unwilling to work on changing her situation, yet expresses great impatience and hostility in living with things as they are.

The phenomenon of constipation is related to non-propulsive contractions of the descending (left) colon and sigmoid colon which occur in the intervals between activations of the gastrocolic reflex. These contractions, which process fecal material into a formed mass suitable for evacuation, are present in the normal individual not subject to constipation. When the contractions are overdone due to excessive stimulation from the autonomic nerves, the stool may become excessively hard and difficult to move forward. The person subject to severe constipation may be aware of abdominal cramps during this contractile state—a condition known as irritable bowel syndrome. Studies have shown that constipation accompanies an attitude of grim determination to struggle and carry on in the face of seemingly insoluble problems. Retention of feces is thus equivalent to the psychological attitude of "holding on" without quitting.[70]

"A. M." is a seventy-one-year-old woman with a history of worsening constipation for twenty-five years. Her diet appears adequately supplied with bulk-producing foods, and her liquid intake is average. Her exercise pattern is excellent. Her children have matured into productive, understanding adults in whom she takes pride. Her husband is quiet, much less communicative than she, and more concerned about objects than persons. This is a matter of frustration for her, as her husband's traits seem to grow stronger with the passage of time. She has also been disturbed as grandchildren in the family assumed lifestyles inconsistent with hers. They have not fit into the traditional "productivity-and-outstanding-citizen" image which she has valued. Her stance, not verbalized, is that of holding onto her own beliefs amid great social change in her family.

Ulcerative colitis is a colon process in which the mucosal lining becomes inflamed, fragile, swollen and subject to easy bleeding, leading to periods of profuse diarrhea with loss of body fluids. These kinds of changes were observed directly in four patients who had a portion of colonic mucosa temporarily exposed on the skin between surgical procedures.[71] One young subject showed typical inflammatory changes as the result of stress: he was observed to sustain a full-blown attack of ulcerative colitis following a hospital pass and a visit home in which he discovered that his bedroom had been taken over by a sister.

A classic study by Engel relates ulcerative colitis to obsessive-compulsive character traits, including excessive conscientiousness, neatness, indecision, conformity, overintellectualization, rigid morality, and worrying.[72] The disease is often associated with anti-colon antibodies. The demonstration of such antibodies has led several investigators to believe that this may be another auto-immune disease in which the immune system, responding to excessive antigen with insufficient antibody, permits the formation of antigen-antibody complexes which act, in turn, as further potent antigens, stimulating greater antibody formation. The resulting reaction is then accompanied by profound inflammatory changes which may, in advanced stages, result in life-threatening colon infections, bleeding, loss of colon function, and, ultimately, death when surgical intervention is not utilized.

The very common problem of diverticulosis, the formation of small appendix-like projections from the colon which can cause bleeding and perforation, may be related to prolonged and excessive bowel activity, especially the development of increased pressure within the colon, as in irritable bowel syndrome.[73] The excessive bowel activity itself results from the excessive hypothalamic nervous stimulation occurring from life stresses and inflexible response patterns, and from the presence of insufficient bulk in the colon.

H.   GENITOURINARY DISTURBANCES

A common problem I encounter in patients, especially women, is that of fluid retention, or edema. In the vast majority of minor complaints of this sort, I find no organic predisposing causes in the form of heart disease, protein abnormalities, or thyroid disease, and no measurable deficits in kidney function.

Extensive studies have demonstrated two extremes of renal function.[74] Subjects whose emotions are characterized by anxiety or aggressive feelings exhibit marked diuresis, a tendency to rid themselves of excessive amounts of urine. Another group exhibits marked retention of fluid during periods of immobility, withdrawal, depression, or high mental concentration. The magnitude of fluid retention in some cardiac subjects during episodes of depression is so serious as to precipitate signs of congestive heart failure.

The kidney functions controlling the exchange of liquid from the system and urine formation—hence the presence or absence of edema—have been shown to be highly responsive to integrative mental functions at the levels of interpretation, reasoning, and attitudes.[75]

"C. K.", a woman of twenty-five, complained of lethargy, weight gain, and depression. No organic cause of symptoms was found after thorough examination and laboratory studies. A trial of a diuretic medication resulted in a seven-pound weight loss in three days, even though edema had seemed minimal at the time of examination. Some years later, after therapy had permitted her to deal with the tension which precipitated her depression, edema was no longer present.

The control mechanisms whereby excessive tension leads to excessive fluid retention include the hypothalamus, the antidiuretic hormone of the posterior pituitary gland, and the hormones of the adrenal cortex (including aldosterone), which regulate fluid and electrolyte balance in the body.

The problem of uncomfortable or frequent urination is, in my experience, commonly experienced by patients, often without any persuasive evidence of infection or other organic problems of the urinary tract. Increased pain, sensitivity, and urinary frequency have been shown to be associated with engorgement and inflammation of the bladder surface (this can lead to bladder ulcerations with bleeding) and is correlated with periods of frustration, hostility, and resentment, usually unexpressed.[76]

The opposite difficulty, that of excessive urinary retention and inability to empty the bladder, has been linked to life situations when the subject is dominated by intense dejection, discouragement, or fear, which often may be completely repressed.[77]

I. ENDOCRINOLOGICAL DISTURBANCES

The commonness of diabetes, a metabolic condition in which regulation of blood glucose levels is impaired because of decreased insulin secretion, has made it the subject of extensive research. The underlying cause of diabetes still eludes the scientific community. The discovery of antibodies relating to the islet (insulin-producing) cells of the pancreas has led to speculation that an auto-immune reaction with destruction of insulin-producing cells may be present in diabetics. The full implications of this discovery are not clear at this time.

In diabetic subjects whose dietary intake and muscular activity were held constant, episodes of elevation in blood sugar, acidosis, and near coma have been induced by exposing them intentionally to stress-evoking circumstances.[78] Observations of diabetics have also led researchers to conclude from attitudes and patterns of life adjustment that they commonly hold a suppressed conviction of having been starved of maternal love.[79]

Hyperfunction (excessive function) of the thyroid gland has been demonstrated in subjects exposed to stress-evoking life situations.[80] Increases in the measurements of thyroid functioning increased as much as one hundred percent in some patients in as short a space as one hour after the start of a stress interview. The incidence of hyperthyroidism in Norway during the first year of World War II was twice that of the previous year and five times greater than that of 1934. Interestingly enough, the nation of Sweden, neutral during World War II, experienced no such dramatic change.[81]

Impairment of the function of the pituitary-ovarian axis, which controls the menstrual cycle in women, has been observed in stressful circumstances. Amenorrhea, or cessation of menstrual function, occurred in a high percentage of women interned in Nazi prison camps in World War II. In most of those women who survived the imprisonment, normal menstrual cycles resumed after the war was over. The pituitary gland thus appears to be subject to input from those portions of the brain transmitting messages concerning stress and tension.

J. DERMATOLOGICAL DISEASES

D. T. Graham has done research shedding a great deal of light on the origin of hives.[82] In my experience, while I always consider an allergic source as the cause of hives, in about three-quarters of the instances where hives have appeared in a patient, I am unable to adequately explain the onset of the hives by exposure to an environmental allergen.

Graham's experiment involved measuring the resistance of small blood vessels in the skin under various conditions. Initially, a subject's arm was struck with a small paddle. The resistance of the blood vessels to dilation was decreased immediately, and the site of the blow began to redden. This corresponds to the body's beginning of its attempts to supply greater amounts of nutrient chemicals and white blood cells to repair the damage done by the blow. After the subject's arm had returned to normal, the procedure was repeated, except that the paddle was stopped just short of the surface of the skin the second time. In other words, a sham blow was delivered to the arm. Again, the resistance of the tiny blood vessels to dilation was immediately decreased, and the area which would have been struck by the paddle became reddened in just the same fashion as it had before. Gradually, the arm returned to its normal state. The whole procedure was repeated a third time, except that the subject was now told that a sham blow was to be delivered. The arm of the subject so forewarned showed no change in the state of the blood vessels.

Graham describes another set of experiments on a subject predisposed to hives.[83] The subject was struck with a paddle on the forearm. A predictable response was noted: reddening and the formation of a small hive. After the arm had returned to normal, instead of striking the forearm with a paddle, Graham introduced as a topic for discussion a very painful family situation. When the subject was asked about his attitude, he replied that he was "just thinking about the things they did to me." The skin at that point again behaved as if it had actually been struck. Resistance to dilation decreased immediately, and hives developed.

These parallel experiments have been interpreted as meaning that a stressful psychological blow can arouse the same bodily defenses as a physical blow, even though there is no actual physical injury. The subjects in these experiments typically expressed the feeling that they were being mistreated and made statements such as "I was taking a beating" or "My mother was hammering on me." They also expressed the feeling that they were under observation and had no response to make—a feeling one would commonly describe as embarrassment.

Eczema is most often explained as an allergic disease, usually thought to relate to allergens (foreign proteins) introduced into the intestinal tract (via food) or the respiratory tract (via airborne pollens, dust). Studies by Graham and Wolf in 1953 showed a clear-cut time relationship between life events (which the patient recognized as emotionally disturbing) and recurrences of their eczema.[84] Itching, a common symptom, increased while subjects were discussing stressful events in their lives.

Graham's subjects expressed the attitude that they were being interfered with and prevented from doing something, but could think of no way to deal with their frustration. Their scratching appeared to be habitual rather than really triggered by itching—similar to a variety of other tension-relieving activities such as table tapping or foot bobbing.

Neurodermatitis is a skin disorder observed mainly over the extremities. The intense itching associated with it is apparently due to excessive discharge of transmitter chemicals (acetylcholine) in the minute space between the terminus of an autonomic neuron or nerve fiber and the sweat and oil glands in the skin to which the nerve leads. Such transmitter chemicals receive the electrical energy from the nerve cell and transmit it to the exocrine gland. When the autonomic nerve stimulation is excessive, the transmitter chemicals are produced in excessive amounts and irritate the surrounding skin. In many instances, small vesicles or blisters containing tiny amounts of fluid are formed. Again, this contributes to our knowledge of how stress, mental activity, and hypothalamic function, through control of the autonomic nervous system, can help cause or worsen such skin diseases.

"C. C." reported to my office with a complaint of a "skin outbreak"—her hands and fingers showed inflamed areas with flaking skin. The newest lesions showed a tiny blister with an inflamed border. "I try not to scratch it, but it really itches," she said. The picture was typical of neurodermatitis. Knowing me, she suddenly said, "I suppose you'll say it's my nerves." I nodded, and asked what was going on. She revealed feelings of anxiety and frustration as her husband had begun not to come home at night or to be gone until near dawn. The change in her skin coincided with the change in her husband's behavior.

Acne occurs typically among teenagers, but is not limited to that age group. The theories concerning cause of acne have varied throughout the years, and have included emphasis on poor diet and improper skin cleansing. Neither explanation seems in my opinion to be adequate to explain the condition. The actual development of whiteheads and blackheads appears to be related to the quantity of oil secreted in the skin and to the freedom with which it gains access to the surface through the ducts of the glands producing it.

Measurements of the quantity of sebum, or oil, have been performed on acne subjects during periods of relative calm and during intense reactions of anger.[85] The sebum increased between two and five times during the periods of anger. The stressful teenage years, combining rapid hormone changes and the need for adaptation to a more adult life pattern and accommodation to the demands of parents and peers, are a fertile time for development of excess tension. Many of my older acne patients too are aware of the worsening of their skin condition when stress and tension are increased.

K. Neurological Diseases

Epileptic seizures have generally been treated in medical circles with medications designed to raise the seizure threshold, so that the synchronous electrical discharge in the brain which is causing the seizure finds a less susceptible subject. Wayne Barker, in patients with recurrent seizures, was able to correlate worsening attacks with periods of situational conflict which engendered suppressed rage.[86] He also was able to experimentally induce seizures in susceptible subjects by making them submit to a stress interview.

Other neurological diseases, including narcolepsy, multiple sclerosis, and myasthenia gravis, have been thought by some to be subject to improvement or deterioration depending upon alterations in the level of stress in the patient's life.

L. Cancer

Cancer—carcinoma, as it is known in medical circles—is one of the most feared topics in the field of health. Much is known but even more is unknown about the process whereby a cell or group of cells start dividing abnormally and grow to take over the function of surrounding cells, spreading eventually to vital organs and destroying the host itself.

In considering the longevity of the life of the body and reviewing the statistics relating to longevity, one quickly discovers that cancer is one of the significant factors in shortened life expectancy. Except between birth and age five and between ages fifteen to twenty-five, cancer is a leading cause of death in nations which keep careful statistical records. In total causes of death, it ranks second only to arteriosclerotic cardiovascular disease (strokes, heart attacks, and arterial disease).

The cause of cancer is as yet unknown. Three theories have predominated in recent years. The first is the virus theory. Many or most varieties of cancer, some medical experts contend, are caused by the invasion of a virus whose DNA (deoxyribonucleic acid) system takes over the function of a normal cell, eventually inducing changes in surrounding cells and becoming the start of a cancerous growth. There is evidence from research that certain viruses can induce tumors in experimental animals.

The second theory infers a statistical relationship between cancer and chemicals, poisons, and pollutants in the environment. The marked increase in a specific type of lung cancer in persons who work with asbestos has been well documented. A rare type of liver cancer has begun to be reported among workers who handle certain plastic and chemical substances. The incidence of cancer on a map of the United States so drawn as to indicate a county-by-county rate of cancer is visibly concentrated in industrialized counties or those associated with high levels of potentially toxic chemicals used in farming and mining.

The third theory regards the relationship of stress, tension, and negative emotions to cancer. For the last several years, the annual meetings of the American Cancer Society have contained records of papers submitted by researchers contending that attitudes of passivity, hopelessness, helplessness, and self-effacement may render persons cancer-prone.

One interesting investigative phenomenon in cancer studies is the unexpected survival of a small group of patients whose cancer has been documented. Many surgeons who have practiced for a number of years can recall one or two cancer patients whose tumor appeared to be non-removable at the time of surgery: since the malignancy is too advanced to be removed, it is biopsied and the wound closed. Confirmation of the presence of malignant disease in these cases is made by pathological examination of tissue removed at the time of surgery and biopsy. In these amazing cases—much to the surprise of the family, the patient, and often the physician as well—the patient, instead of surviving a few months or weeks as anticipated, lives on and on, apparently cured of disease and requiring no additional treatment. Some of these patients have been subjected to reoperation, either to confirm the absence of malignancy or for other diseases. The second operation in these patients shows complete disappearance of the original cancerous growth. The astonishing survival of this small number of patients has been the subject of great research interest. The explanation for this phenomenon is no more well understood by scientists than is the secret of the origin and continuation of the cancerous growth itself.

David Kissen concluded in a paper in 1964 that cigarette smoking and a certain personality type both appear to be involved in the development of lung cancer.[87] He found that the less adequate the outlet for emotional discharge, the greater the chance that cigarette smoking will induce lung cancer.[88] His lung cancer victims tended to be unable or unwilling to express emotions, consciously concealing or bottling up their emotional difficulties rather than talking them over with someone.

In a prospective study, Dr. Kissen found that lung cancer patients reported more adverse circumstances in adulthood, less rise in emotional response to those situations, and a higher incidence in their childhood of the death of a parent or an unhappy home situation when compared to control subjects.[89] The adverse adulthood problems tended to relate to work and interpersonal difficulties, particularly marital strife of long standing.

Bahnson concludes that there is ample evidence in many cancer patients that a traumatic loss or separation during adulthood mounts a devastating effect on the patient, echoing the early despair experienced by the child in relationship to its parents. Thomas and Duszynski also found a striking relationship between malignant disease and lack of closeness to parents in childhood.[90] Persons who are cancer-prone, Bahnson infers, have primitive but unsatisfying relationships with their parents, with many years of rehearsal tolerating an ungratifying reality, and then try to maintain in adulthood an equitable and realistic relationship to society. The cancer-prone person does not seem to show any regression in behavior when faced with stress, other than turning emotionally inward. The negative consequences are then applied to his own body instead of being cathected outwardly in terms of emotional expression in society.[91]

Bahnson describes this process in the following way. An individual encounters a change in his environment in which the loss of an important object or person occurs. An experiential phenomenon then occurs within the individual. Stimulation of the hypothalamus and areas of the surrounding primitive brain, resulting from the perceived stress, may be associated with a reduced psychobiological defense. This may occur on the basis of the body's control of the immune mechanism as discussed in the previous subchapter on factors in resistance. Changes then occurring through the autonomic nervous system controlled by the hypothalamus, hormonal changes in the adrenal glands controlled by the pituitary and hypothalamus, and biochemical reactions in the immune system all interact with bio-organisms, possibly viruses, resulting in the production of a malignancy.

Bahnson postulates that the experiential phenomenon of despair or depression that results from the perceived loss varies greatly from one individual to the next. Characteristically, a majority of cancer patients fail to show the reality-distorting aspects of the mourning process, stoically maintaining their life routines unaltered throughout the process, as if to deny the impact of the loss.

Kidd[92] and Sommers[93] have suggested that latent cancer cells are often present within body tissues, and that their sudden proliferation may be a function of the diminished immune resistance at any given time. Evidence is accumulating that resistance to cancer is indeed immunologic in nature.[94] The evidence that the host may also react against tumor-specific antigens is also impressive.[95]

LeShan and Worthington found four consistent factors in personality studies on cancer patients: the loss of an important relationship prior to the development of the malignancy, inability to express hostile emotions, unresolved tension concerning a parent, and sexual disturbances.[96] The latter was considered a major cause of cancer by Dr. Wilhelm Reich and his followers.[97] Klopfer related prolonged survival of cancer patients either to a successful denial of reality or, more rarely, to a mature, calm acceptance of reality; he related short survival in cancer patients to excessive defensiveness with a high degree of subjective distress.[98]

Other postulated mechanisms by which the psyche may influence cancer will now be considered.

The constriction of the small arterioles, discussed in the section on high blood pressure, may slow down the blood flow through these vessels, permitting an easier escape of circulating tumor cells through the lining of the blood vessels into surrounding tissues. More rapid clotting of the blood, influenced by adrenal gland hormones, increases the probability that circulating tumor cells will be trapped in small clots and adhere to and penetrate capillary walls.

Assuming that immune mechanisms maintaining a constant surveillance of the body cells play a significant role in resistance to the spread of cancer, the known influence of adrenal steroids (hydrocortisone) to suppress immune responses may be a very important factor in certain stress situations. The tendency of the adrenal's cortisone chemicals to suppress the activity of the white blood cells in order to destroy foreign invaders and to suppress as well the accompanying acute inflammatory reaction is also significant, since the adrenal cortex activity is controlled by the hypothalamus, in turn influenced by mental processes. In certain animal malignancies, the estrogen and progesterone hormones significantly affect the progress of the cancerous virus. These hormones are also controlled, at least in part, by the hypothalamus in mammals.[99]

Studies have shown that cancer of the cervix in women occurs most frequently in patients who are highly motivated to sexual activity but are prevented from achieving orgasm by an inordinate need for autonomy.[100] Cancer of the prostate in males is especially frequent in cultural groups in which the men frequently engage in lovemaking without actual coitus.[101] The increased incidence of breast cancer has been related to a decrease in the practice of breast-feeding in the last several decades.

The Surgeon General's 1964 cancer report related the incidence of lung cancer and tuberculosis to a high rate of migration, urbanization, and socio-economic deprivation. Cancer of the stomach is definitely related to poverty, the report declared. Currently it is one-half as common as it was at the height of the Depression in 1930.

It is pointed out by Boothe that there is no cancer among the Ute Indians, a population whose tuberculosis-prone members died out when the tribe lost its freedom in the 1800s. Boothe believes that of those persons possibly genetically predisposed to cancer, the loss of an important object relationship is experienced as an irrevocable blow to their need for rigid unilateral control over their objects, resulting in a conscious or unconscious depression which is then somatized in the form of a malignancy.[102]

Simonton, a radiation therapist, believes that cancerogenic (cancer-producing) viruses are experienced by all of us many times during our lifetime. It is his belief that each of us resists these cancer-producing viruses for the most part, but that on rare occasions the factors in our surveillance system (resistance and immunity) are somehow decreased, rendering us susceptible to their invasion into our system.[103] (Further reference to Dr. Simonton's work is made in Section III.)

M. Pain

Pain is a prominent factor in many of the disease syndromes discussed in previous parts of this chapter. Pain is the unpleasant sensation experienced as a result of injury, disease states, or emotional disorders, resulting in suffering or distress on the part of the organism. Anti-pain medications, like other groups of drugs, are commonly prescribed by physicians to reduce awareness of pain. Pain plays a prominent role in many of the syndromes of distress which, at one time or another, require patients to be hospitalized. It also plays a prominent role in the syndromes which cause people to lose time from work and productive activity. Pain, for instance, is usually listed as the major reason why patients suffering back injuries in industrial accidents fail to return to work. Fully forty percent of those workers suffering from such injuries fail to return to employment and remain chronically disabled. Between fifty and seventy-five percent of the medical costs of workmen's compensation goes toward treating persons having chronic pain as a result of accidents.[104]

Pain is a means by which important data is conveyed to the centers of sensation and thought; thus, the purpose of the pain mechanism is to protect ourselves from further injury. The individual who touches a hot stove, because of the sensation of pain, quickly responds with withdrawal of his hand.

My observation concerning the pain threshold (the level of sensation which in any given individual arouses the feeling termed pain) is that the establishment of the pain threshold originates in early childhood. Newborns are endowed with certain basic awarenesses of painful stimuli and are supplied with a primitive system to begin to cope with those stimuli. Thus, the infant cries when he experiences hunger and pulls away his leg when a misplaced diaper pin jabs it.

I have always been impressed with the fact that some persons tolerate pain extremely well and others very poorly. I find that pain is poorly tolerated when the tension level is excessively high, and much better tolerated when the tension level is within manageable limits. One can often observe two children side by side, subjected to the same injury: one will protest long and loudly as the result of experiencing great pain, while the other seems to experience little pain. The total pain experience is in large measure a learned response, supplementing basic instinctual patterns with which we are endowed at birth.

In addition to these factors, pain is significantly intertwined with emotional experience. Psychologists speak of the secondary gains afforded by experiences of pain and other similar phenomena, by which they mean that a person subject to pain may discover numerous rewards in that experience. Thus, a woman may find that experiencing pain enables her to avoid sexual intercourse with an undesirable partner. She may learn that in this way she gains the secondary benefits of controlling her situation and escaping from an unpleasant experience she is otherwise unable to deal with.

The pain experience may also be a self-limiting adaptation to escaping a difficult job situation. I have had one male patient who conditioned himself to escape the wrath of his boss by developing painful abdominal cramps and diarrhea at stressful times, whereupon he retired to the lavatory. Likewise, painful stomach aches have been known to conveniently enable a child to avoid unpleasantness at school.

Bodily injury due to accidents, illnesses, or surgery of course causes pain. Such a stress demands an adaptive response from the system. If an individual's tension level is already high, it will rise even higher with the onset of injury, causing more distress.

Pain always seems to be aggravated by other stressful stimuli. A chronic headache sufferer will, for example, cope with the situation fairly well until there is significant stress in his marital relationship or the threat of some change in his employment status. Studies by Graham showed that pain in peripheral tissues (fingers) depended not only upon the decreasing skin circulation induced by low environmental temperatures, but also was significantly affected by the distress and consequent feedback stress of severe anxiety and anger.[105]

Studies in one experimental subject demonstrated a lowered pain threshold in the stomach (with typical hunger pains of peptic ulcer even when no ulcer was present) during a period of sustained emotional conflict.[106] Ongoing family disturbances often arouse pain. A patient of mine with a pattern of chronic headache and dizziness realized after charting the events in her life that her headache pattern worsened each time she was upset by what she considered unacceptable behavior in her teenage child. In her case, a destructive cycle was perpetuated by the teenager, who recognized that his control of a situation could be enhanced by incapacitating his mother with pain whenever he engaged in errant behavior or threatened to do so.

Chronic pain syndromes, in my experience, nearly always are intertwined with some aspect of negative emotional expression. At least one of the following states is usually present in persons with chronic pain problems: depression, anger, anxiety, fear, feelings of worthlessness, or paranoid distortions. It is most difficult to ascertain which may come first—the injury and initiating source of painful stimuli, or the emotional climate of the individual subjected to the painful stimulus. In any event, successful treatment of the pain itself appears virtually impossible unless these negative emotional states are also dealt with.

A variety of approaches for dealing with stress and excessive tension will be discussed in detail in Section III of this book. Many of these same approaches are applicable to pain. We will also discuss there the outstanding ability of certain individuals to deal with pain successfully via internal adaptive mechanisms, the potential for which is present in all individuals at all times.

N. Fatigue and Lethargy

These are among the most common complaints of patients. Rarely is any organic cause found for these symptoms. A sense of being tired and a feeling of lack of energy are probably experienced by everyone at some point in their lives. We know, for instance, that prolonged physical activity exhausts ready supplies of energy within the system and leads to awareness of great exhaustion and tiredness. The broader question, however, is why so many people experience symptoms of fatigue when they have *not* engaged in any great physical exertion or activity.

Many theories have been advanced to explain these symptoms. One certainty is that the energy transfer systems within the chemistry of each body cell must be supplied with adequate nutrients in order to accomplish their energy-transferring function properly. Energy within the body is the ability to accomplish work and to maintain body temperature. As nutrients are absorbed from food, they are chemically changed into forms that can be absorbed within the working cells of the body. When these nutrients are absorbed and chemically combined in various ways with oxygen in the system, the process called oxidation supplies immediate forms of energy. Energy may also be built up and stored by the conversion of low-energy-storage chemical compounds to high-energy-storage compounds. In this way, it can be kept in reserve and made available for use later on by the reconversion to low-energy compounds, which release the stored energy.

All of these chemical reactions require certain chemicals to cause or permit the reactions to take place. These chemicals are catalysts (enzymes), coenzymes (vitamins), and mineral activators. In the main, these chemicals are not actually used up in the chemical reactions, but a deficiency in the catalysts, coenzymes, or mineral activators means that energy transfers take place with less than ideal efficiency and frequency. Adequate protein, vitamins (especially the B-complex vitamins), trace minerals (manganese, magnesium, copper, zinc), and iron are especially important in the proper transfer of energy.

Chronic feelings of exhaustion may also be associated with lack of physical reserve. It seems to make a great deal of difference whether activities such as housecleaning, lawn mowing, or walking short distances are the maximum amounts of exertion experienced or whether activities requiring considerably greater amounts of exertion are undertaken at other times. Personally, I sense much greater energy levels for everyday activities during periods when I am exercising regularly and up to my full physical capacity. The reserve available for activities requiring less than maximum exertion seems much better when energy has been maintained at a high level by strenuous and regular activities or exercise.

I find it very interesting to speculate about what parts of ourselves appear naturally to have the most energy. In terms of transactional analysis, it seems to me that the Child ego-state harbors the most energy. Vigorous and spontaneous expression of energy seems far less typical of Adult and Parent states. This correlates well with the experience of many of my tired and exhausted patients, who usually involve themselves in dutiful Adult and Parent activities nearly to the exclusion of the Child's pleasure-oriented activities.

I personally experienced this phenomenon several years ago when I became aware that my energy level on Monday, Tuesday, Thursday, and Friday mornings was much lower than it was on Wednesday. During that time, I was taking Wednesdays off to hike and fish in the summer and ski in the winter. My spontaneous Child's anticipation of enjoyable activities on Wednesdays determined my high energy level on those days. This was in marked contrast to the Parent and Adult activities which occupied most of my other time, during which a feeling of lower energy prevailed.

I have also observed that energy levels drop when we get into a rut. Repetitive, tedious activities generate emotional feelings which erode our energy level. Industries have discovered over the last several decades that coffee breaks and variety in assignments increase workers' energy and productivity.

Excessive tension decreases energy levels in several ways. First, the tension itself is related to such self-destructive habits as lack of exercise and inadequate nutrition. Second, excessive tension induces those predominantly negative emotions—depression, sadness, anger, fear, anxiety, and guilt—which drag down the energy level, while happiness and joy are reflected in high energy levels. The hypothalamic responses to excessive tension include the expending of large sums of energy in unhealthy responses of the autonomic nervous system—abnormal and rapid heart rates, hyperventilation, excessive and painful muscle contractions, or overactivity of the intestinal tract, for example. The autonomic nervous system may also decrease energy by excessive stimulation of nerve pathways leading to the pancreas from the hypothalamus, increasing insulin output and lowering blood sugar levels to a point where proper mental and physical functioning are not possible.

Experiments have shown that the amount of lactic acid present in the system is higher in states of fatigue than it is in normal states. It is also present in excessive amounts in persons with high anxiety levels, and fatigue and exhaustion are commonly seen together with anxiety. Conversely, lactic acid has been shown to be greatly decreased in states of relaxation.[107]

Excessive tension may interrupt a rewarding sleep cycle. The distressing emotions associated with exhaustion or even sleepiness during waking hours are paradoxically associated with sleeplessness during nighttime hours. "I wake up more (or as) tired as when I went to bed" is a typical statement of the exhausted patient. Such a person finds it difficult to relax, even during a rest period.

An automobile whose engine is never actually started yet whose ignition is left turned on will soon be found to have exhausted its reserve of battery power, and therefore cannot move. Human beings, like cars, remain charged with energy when they keep moving; they are restored when they rest properly. If, however, they are constantly tense and in a state of anxious expectation, their systems are "turned on" but run down eventually because their energy outlets are blocked. Tiredness, exhaustion, and fatigue, then, are clearly related to a state of excessive tension within the system.

Chapter 4

EMOTIONAL DISTRESS

A brief and universally applicable definition of emotion is difficult to give. Great confusion has arisen in medical and psychological circles because of the seemingly close association between overt emotional disturbances and physiological dysfunction. One widely accepted but erroneous proposition persists, namely that emotions are the *cause* of bodily reactions. Clearly, however, an emotion is a *symptom* or *manifestation* of the way an individual's system handles tension. Chapter 12 in Section II will shed more light on this confusing question.

Some authorities equate an emotion with an internal sensation which may be pleasant (positive) or unpleasant (negative). Internal sensations of physical states should be excluded from this definition. One way to separate the two is to refer to an emotion as a feeling state.

Emotions may also be looked upon as functioning but often repressed aspects of the interpretation of one's life experience. Bodily changes, however, appear to result from the system's total conscious and unconscious evaluation of the life experience, which occurs with or without the experience of emotions or the expression of the feeling state.

The best working definition of an emotion, then, would probably be that it is a feeling state occurring because of one's conscious or unconscious interpretation of a life experience.

This chapter on emotional distress deals with functional states associated with unpleasantness, that is, when negative emotions predominate.

Fear, anxiety, depression, sadness, anger, disgust, helplessness, and guilt are emotions or feeling states experienced by nearly all persons at one time or another. When we experience our feeling state as rooted predominantly in one of these emotions, or when there is a lack of balance with positive feeling states, emotional distress exists. For the most part, the disturbances discussed here can be classified as neuroses.

A.   ANXIETY, FEAR, AND PANIC

Anxiety neurosis is a very common condition characterized by a state of uneasiness and distress about uncertain, non-specific, or vague threats. Worry, by contrast, usually involves a specifically identifiable threat.

Adapting Plutchick's classification of emotions, fear and anxiety exist in the same emotional spectrum, fear being severe and anxiety milder.[1] Panic describes an extreme state of fear.

Anxiety generally has specific antecedents, though much of the time these are not consciously identifiable. It is associated with a wide spectrum of physical symptoms—pounding heart, dry mouth, sweaty palms, blushing skin, shortness of breath, upset stomach, nausea, vague feelings of unsteadiness or faintness, and choking. Patients complaining of the latter symptom, where nothing organically abnormal can be found in the throat or larynx, are known to every physician. (Interestingly enough, the word "anxiety" comes from the Latin *angere*, "to choke".) All of the above-mentioned physical symptoms accompanying anxiety indicate that the body is in a way "choking" from the excessive presence of emotion. Negative emotions are clearly a response to disturbing information presented to the system (whether or not that information reaches consciousness), as affected by will, desire, and motivation.

I see a great number of patients who present with physical complaints in which accompanying manifestations of anxiety and fear are clearly apparent, or who present with that vague uneasiness that we call anxiety, unaccompanied by specific physical symptoms. They often describe a sense of shaking inside, a fear of impending disaster, a sense of panic about a certain situation (phobia), a restlessness within the limbs or trunk of the body, or simply "nervousness."

High levels of stress and tension are undoubtedly present when anxiety is manifest. It is extremely common for a patient to tell me, "I don't have anything to be anxious about." Yet while such a patient is usually being honest as far as his conscious awareness is concerned, the sources of stress within his unconscious sphere contain stimuli as potent as those within his consciousness.

B. ANGER, HATRED, AND RESENTMENT

The spectrum of angry emotions is experienced by everyone. So common a group of emotions would seem to pose no specific problems. When experienced in excessive amounts, however, hatred, resentment, and anger can be quite debilitating. Such negative emotions are fed back through the system in the form of a wide range of physical symptoms. "Certainly, for every patient, his prompt and full appreciation of the truly poisonous and destructive nature of hate, resentment, jealousy, frustration, envy and fear is of crucial importance," Dr. Harold Wolff has stated.[2]

The many physical distresses related to attitudes of hostility and too great anger have been mentioned in Chapter 3. I often observe aggravation of distressing physical states—including diarrhea, migraine and muscle contraction headache, hypertension, diabetes, ulcerative colitis, and all manner of bodily malfunctions where pain is a factor—when anger soars out of control.

Missildine describes the angry personality as one having a tendency to fly into temper outbursts and to act impulsively. Such an individual frequently infringes on the feelings and rights of others; they are usually involved in dictatorial interpersonal relationships in which the mutuality of interpersonal problems is not recognized. In addition, persons with impulsive behavior frequently are unable to move consistently toward their adult goals. Over-submissiveness by parents often lurks in the childhood background of such aggressive individuals.[3]

C. Depression

Depression is best viewed as a complex of emotions including anxiety, fear, anger, and sadness. Deckert feels that depression always incorporates some elements of all these primary emotions.[4]

In recent years it has become apparent that depression is possibly the most serious emotional problem of our times, while also being one of the least understood. The National Institute of Mental Health has published statistics indicating that eight million people per year in the United States alone may suffer depression severe enough to be reported to a physician. In 1972, more than one-quarter of a million Americans were hospitalized for depression. Of great significance, of course, is the frequent outcome of serious depression in the form of suicide. Estimates of suicidal death in the United States range up to fifty thousand per year. Some surveys show that one out of every two people acknowledges depression in themselves at least some of the time.

The bodily manifestations of depression include insomnia, appetite changes, restlessness, inability to concentrate, crying spells, headaches and backaches, nausea and vomiting, constipation, and accumulation of fluid in the tissues. Numerous references also point out the possible relationship between chemical changes in the body, including hypoglycemia, and the activation of feelings of depression.[5]

To borrow a phrase from transactional analysis, the depressed person exists in an "I'm not O.K." state. It is probably based upon a replay of old memory tapes in which the child felt powerless in relationship to his parents.[6] Interestingly enough, while depression is commonly experienced in reaction to events associated with loss or the threat of loss, it may also be experienced after events which society recognizes as signs of success, such as a business promotion, the birth of a baby, or an outstanding achievement or award. Thus, the depression is related to the amount of excess tension evoked by stressful stimulus, whether that stimulus is positive or negative.

D.   FEELINGS OF HELPLESSNESS AND INADEQUACY

The sense of self-worth is established by the age of five and one-half in the internal speech developed up to that time.[7] It is established by parental models who have demonstrated: (1) total acceptance, care, concern, attention and interest, affection, and a calm, assured demeanor; (2) definable apparent limits; (3) latitude for dissent and individual expression; and (4) a sense of high self-esteem on the part of the parental models themselves. Feelings of inadequacy and helplessness commonly result when positive regard for a child is insufficient or lacking.[8] Over-coercion, over-indulgence, neglect, and rejection by parents leave children with feelings of a lack of resources and painful loneliness.

Deficient ego-strength (self-esteem) is linked with many physical distress states, among them cancer and poor immunologic response. Bahnson established the feeling of despair (hopelessness and helplessness) as a common characteristic of cancer-prone patients.[9] This effect may be mediated through the immune response mechanism (see Chapter 3, subchapter L).

Patients with below-average self-esteem were noted to take much longer to recover from infectious mononucleosis, for example, as compared to patients having average or high self-esteem.[10] This is also linked with a decreased response of the immune system acting in surveillance or defense of the body against foreign invaders.

E.   GUILT

Guilt may be viewed as the emotional distress resulting from continual external or internal demands for attainment of certain high standards, when those standards fail to be met in actual accomplishment. Guilt frequently implies an extra degree of sensitivity to or awareness of one's own shortcomings, often linked with perfectionism. The pattern of self-blaming includes continual comparisons between higher and lower levels of performance. It may result in wasted hours of mental reconsideration of something one has said, done, or thought.[11] Thus, huge sums of time and energy from the pool of energy available to an individual are dissipated.

Fritz Perls considers guilt as intertwined with resentment.[12] To deal with the resentment, allowing it to escape, and to deal with the perceived demands relating to the guilt, may bring resolution of such feelings.

Guilt feelings can accompany many physical distresses. For example, in cases of lupus erythematosus an unusual need for activity and independence has been identified. This behavior is considered a denial of the guilt-provoking wish for maternal closeness.[13]

Chapter 5

MENTAL DISTRESS

We have previously examined certain distresses called neuroses in which aspects of thinking, feeling, and behaving become abnormal. The layman's term "nervous breakdown" may apply to distresses which therapists call neuroses or, in more severe cases psychoses. In the latter, the sufferer has lost some of his ability to interpret reality. (The differences between individuals in terms of belief about their own reality will be discussed in later chapters.)

The commonest forms of psychotic behavior include depression or melancholia, in which there is a degree of loss of contact with reality; manic disease, in which the patient experiences episodes of euphoria and manifests overactive, highly stimulated behavior; and schizophrenia, in which the patient lives in his own fantasy world, having bizarre beliefs about himself and others which are unrelated to the reality experienced by others.

When tension levels become excessive, retreat into psychotic behavior in a way serves as a defense for the patient. I have said previously that the system works incessantly to keep tension within manageable limits. In the case of psychotic behavior, extreme measures are required to achieve that end.

Those measures include forms of behavior and thinking that deny reality. The tendency for those predisposed to psychotic illness, in my own experience, is clearly related to life stresses and consequent increasing tension, coupled with an inability of the system to keep that tension within manageable limits.

Obsessive and compulsive behavior also functions in a defensive way by permitting tension to find outlets in a series of harmless repetitive thoughts or gestures instead of being channeled into problem-producing anxiety. The mechanisms whereby excessive tension is diverted into compulsive thinking or obsessive behavior from a source which would otherwise cause unacceptable anxiety are usually unconscious.

The perfectionism resulting from being conditioned to strive for excellence leads to a pressured existence for the person so afflicted. Parental reminders to do better and try harder remain in the system as internalized commands and foster a methodical, strenuous approach to detail, often to the point of exhaustion.[1] The simple fact, of course, is that nobody is perfect. This conflict alone—"Be perfect" versus "No one can be perfect"—is sufficient to generate potentially intolerable tension.

The perfectionist feels uncomfortable if he does not try hard. Since his rewards and positive strokes in childhood came from accomplishment, he believes that if he tries hard enough, he will finally be able to accomplish enough (perfectly, of course) to get the recognition and acceptance he craves. He withholds approval from himself because of his constant feeling of not having accomplished enough. Ironically, the perfectionist who has achieved everything on his list will often compulsively add more to it so he can continue to strive hard.

Hysterical reactions, generated from the tension of conflicting motives, may be a means of working out that tension, thus avoiding an anxiety-producing result. Hysterical reactions can take the form of a sudden inability to move a limb, tremors or spasms afflicting a group of muscles in the upper torso or limbs, symptoms of false pregnancy, pain, deafness, blindness, or sleep. They may also be responsible for the loss of a sense of smell or taste, loss of the voice, or of the ability to swallow. Again, the source of conflict exists at an unconscious level and is frequently unrecognized and denied by the patient at the level of consciousness.

Another manifestation of mental distress occurs when mental functioning is blocked in terms of decreased memory. (I am not referring here to severe memory disturbances, which can be signs of psychoses.) The nature of memory and the definition of it in higher mammals has been a subject for speculation and experimentation by scientists for centuries. The experiments of Dr. Wilder Penfield, a neurosurgeon in Montreal, over a period of fifteen years, have shed great light on the nature of memory and will be considered in Chapter 7.

In my own experience, it is extremely common for a patient to come to me listing a series of complaints that include the problem of decreased memory. I rarely find any organic cause. I have correlated most of these cases with a recent increase in stress and a resulting excessive level of tension. In most instances, when tension returns to a manageable limit, the memory problems disappear.

All of us have experienced the immediate effect of tension when attempting to remember the names of two individuals whom we are introducing, one to the other. The tension seems to result from the conflict over recalling the name of each person (whom we may actually know well) versus the social censure we believe to be present if we fail to remember their names. The level of tension may be sufficiently high to then upset the recollection mechanism.

Chapter 6

SELF-DESTRUCTIVE HABITS

Habits are the result of conditioning to a set of stimuli over a period of days, weeks, months, or years, resulting eventually in a stereotyped and unconscious series of electrochemical events within the system leading to an emotional experience and/or to a muscular or glandular response. Most habits, if traced to their origins, begin with some type of conscious response. As time progresses, the shortest pathways are found through the brain substance to transmit the energy from the initiating impulse to the areas of the brain which control the output response. Also as time progresses, the initiation and continuation of this chain of electrochemical events within the brain and spinal cord require less and less conscious attention and eventually become unconscious responses. When the pattern of response becomes completely unconscious, we call it a habit.

A good example of habit formation is the case of a five-year-old learning to ride a bicycle. Initially, he has some vague idea of how to proceed, having watched others riding bicycles. He then puts his idea into action one step at a time, consciously weighing each of the steps necessary to eventually become an accomplished bicycle rider. He grips the handlebars, puts one foot on a pedal, swings his other leg over the seat, pushes himself forward, and begins to pedal. All of these events contribute to his experience, which is fed back to him in terms of moving forward, balancing or not balancing, and the muscular effort required of his lower limbs. At some point, he will experience failure, including falling off the bicycle and perhaps even injuring himself. He connects this failure with something he has or has not done and resumes riding with the aim of consciously correcting the particular bit of behavior which resulted in his fall. After much repetition, he makes the proper electrochemical connections through the brain. These become more and more automatic as the energy discovers its pathway through the brain by gradually making chemical changes in the double helix DNA (deoxyribonucleic acid) molecule of the control center of each neuron's nucleus as the energy is received. It is these keys in the DNA which appear to be the determinants for the pathway and transmission of the electrical energy in such a way that a predictable output in the motor cortex results from a consistent input.

Thus, over a period of days and weeks, the youngster becomes more and more facile and coordinated in riding his bicycle. Finally, he is able, without any conscious thought, to merely initiate the process of riding and to devote his field of consciousness to other matters entirely, carrying out, in a very stereotyped and habit-based way, his cycling activity.

Overeating, leading to problems of overweight and obesity, is an example of the exaggeration of a life habit responding to the instinctual drive for self-survival. Experiments in animals and humans reveal that there exist, in the old brain adjacent to the hypothalamus, two centers relating to hunger and satisfaction. These two centers are stimulated in sequence: the hunger center is stimulated by chemical changes within the system, including blood sugar levels and the levels of certain hormones. As a result of this stimulation, we seek food to eliminate the distressing feelings of hunger in the abdomen and elsewhere. Once food is taken into the system, the blood sugar level rises and the associated hormone changes are turned off, with a resulting stimulation of the satisfaction center, which decreases stimulation of the hunger center, in turn causing us to stop eating.

The normal hunger-food-satisfaction cycle can be adversely affected from energy input from the neocortex or higher brain centers. These centers are capable of responding to such sensory data as the attractive appearance of food in magazines and television advertising; past conditioning influences, such as the obligatory eating of one's mother-in-law's cooking or the gourmet fare offered by the boss's wife; and to other influences of the limbic brain, including boredom, anger, loneliness, and anxiety. In the latter instances, these inputs or demands on the system upset the balance of the hunger-food-satisfaction cycle and, depending on one's internal state, may raise tension to more than comfortably manageable levels. When this happens, the system seeks to solve the excessive level of tension in the direction offered by the combination of hereditary factors, past conditioning, and present awareness which offers the most relief.

Overweight, then, obviously results from the tipping of the scales in the direction of solving the excessive tension by eating more than is necessary to merely supply the physical body with sufficient calories for maintenance of body temperature and expenditure of physical energy. This response frequently has a history which extends back into childhood, typically involving parental injunctions to be "good" by cleaning up one's plate.

Several examples of overweight patients whom I have worked with will illustrate this negative response. One patient recalled that when she was five or six years old her mother urged her to eat heartily in order not to become sickly, like a skinny cousin. The mother was thus perpetuating the myth that slimness is a sign of disease.

Another patient recalled the experience while she was ten or eleven years old of seeing her mother grow emaciated due to the presence of a malignancy. She even recalled making a conscious decision, having linked her mother's thinness with illness, that she would never permit herself to be in the same situation.

An overweight man recalled that his father used to tell him repeatedly that he must eat his meat, spinach, potatoes, and gravy in order to grow up to be strong. One can easily see how this idea that size equals power continues to exert a strong influence in the form of a persistent habit of overeating.

In addition to the "clean plate" syndrome previously mentioned, many adults eat inappropriate quantities of food as if recalling a parent's guilt-provoking statement that "It isn't fair for you to waste food when there are starving children in India." In some cases, excessive food is indirectly forced on children as a prerequisite for having desserts. In still other instances, having the stomach filled with food seems to be a substitute for having emotional needs fulfilled through warm contacts and affection from parents.

The medical significance of overweight has been pointed out by a research project undertaken by the Methodist Hospital in Indianapolis.[1] This study indicates that overweight plays a measurable role in many diseases, including heart trouble. The results indicated that the likelihood of death from heart disease increased about two percent for each ten percent increase over ideal weight. In fact, longest life survival with heart disease was best correlated with being ten percent underweight. This probably means that the normal weight tables which we have been using for several decades are really ten percent over truly ideal norms.

The solution to excessive tension which eating offers is, of course—as are all self-destructive habits—only a short-term answer. Indeed, many overweight patients tell me that quickly on the heels of the tension reduction that comes with eating is an increase in tension in the form of guilt. In Section III, I shall discuss means of increasing awareness of short- and long-term goals and of what is happening when we overeat without realizing it.

A beautiful example of the unconscious association of weight and the desire for strength appears in *The Masculine Principle—The Feminine Principle and Humanistic Medicine*.[2] A life-threatening case of obesity is presented in which "Harold", an obese teenager, was followed for several years by his physician. The obesity was so gross that it threatened to lead to heart failure. The boy finally came to a basic positive decision regarding himself, gained gradual understanding of unconscious factors and accomplished weight loss with the help of his physician.

Improper nutrition is as self-destructive as habitual over-eating. The essential amino acids (essential because the body is unable to build its protein chemicals without them) are supplied in protein form in most Western countries largely through fish, poultry, and animal meats. Vegetable sources of protein have generally been neglected until recent years. One apparent reason why vegetable proteins may be as good as or better than animal proteins is that animal protein sources in the form of meats are usually prepared through long periods of cooking at high temperatures. American cooking techniques—broiling, for example—tend to degrade the chemical structure of the protein, in this way destroying some of the meat's value. Vegetables are usually prepared more quickly (brief steaming being better than boiling in water) and are frequently consumed in their raw state, thus preserving more nutrients.

Many arguments have been advanced in recent years for the use of vegetable rather than animal fats in the diet. It appears to be true that a diet which emphasizes polyunsaturated fats, particularly found in vegetables, rather than polysaturated fats and oils from animal sources is a healthy one. The is especially important for persons who have elevated cholesterol levels. The average American diet contains approximately forty percent fat. The fat content of the diet in areas of the world where many American metabolic and degenerative disease problems are absent is in the range of ten to fifteen percent.

Many American diets are too high in carbohydrates and sugars. In the United States, between the late 1800s and the 1960s, the pattern of carbohydrate consumption changed radically.[3] During this time, there was a fifty-four percent reduction in intake of complex carbohydrates and a fifty percent increase in use of simple sugars. The elevation of serum triglycerides (a serum fat related to proneness to arteriosclerosis) is known to be related to both a high alcohol intake and a high carbohydrate intake, particularly simple sugars. Clearly the American diet could benefit from a reduction in the percentage of carbohydrate intake, especially of simple sugars, and from a greater reliance on unrefined carbohydrate sources for a significant portion of dietary calories. Taking in more of our foodstuffs in raw form, as fruits and vegetables, would provide the added advantage of bulk in the diet in forms that would seem to be of benefit in preventing diverticulosis and irritable bowel syndrome.

Vitamin supplements, particularly those including a variety of essential minerals including trace minerals, may be necessary if the diet does not contain sufficient amounts of freshly prepared vegetables and fruits. In only rare instances is the taking of vitamins a problem, since most of the vitamins commonly available contain high amounts of vitamins B and C, which are water-soluble. Generally, multivitamins contain limited amounts of vitamins A and D, in which overdosage is a rare but theoretical possibility if suggested amounts are exceeded.

Since the introduction of tobacco to America in the 1600s, the habit of smoking has reached a peak in this century. Indeed, in spite of the known malignant nature of the smoking habit and in spite of the warnings issued as a result of the Surgeon General's report in the 1960s linking smoking and cancer, the amount of cigarettes and other smoking materials consumed each year in North America continues to increase. Repeated studies correlating death statistics with smoking habits indicate that one-pack-plus-per-day smokers shorten their life span on the average by about seven and one-half years. The Methodist Hospital study also indicates that a high percentage of specific respiratory diseases (pneumonia and bronchitis), gastrointestinal problems (ulcers), strokes and heart attacks are linked to the smoking habit. In my own practice I see an increased incidence of emphysema, throat infections, sinus difficulties, and asthma in smokers as compared to non-smokers.

Recent statistics have indicated a shorter life span for the American population as a whole compared with the survival rates of adherents of certain religious groups, including Latter Day Saints (Mormons) and Seventh Day Adventists. While the statistics do not shed light on all of the differences between these groups and the population as a whole, it is thought that the strict rules of these churches prohibiting the use of tobacco, alcohol, and stimulants (coffee and tea) are significantly related to the longer survival of their members.

Seldom does a smoker tell me that he is happy with his habit. A vast majority of such patients tell me that they would like to quit; however, a vast majority also tell me they are not yet ready to do so. It has been my observation that patients with a well-established smoking habit find it very difficult to relax.

These patients describe to me uneasy and restless feelings, boredom, anxiety, and an urge to keep moving, with a strongly established habitual tendency to reach for a cigarette to obtain relief from these feelings. The excessive tension they experience finds a temporary solution in the act of smoking. The chief problem of solving tension in this way, of course, rests in the statistical increase in proneness to disease.

Although smoking is said to be capable of causing a psychological dependency, I have also seen withdrawal symptoms such as nausea, vomiting, abdominal pains, headaches, and dizziness, indicating to me that for some patients the smoking habit may actually be a physical addiction.

The well-ingrained smoking habit has roots so deep within the unconscious that its origin is not readily apparent. Some potential causal factors are rebellion against parental controls, imitation of parental models in families in which parents smoke, a wish to be accepted by peers, and a desire to give the appearance of sophisticated maturity. Psychoanalysts have also proposed that smoking is the extension of an unsatisfied sucking instinct deriving from infancy and projected into an oral habit in adulthood.

Whatever the origin of the smoking habit, it is quite apparent that the degree of dependency upon the smoking habit parallels the degree of tension in the smoker. Many patients report to me that their increased smoking is directly related to stressful situations in which they experience increasing tension.

One last comment on this subject involves the explanation for the chronic cough smokers often experience. Many previous investigators have shown that the presence of smoke in the lungs of experimental animals paralyzes the cilia (hairs) projecting from the cells lining the tracheal and bronchial passages. The function of these hair cells is to move upward the mucus of the lubricating cells of the respiratory tract, produced in an amount of approximately one and one-half quarts per day, from the fine radicals of the lung flowing over the vocal cords, and from there to be automatically swallowed and enter the stomach. This is accomplished by a coordinated beating action of the hair cells in fast upward strokes. The effect of smoke products from cigarettes is to poison the hair cells with which the smoke comes into contact, thus rendering the beating action of the cilia ineffective for a period of forty minutes after the smoking of one cigarette.

Smokers are most aware of a cough when arising in the morning. This is probably because the mucus collected during a day of persistent smoking has become more mobilized during the night as the hair cells return to activity, collecting the mucus for an assist with a few vigorous coughs in the morning before being poisoned again by the first cigarette of the day.

Much has been written in recent years regarding the relative disadvantage for the physical body of the use of alcohol versus hallucinogenic drugs. I shall not enter into that argument here. It seems clear, however, that both are related to a need to escape from tension. The life history of the drug addict or alcoholic typically includes stressful incidents in young adulthood, including the need to gain peer approval and to seek "forbidden" pleasure, in rebellion against parental injunctions. The short-term solution to adolescents' problems offered by alcohol may in later life also be used to solve problems involving excess tension. For example, attempting to make a sale over a business-man's lunch, a salesman struggles with the fear that not drinking with his client may cost him the sale, and proceeds to drink excessively. Claude Steiner discusses the scripts and counter-scripts found in the minds of many alcoholics in his book *Games Alcoholics Play.*[4]

Death from cirrhosis of the liver is now the fourth highest cause of death in America. While death from cirrhosis is obviously most common in chronic alcoholics, the rise in the incidence of death from cirrhosis begins to occur even at a consumption level of one to two drinks in a two-week period.[5]

The destructive nature of hallucinogens, amphetamines ("speed"), sedatives, and narcotics is fully documented by the emergency room records of any large city hospital. The deaths, illness, profiteering, social disruption, and crime linked with drug and alcohol usage point out the necessity for modern society to find innovative solutions to the stress and tension that perpetuate this vicious cycle.

Two more self-destructive habits I include in this chapter are the "habit" of under-exercising and of not wearing automobile seat belts.

The relationship of physical exercise to health is fully discussed by Evarts Loomis in *Healing For Everyone.* [6] Suffice it to say that physical distresses result from the kind of world in which we expect to live with maximum physical comfort and minimum physical challenge. These distresses are terribly apparent when we attempt to run for a bus, climb four or five flights of stairs, hike in the summer, or go hunting in the fall when our bodies have not been challenged on a regular basis. In Section III, exercise will be discussed in detail.

Studies conducted several years ago by the National Safety Council showed that the use of automobile seat belts is a very effective means of reducing death and injury on the highway. Statistics indicated that overall, in a potentially fatal accident, a driver or passenger had a forty-one percent better chance of survival if he was wearing a properly applied seat belt. The National Safety Council also indicated that less than fifteen percent of automobile riders regularly used seat belts at the time of the survey.

I now use this question in my routine health questionnaire for all my patients. About eighty-five percent of those who complete the questionnaire indicate they do not routinely use seat belts. When I ask them why, a few indicate claustrophobia or some theoretical reason why they do not wish to have them on. The vast majority indicate it is either forgetfulness or "inconvenience" which prevents them from fastening their seat belts as they enter their automobile. I would term all these reasons highly self-destructive, whether consciously or unconsciously so.

A FUNCTIONAL MODEL OF MAN

Experts have estimated that the human body consists of one quadrillion cells.[1] Of this number of cells, approximately seven to twelve billion exist as the brain and central nervous system.[2] The average nerve cell or neuron has an estimated five thousand direct connections to other nerve cells. The number of potential pathways of nerve messages within the brain is calculated at ten to the two-million-seven-hundred-and-eighty-three-thousandth power. The mere number of zeros in this number would require two thousand book pages to be recorded.[3]

The computer-like function of the human organism has been emphasized by Dr. Thomas Harris in *I'm O.K.—You're O.K.*[4] A computer can be thought of as having input, processing, and output systems. As human organisms we have a capacity to receive input data, to process it, and come to output in terms of action.

I present here a model of the message process system for purposes of understanding human functioning and the potential basis for changing or modifying ourselves.

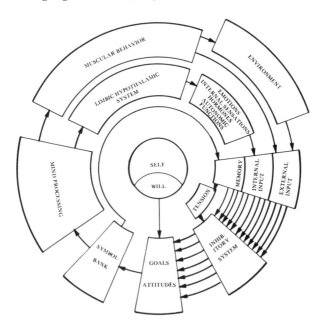

Fig. II.1 A Functional Model of Man

Source: Anderson, Robert A., Unpublished material, March 1976.

   As with any model, a simple representation of so complicated a subject as the human organism is subject to over-sim-
plification and lack of accurate detail. Nevertheless, this model
has been very helpful for many of my patients, clients, and
students, providing a framework for intellectual understanding
of what is involved in making changes to improve their overall
health. (For those interested in further scientific insights into
neurophysiology, a paper by Robert H. Riffenburgh is very helpful.[5])

Chapter 7

PERCEPTION OF DATA OR STIMULI

Three sources of data or stimuli are apparent.

First, we receive data through our five senses: visual, auditory (hearing), gustatory (taste), olfactory (smell), and touching senses—pain, tickle, sharpness-dullness, temperature, and pressure. This sensing of external data may be distantly environmental (for example, spectator sports, television, or tape recordings), or may be participatory, that is, we may be aware of our own muscular behavior and its participation in the immediate environment. Thus, we hear ourselves talking, see ourselves moving, gesturing, running, smiling, and in a mirror we see ourselves communicating verbally and nonverbally.

Second, we are aware of internal physical sensations and emotions. The sensations of thirst, a full bladder, a hungry stomach, heartburn, bowel cramps, a tight neck, a twitching muscle, a thumping heart, air-hunger, or a muscular "charlie horse" are examples of the former. Kinesthetic or propriocep-tive receptors within our locomotor structures (tendons, liga-ments, and muscles) give us feedback to tell us the position of our limbs, head, and trunk. Even with our eyes closed, our kinesthetic receptors tell us that our arm is raised in a certain position. Likewise, we may either readily or with difficulty be aware of emotions within ourselves—fear, anxiety, anger, joy, disgust, sadness, or guilt.

The third source of input data involves the phenomenon of memory. Although exact mechanisms are still unknown, memory may be thought of as an electrochemical phenomenon, dependent on computer-like functioning of electrical patterns between groups of cells, mediated by the DNA (deoxyribonucleic acid) storage molecules in each cell of the brain.[1] It is now believed that permanence in memory is accomplished by the patterning of chemical bonding between the paired spiral chains of atoms within the helix of the DNA molecule.

Thus, the pattern of a certain recollection must involve the serial and simultaneous stimulation of a precise pattern of neurons which were chemically altered at the time of the original experience by the input data and its accompanying energy.

The brain experiments of Wilder Penfield, Canadian neurosurgeon, enabled him to conclude that a specific site in the brain, when stimulated electrically, reliably and repeatedly invoked the same single memory.[2] We may thus assume that each specific memory we retain has an anatomical triggering location within the brain. Penfield also found that a remembered event, when electrically elicited, evoked at the same time the emotions and interpretations associated with that event. Day-to-day stimuli may in the same way evoke a *déja vu*—a reliving experience which is quite spontaneous.

I have a favorite tree which I pass on the way to work—favorite because it reminds me of a tree I used to climb as a child. This memory triggers recall of happy events at that time in my life and of spontaneous expressions of myself as a "free" child out-of-doors.

The initiating stimulus for a particular memory may even be the emotion associated with it. A patient once told me that the pleasurable emotional state he experienced in listening to a Beethoven symphony regularly triggered the memory of a similar feeling in childhood when he was anticipating the visit of a favorite grandparent.

Consider for a moment the chains of thought we all experience. I may walk past the door of a music shop and hear the strains of a familiar tune. The incoming data of the musical theme may then trigger the recollection of the entire musical number, even though I briefly hear only the theme. The orchestration, soloist, and even the circumstances in which I first experienced the music, with the emotions accompanying that experience, may also be recalled as a result of my hearing the theme alone.

Many authorities now believe that memory is permanent and that data once received remains indefinitely and indelibly stored.[3] Penfield also concluded that new experiences are immediately classified with similar past experiences, though with enough separation so that judgment of similarities and differences is possible as a result of the pattern of storage.

The bulk of such data is stored out of the range of normal conscious recall. The field of consciousness of incoming data is relatively narrow; surrounding it is data readily available when triggered by another incoming item, in a functional location termed by Assagioli the "middle unconscious".[4]

Jung was aware that as he progressed in his understanding of human function it became more and more difficult to distinguish between internal and external data. Certain images (stimuli or inputs) are indeed derived from the material external environment, and others, just as real, come from mental sources (memory of words, concepts, images, ideas, beliefs, and emotions).[5]

The "realness" of internal stimuli from the memory bank can be appreciated by recalling the impact of any frightening dream. We say to ourselves, "It was so vivid, it seemed as if it was really happening." The images in dreams originate in the unconscious, and may profoundly affect the entire emotional system, causing fright and panic, and the entire physical system causing rapid heart beat and respiration, dilated pupils, elevated adrenalin level, and tensed muscles—the "real" physical consequences of nightmares.

Dr. Raul Hernandez-Peon, at the University of California at Los Angeles in the late 1950s, derived data from experimental psychology which profoundly influenced the thinking of neurophysiologists.[6] His work was so important that I will review it here.

A tiny electrode was surgically implanted in the eighth, or auditory, nerve of a cat. (The eighth nerve is the nerve leading from the ear to the deeper portions of the brain, with eventual connections to the auditory cortex where hearing actually is experienced.) The electrode was connected to an electrical lead fastened in the skull and then connected by a flexible wire to a transmitter, a recording device, and eventually to an oscilloscope screen. The wire was flexible, permitting the cat to move about freely. The animal was then placed in a soundproof room. Then, through a loudspeaker in the wall, a click was sounded. A few milliseconds later, a "blip," or electrical discharge, was recorded on the oscilloscope screen. Thus, the same energy of the click moved the bones of the middle ear, moving in turn the round window, activating the cochlear fluid and stimulating the hair cells of the inner ear, finally stimulating the eighth nerve endings—whose electrical impulse, as it passed toward the brain, ultimately recorded the energy on the oscillograph attached to the transmitting apparatus. This impulse was shown to be reliably reproduced with each click.

Next, a large, clear jar was inverted over two capering white mice and placed in the center of the room. The cat turned its full attention to the mice. Once again the click was sounded; this time the electrical impulse was not present on the oscillograph. The investigators concluded that somehow the attention the cat gave the mice inhibited the auditory mechanisms at the level of the ear itself. A distracting painful shock, as well as a fish aroma, both commanding the attention of the cat, likewise could extinguish the auditory response, just as the attention to the mice had done.

The concept of an inhibitory portion of the nervous system was further validated when Dr. Robert Galambos of Yale University reported in 1956 that he had surgically severed the efferent (directed outward from the brain) olivo-cochlear nerve bundle, thereby obliterating the inhibitory phenomenon demonstrated in the experiments at U.C.L.A.[7] Dr. Galambos has subsequently introduced evidence in humans showing that the change in auditory perception when attention is focused elsewhere is a central rather than peripheral phenomenon.[8] With either the peripheral or central concept, the attention phenomenon profoundly affects perception by a sensory organ.

We may, therefore, conclude that humans have a modulating system whose function it appears to be to screen out from the thousands of potential bits of input data relating to each of us at a given point in time a smaller number of items which we are capable of handling.

George Miller of Harvard has calculated that the human being processes seven plus or minus two items of data at a time.[9] Whether the number seven is the exact integer involved in intake and processing functions is open to question. The significant point, however, is that the system places some finite limit on taking in and processing data—a relatively small percentage of the total potential input available from memory and other internal and external sources.

If, then, we are governed by some process by which we accept only a small percentage of potentially available data, it is very important for us to be in touch with the controls of that process so as to be able to receive the data necessary for a healthier existence.

The major controlling influence in data selection is tension. Tension, the result of conflicting bits of information on the same subject within the mind's processing, may be modified by cognitive manipulations such as repression, projection, and rationalization, serving to change the memory's interpretation of the conflicting data.[10] Since the system functions constantly to keep tension within manageable limits, data may be inhibited so that conflict is held to a minimum.[11]

In situations of severe stress and tension, an individual's ability to use rationalization, projection, and repression may be exceeded. The inhibitory system is then called into play to modify his perceptions. Tension may induce a profound alteration in self-perception: "selective screening of sensory data admits some things while filtering others so that experience as it is perceived through one set of socially patterned sensory screens is quite different from the experience perceived through another."[12]

The ultimate example of inhibiting data is the psychotically ill person who, by definition, is out of touch with reality. Admitting certain data would lead to unbearably high tension levels; therefore, the threatening or noxious data is inhibited and completely screened out in such a case. The victim of amnesia may be utilizing the same protective sort of phenomenon. To remember certain feelings or events would lead to too much conflicting data and a tension level impossible to handle.

The level of tension present at any given moment profoundly influences the operation of the inhibitory system. Tension requires us to give our attention to the matters in conflict, since the system constantly seeks to adapt to keep tension within comfortable limits. The cat attends to the mice and inhibits auditory input. Its greatest tension at that time is instinctual, derived from the apparent genetic stress of the necessity for hunger and survival, inducing a foraging response. Thus, only its attention to food-gathering activity meets the stress and reduces the tension; the mere clicking sound in the laboratory is excluded from the cat's concern.

Anatomically, the screening of data is done largely by the reticular system and the limbic portion of the brain. The reticular system is a loosely woven network of nerves extending from the brain stem upward into the old brain and possessing inhibitory and activating functions. The limbic brain inhibits irrelevant stimuli and functions in the habituation to stimuli; it is an essential component of the inhibitory or filtering system participating in selective responses to stimuli.

Any complex form of attention, voluntary or involuntary, requires the selective recognition of one relevant stimulus and an inhibition of response to irrelevant stimuli. This contribution is made by the reticular system (which determines wakefulness) and by the limbic cortex, along with activity of the frontal brain.[13]

Investigations have repeatedly shown that the cerebral cortex, besides being involved in specific sensory and motor functions, also assists in performing man's activating functions. Every specific afferent (inbound to the brain) or efferent (outbound) nerve fiber is accompanied by a fiber of the nonspecific activating system. The stimulation of individual areas of the cortex can evoke both activating and inhibiting influences in lower brain structures by means of descending fibers running from the prefrontal cortex to the thalamic nuclei and the brain stem. In this way, the highest functioning levels of the cortex, via the formation of intentions and plans, recruit the lower systems of the reticular system in the thalamus and brain stem, modulating their work and making possible the most complex forms of conscious activity.[14]

The medial zones of the cerebral cortex are also closely connected with the reticular formation of the brain stem. The principal function of these brain zones is regulation of the general state and modification of the tone and control over inclinations and emotions, as well as the activating or inhibiting of cortical activity through recruitment of the energy of the reticular net. These zones constitute first functional unit of the brain along with the reticular system, according to Alexander Luria, Russian neurophysiologist.

The "orienting reflex" relating to attention is highly selective in receiving stimuli from the external world and forms the basis for directive and selective organized behavior.[15]

Luria's second functional unit of the brain participates in perception, analysis, and storage of information. The third functional unit exhibits regulation and verification of activity, elaboration of intentions and plans, and sets the stage for the carrying out of these intentions.

A person subject to tension levels well above normal will tend to inhibit more new data and more noxious data than one whose tension level is at a relatively manageable level. For the latter person, new data—even if unfavorable or unwelcome—poses less of a threat because of his lower tension level, which enables him to cope better with such stimuli.

Chapter 8

ATTITUDES AND GOALS

The next step in the processing of data in the human system is application by attitudes and goals. An attitude is a "mind-set" which exists in a basic continuing frame of reference in regard to one's own self, situations, other persons, and relationships. As the attitude of a space craft describes how it is oriented in relation to the earth, the moon, other celestial bodies, and its source and destination, so too attitude in the functional model for man describes his orientation to other persons, relationships, his source, and his goals.

The attitudes a person has influence the further processing of data in the following way: incoming data crossing the threshold of the inhibitory system are filtered through the "attitude screen." The data used is compared, matched, and contrasted to data already in storage for the best "fit". This process is generally done in a stage of brain activity called the "Alpha" stage (see Chapter 16). New data is immediately classified with past experiences that are similar, with enough separation, however, so that judgment of similarities and differences is possible.

The data so triggered from the data bank or memory will tend to be positive if the attitudes held are generally positive. If the attitudes are generally negative, the data retrieved will tend to be negative.[1] This secondary data is feedback input from memory, modifying the tension level with the passage of information through the feedback loop. It is my belief that people usually retrieve more negative than positive data from their memory banks because they maintain negative mind-sets most of the time.

As I arrive home from my office, I am confronted with a set of new data: my wife's car is not in the garage; the garage door is closed; the lawn has not been mowed; the weeds along the drive are a bit higher than they were yesterday.

These bits of data, recorded and received across the threshold, trigger related data from memory; the type of data depends on the attitudes I hold at the moment. Holding a positive attitude toward my wife, I then retrieve the data that she is already about her business of teaching a class in her own competent way on Wednesday nights, which we had previously agreed was the best night for the family. Were my attitudes negative, then I might retrieve awareness of the negative aspects of the situation, namely, heating my own dinner, postponing interchange with my wife until late, and managing the household until offspring are settled for the night.

The garage door is closed; this means no one is home. If positive attitudes prevail, I retrieve data that my sons are occupied playing and learning baseball and my daughter is constructively occupied working at her first job; if negative, I retrieve concerns about the progress of my sons under their respective coaches and concerns over irregular meals when baseball intervenes; I retrieve concerns over my daughter leaving her place of employment late at night.

All of the data retrieved may be valid. In my experience, however, most of us seem to retrieve more negative data than positive as a result of being in a negative mind-set or attitude the greatest portion of the time.

Balancing the selectors for data retrieval by a shift in attitudes toward a more positive balance surely has beneficial effects.

I have had occasion to be among a group of friends when news of a possible job promotion was transmitted about someone previously known to the members of the group, but now moved away. As members of the group responded to this news, it became apparent that not only was each person interpreting and extrapolating from what they heard, but that each has actually heard the news differently. "I don't understand how he can get promoted so quickly, knowing John," said one. "John just can't handle vice president," said another. "They'll never do it when they investigate carefully," said a third person. The first two actually thought they heard that John was promoted, while only the third heard—correctly—that a promotion was a possibility.

Similarly, if a group is asked to tell what they remember about a movie they have all seen, each person will remember a different scene. Many will agree on the details of a series of scenes, but will also disagree about details of other scenes. Their varying attitudes, stemming from different psychological make-ups and conditioning, have permitted them to receive differing bits of data.

I have had more than one school principal tell me of a mother who, when told of a destructive act committed by her child in school, refuses to permit that data to enter, continuing to behave as if everyone knew her child would "never do such a thing." That basic attitude about her own child continues to retrieve data from her own experience which is saying that "it cannot have happened." It may take several repetitions or testimony by witnesses for the mother to "hear" the unpleasant facts.

The goals we set determine specifically what our direction will be. Goals concerning individual matters will, in the main, conform to overall attitudes because tension will rise to intolerable levels if there is marked inconsistency. Goals are extremely important in the scheme of function, since a great deal of human activity is initiated by intentions and plans, by predictions and programs which are formulated during man's conscious life.[2]

It has been pointed out that all responses are goal-oriented.[3] The goals may be operative on a conscious level, and may also exist on an unconscious level. Thus, as much as possible, we need to be aware of what our goals are. Probing the unconscious is one means of decreasing both physical and emotional distress.

Goals commonly start as a conscious or middle unconscious (periconscious) process, but subsequently become deeply unconscious and part of the habit pattern. The process of habituation is permitted by the brain structures of the limbus and reticular formation which, by comparison, show that a given stimulus, when repeatedly encountered, is decreasingly novel and requires no special mobilization of the organism as a result.[4]

A five-year-old receives a bicycle for Christmas, for example. His goal, of which he may or may not be consciously aware, is to keep up, catch up, or compete with the six-year-old next door who already has a bike. Because of the presence of the bike, the five-year-old determines that he will learn to ride it by watching and imitating the older boy and by trial and error (positive and negative reinforcement). All of the conscious step-wise synaptic (cell to cell) connections finally enable him to proceed in wobbly fashion for twenty feet down the driveway before halting. Because of the work load of this laboriously conscious step-by-step process, the brain then somehow finds the shortest route from neuron to neuron and the nerve cell responses become habitual and fixed. Thus, a fixed system of pathways is established which controls the formation of a series of coordinated physical movements we call a habit. As the process is refined, the habit is established in the nervous system and muscles, without further conscious thought required. In fact, once the habit has reached the fully unconscious level, the mind may be turned to many other thoughts and mental activities, even while the bike riding process is going on. An infant learning to walk and an adult learning to drive a car follow the same pattern of habit formation.

The goal associated with a habit is thus part of the more or less automatic process as well. As the boy's initial goal of bike riding is met, for example, the habit may become associated with other goals, such as "having fun", "going to the store", or "getting exercise". The habit remains a nerve cell legacy and may be performed even if the original goal is later invalid or not recalled at the conscious level.

We may thus be the recipients of our past conscious goals through habit formation. Unfortunately, many habits may continue a behavior which is counterproductive to our health.

Nearly all habitual smokers agree that the habit is not healthy for the body. The habit frequently starts in the late teenage years with goals of acquiring status and approval in a peer group. Later, when these goals have either been met many times over or, on the other hand, seem to be invalid, the habit remains— in this case, an unhealthy habit.

Returning again to the demonstration of the importance of attitudes in the retrieval of data and subsequent output, the studies made by Rosenthal and Jacobsen in 1968 are very revealing.[5] Five students were selected at random from each class in an elementary school of a lower-class neighborhood in southern San Francisco. The students were all given tests, reportedly designed to predict academic promise. Their teachers were then told that on the basis of these tests the selected students were very likely to make rapid progress. In actuality, the designated students had no more potential than any other of their classmates, but the teachers were not informed of this.

During a later period of the Rosenthal-Jacobsen study, the five students made great intellectual gains compared with control students. Since there seemed to be no other variables, it must be assumed that the attitude of their teachers in some way enabled this totally unsubstantiated prophecy to be fulfilled. This is a striking demonstration of the profound effects that positive attitudes can have upon the eventual outcome of reality.

The question frequently arises as to whether attitudes exist within the field of consciousness or whether they are stored within realms of the unconscious. I return again to the premise that present behavior is determined by a complex combination of heredity, conditioning within the cultural milieu (including all of an individual's previous experiences), plus the state of present awareness.

Many patients with the same manifestations of distress are found to have had in common certain experiences in their conditioning. Exposure to the negative attitudes and behavior of parental models frequently results in the development of unhealthy attitudes later in life. Nor is the effect of conditioning limited to the past, a fact which holds open the possibility of change as the result of certain experiences in adulthood. Much of this entire process proceeds unconsciously, and although some attitudes may be conscious and easily verbalized, in my experience they are most often beyond the patient's own recognition.

Many investigators now believe that all incoming data once received for storage is never forgotten. It frequently is stored in the unconscious functioning parts of the brain, but may exert its influence from there as in the case of unconscious goals and may, under hypnosis or the use of pentothal, be recalled into conscious memory. Subjects are often surprised at material they are able to recall under such conditions, yet cannot recall the original circumstances under which they acquired such material.

Finally, it is apparent that functional goals and attitudes, as important as they are, cannot be understood without an equally thorough understanding of another highly significant controlling factor, the will, as exerted by the self. That factor will be discussed fully in Chapter 11.

Chapter 9

DATA PROCESSING

Following the process of selection of ideas, concepts, and images, as matched with incoming data and influenced by set attitudes, the intellect uses this data for study, comparison, the application of reason, and a conclusion in the form of a final decision. Luria presents evidence that learning is a process of formulating one's wishes and intentions independently, first in externalized speech (particularly prior to age five) and later in internal speech.[1] The role of internal speech (beginning at five and a half) is that of organizing new links of thought.

Much of the translation of plans, goals, and intentions depends upon the participation of an individual's internal speech. Every goal is defined by a program of internal speech which activates the processing of data leading to attempts at meeting the goal.[2]

The limbic brain closely related to the reticular system receives a new stimulus and functions to compare the new with the old, determining whether the organism must mobilize to respond to a truly new stimulus or verify that the input is not really new. Repeated similar stimuli permit habituation, a state in which the organism is not consciously aroused to respond to an input because comparison verifies from memory some previous exposure to the same input.

In further processing of data we are dependent on the cumulative experience from past conditioning which is available in our memory for matching when we are confronted with a new input. The example of a class of fifth graders going to a farm illustrates this point: a few of the children, on seeing a steer, may because of some previous farm experience "see" a familiar farm friend; a few might have seen a movie of a bullfight and therefore will "see" a potentially raging animal, and experience fright; others may have read about the sources of beef and will "see" a food source.

The temporal lobes of the brain seem to be the receptors for the input. Coordination of information and the matching of possible responses is a function of the association regions of the parietal, occipital, and temporal lobes (portions of the brain above and behind the ears, beneath the temples and the back of the head). The sequence then moves to the frontal brain to instruct recall of past results, including associated emotional imagery. Messages proceed to the storage area of the temporal lobes for the response list, and are then transmitted to the frontal region for a weighted evaluation of all possibilities. Simultaneously, this step is transmitted to storage and to the association regions for the choice of response and transmission of the decision to action and storage centers.[3]

This technical explanation may be summarized briefly as receipt of the stimulus, correlation with related data, matching of possible responses, recall of past results and emotions, checking of the response list, evaluation, choice, decision, and transmission to output. The application of the above data processing depends upon the items available for comparison and the items in previous experience, plus the application of organized internal speech to eventually formulate conclusions which are refined by reflection into a final processed message ready to stimulate output centers.

Chapter 10

THE OUTPUT SYSTEM

The output system consists of the doing and feeling parts of the system. When messages from the processed data are concluded, they may stimulate the motor area of the cerebral cortex or the limbic, reticular, and hypothalamic centers in the old brain.

Muscular Behavior

In numerous experiments with animals and stimulation studies in humans at the time of brain surgery, each group of motor cortex neurons has been shown to have specific control over a small group of muscles in the muscular system. The efferent (outgoing) electrical messages proceed from the motor cortex in the brain through a series of neuronal connections or synapses into the cranial nerves and spinal cord to stimulate formation of chemical complexes at the termination of the last nerve cell in the chain called the motor end plate. Transmitter chemicals in turn carry the message from the end of the last nerve cell to the surface of the muscle fibers themselves. The chemical complexes making up the muscle fibers then undergo changes, causing the fibers to shorten. As groups of muscle fibers shorten, muscle contraction occurs, resulting in what we recognize as movement of body parts. All such muscular behavior can be described in terms of motion or nonmotion of body parts.

The muscles so controlled by the motor cortex are called striated (voluntary) muscles because of their appearance under the microscope. The strength of the response of striated muscle fibers depends upon the strength of the nerve stimulus originating in the motor cortex. Since the electrical messages proceed along the nerves at uniform rates, strengthening of a stimulus is accomplished by stimulating more nerve fibers, known as recruiting additional nerve pathways, to give a greater total electrical impact to the transmitter chemicals at the end of the nerve. The stronger the electrical stimulus, the greater the percentage of muscle fibers stimulated into contraction and the more powerful the motion.

The Limbic System and Emotions

The hypothalamus and limbus are closely related neurological structures located in the center portion of the skull (cranium) in areas of the brain that were developed early in man's evolution. The limbic brain includes the deep parts of the frontal and temporal lobes and the primitive areas called the diencephalon. Emotions are without doubt significantly related to this limbic brain.[1]

Other portions of the brain also participate in the elaboration of emotions. How this occurs is not precisely known, though it may be that certain chemicals produce certain emotions. Still other contributions to the emotions are made by the endocrine system.

An idea in the mind produces changes leading to emotions, not the other way around. Emotions result from the processing of data beginning with the stimulus.[2] Indirectly, of course, the experience of the emotion and the accompanying physical expression become input in the feedback model, and we experience them as a new stimulus. Commonly experienced potent emotions are depression, sadness, anger, anxiety and fear, guilt, helplessness and a sense of inadequacy, disgust, and joy.

The Hypothalamus and The Endocrine System

The hypothalamus is the center which governs the endocrine system. The hypothalamic brain controls the pituitary or "master" gland. This gland, located in the middle of the head adjacent to the brain, consists of a posterior portion and an anterior portion. The posterior portion is directly stimulated by the hypothalamus to produce certain hormones secreted directly into the bloodstream, influencing kidney urine production, causing contraction of the uterus during childbirth, and contraction of arterial muscular walls.

The hypothalamus also controls the anterior portion of the pituitary gland, which produces HGH (human growth hormone). As its name implies, this chemical is a significant factor in carrying out the genetic and nutritional possibilities for growth of the human body as well as other somatic (bodily) functions.

The anterior pituitary gland in turn produces specific tropic (stimulating) hormones or chemicals which, as they circulate through the bloodstream, stimulate the ovaries, testicles, adrenal cortex, thyroid, and breasts. Each of these then produces, respectively, female hormones (estrogen and progesterone), male hormone (testosterone), cortisone and related chemicals, thyroid hormone (thyroxin), and prolactin (leading to milk secretion in the breasts after childbirth).

In addition, direct hypothalamic nerve connections have been demonstrated to the islet cells of the pancreas (producing insulin and glucagon, which regulate blood sugar); to the adrenal medulla, the center portion of the adrenal gland producing epinephrine or adrenalin; and to the pineal gland in the center of the brain. The precise relationships and possible controlling factors of the pineal gland (participating in the production of skin pigment and the time-clock cycle relating to the onset of puberty) are as yet unclear.

The hypothalamus in experiments with animals has been shown to profoundly influence the immune responses of the thymus and lymphatic system (resistance factors).[3] Psychosocial phenomena may modify immune processes by way of central nervous system mechanisms which are intimately involved in immune processes. The hypothalamus, most likely through its control of neuroendocrine (hormone) and autonomic nervous system activity, plays a significant role in allergic and immune phenomena. In view of the close relationship between the hypothalamus and the central nervous system mechanisms controlling emotions, a possible basis is provided for the understanding of the physiology and chemistry involved in the mediation of immune and allergic processes by psychosocial phenomena.

It seems likely that somatotropin (growth hormone), whose production by the anterior pituitary gland is controlled by the hypothalamus, or some other as yet unidentified hormone of the anterior pituitary gland, may be the link by which the hypothalamus exerts its influence on the thymico-lymphatic surveillance system.[4]

In addition to the many functions already listed, the hormones, as previously noted, contribute to the emotions. The secretion of adrenalin, for example, is associated with a feeling of excitement and anticipation of action. Lactic acid, implicated as the cause of anxiety, is produced by most cells as a breakdown product of metabolism (the taking-in of nutrients, the production of energy, and the dispersal of waste products).[5] The secretion of testosterone is associated with increased feelings of aggression.

The major hormone functions include the cortisone family, which regulate the balance of electrolyte (salt and potassium) and water content; thyroxin, which regulates the rate of metabolism or energy output in the body's cells; testosterone, which causes development of the male genital organs at puberty and contributes to the male sex drive; estrogen and progesterone, which initiate the development of the female genital organs at puberty, regulate ovulation and the menstrual cycle, and contribute to female sexual drive; and adrenalin, which excites many essential body organs to a greater level of activity in what is known as the "fight or flight" reaction. In addition, cortisone and its related chemicals exert a suppressant effect on inflammatory activity within the system.

The endocrine system with the pituitary operates within the system in a balanced fashion by means of a feedback mechanism. To illustrate this mechanism, I will describe what happens to regulate metabolism through the function of the thyroid gland.

The anterior pituitary gland secretes TSH (thyroid-stimulating hormone) into the bloodstream at a certain rate. The thyroid gland, if functioning properly, responds by producing thyroxin. The thyroxin in the bloodstream, in turn, influences the hypothalamus and pituitary gland, and when the right amount of thyroxin is reached, the hypothalamus reduces the amount of TSH produced by the anterior pituitary. In this feedback fashion, further small adjustments occur until a balance is achieved.

This balanced system is capable of responding to additional amounts of stress and corresponding increases in tension. Let us look at what happens in wintertime in temperate climates, for example. Due to the decrease in temperature, the stress from being cold places the system under increased tension. The system, ever working to keep tension within manageable limits, sends increased stimuli to the processing system, in turn stimulating the hypothalamus to greater activity, in turn producing more TSH in the anterior pituitary and leading to increased production of thyroxin. The thyroxin then stimulates a greater level of metabolism and we become warmer.

The increased thyroxin level, in the meantime, feeds back information to the hypothalamus to keep the TSH level from going too high. In this way, balance is again achieved, but this time at a higher level of metabolism. Indeed, on measuring thyroxin blood levels in large groups of persons, higher levels are found during cold winter weather.

The Hypothalamus and the Autonomic Nervous System

The hypothalamus is also the center for autonomic nervous system activity. This portion of the nervous system consists of specialized fibers stimulating exocrine glands and smooth muscle functions.

Examples of exocrine gland secretions are sweating; skin oil lubrication; salivation; mucus in the intestinal tract; stomach acid; digestive enzymes in the stomach, intestine, and pancreas; tearing; bile secretion; respiratory tract mucus secretions from the nose, sinuses, and bronchial passages; and secretions of the prostate and vagina.

Examples of smooth muscle functions include movements in the iris of the eye and in the respiratory apparatus and diaphragm; heart contractions and changes in the heart rate; the formation of goose pimples; swallowing; intestinal, gastric, and colonic propulsion; propulsion of urine from the kidney to the bladder; emptying of the bladder, in part; and muscular control of the caliber of blood vessels.

These functions have, for some decades, been thought to have been autonomously performed by the unconscious brain. We now know from many sources of experimental work that this is not entirely true. A striking example of voluntary control of internal autonomic functions was reported by Dr. Elmer Green and his colleagues in 1970. In this report, the authors describe the details of measurements made on Swami Rama, who demonstrated the ability to voluntarily control his heart rate by shifting his normal heartbeat to a state of atrial flutter (three hundred beats per minute) for seventeen seconds. He also demonstrated control of the major circulatory vessels in one of his hands by voluntarily changing the temperature of two different areas two inches apart to a temperature difference of nine degrees Fahrenheit between them. The cold portion turned gray and the warm portion pink. Such profound control over autonomic nervous system functions by certain individuals impressively demonstrates that this is one area where most persons have vastly undeveloped potential.

The last function of the autonomic nervous system consists of sensory elements recording internal sensations from organs served by this part of the nervous system. Stretching of the small or large intestine, for instance, produces a feeling of cramps and pain in the abdomen. Stretching of the stomach, on the other hand, produces the sensation of fullness that one has after eating. Other feedback sensations include those from the urinary system, from the lower bowel, heart sensations, and pain from stretching of the pleura (the lining around the lungs).

Thus, the hypothalamus and associated areas of the brain lead to the experience of a variety of emotions, internal sensations in the physical organs served by the autonomic nervous system, hormone functions, and smooth muscle and secretory functions of all autonomically innervated structures.

Chapter 11

THE SELF AND THE WILL

As shown in my diagram of the functional model of man, the self and the will, centered on the chart, set the goals and attitudes for the entire system. Jung, Maslow, and Assagioli, have all explored and documented the existence and essential nature of an inner self. Jung described the self as the center of the psyche and the inventor and organizer of the individual.[1] Maslow emphasized the importance of actualizing the self in his volume *Motivation and Personality.*[2] Assagioli presents an excellent working diagram for the understanding of the conscious and the unconscious and the existence of the self.[3] He distinguishes between the self as the point of awareness, and the personality manifesting physical, mental, and emotional existence. Further, he distinguishes between self, the center of our consciousness and awareness, and the contents of our consciousness as it exists within the personality. This center of consciousness differs from both the contents of consciousness and the realm of the unconscious.

It is rather obvious that three distinct realms of personality exist: we have a physical body, with its own organ systems, behavior, and visible form; we have a mind, which is the description of our mental and intellectual functions of data receiving, storage, and processing; and we have an emotional self, with a variety of manifestations in varying balance at different times in our lives.

It is therefore possible to take the stance of a neutral observer in visualizing these three personality levels. This neutral observer position is one key to beginning to experience the self. It is the self which is closely associated with and generates the will. The will, in turn, sets and maintains attitudes and goals.

I have experienced in myself and in many patients the inability to break a negative habit when a choice was made to *will* a change; "will power" then became pitted against the established habit and no change occurred. Unless a significant goal is established at conscious or unconscious levels, such efforts are likely to fail because the will simply does not function in changing behavior directly. Only by referring to appropriate attitudes and by setting definite positive goals can the correct sequence of processes by activated, leading eventually to a change in behavior or emotional experience.

The significance of the inner-centered self and its delegated agent, the will, has been thoroughly explored in *The Act of Will* by Assagioli. When an individual either gradually or suddenly awakens to the discovery of the self, the revelation of that self-awareness and the realization of the existence within of the ally of the self, the will, give him a new feeling of security and joy and a sense of wholeness.[4]

Often, after discussing a particular distress with a patient, I conclude that the easing of the distress requires some change to be made on his or her part. Most patients, at this point, reply that they have no will power. In actuality, they are already expressing their will in terms of the thinking, feeling, and behaving patterns determining the way they experienced the original distress. Dr. Harold Wolff states that in relating stresses to behavior, the relating parts of the human response are integrated as goal-directed responses, and that they are the product of integration, selection, arrangement, and organization. The reason this may be difficult to accept is that an individual's goals are frequently unrecognized and reside at the level of the unconscious.[5]

Thus, as previously stated, our present behavior and feelings are the result of heredity, conditioning, and our present level of awareness. Effective therapy stresses increasing awareness of the goals, attitudes, and controlling influences to which the self is subjected.

One of the reasons many persons visualize themselves as not having willpower is that the term conjures up a picture of a grim, forbidding force crushing all resistance in its path. Actually, the use of will in this kind of repressive fashion, without considering the other needs of the organism, frequently results in temporary success in altering behavior or thought, with about 95 percent ultimate failure rate as the strength of the willful expression fades with time and as the other unmet needs of the individual come to the fore. A patient declaring in this forceful fashion that he is going to lose weight, begin exercising, or quit smoking will probably resume his old pattern at a later time.

The true function of the will, then, is not to act against the personality by forcing the accomplishment of one's purposes.[6] The true function is to express the purposes of the inner self. This is accomplished through the setting of attitudes and goals and maintaining them in consciousness until they become habitual, residing in the unconscious and influencing us from that level. (This will be discussed further in Chapters 21 and 22 as ways of dealing with excessive tension.)

The multitude of distresses experienced by modern man are, I believe, partly due to the overpowering degree of control over nature which science has supplied over the last hundred years, and partly to the lack of development of the inner realms of the self and its agent, the will. As I pointed out in the early chapters of this book, man's external life, while becoming richer and more stimulating than ever before, has also become more complicated and exhausting. These new stimuli have led to the overdevelopment of science and the external life at the expense of the inner self.

The self may be described as a point of existence from which observation of the total personality is possible. In your mind's eye you may picture your physical self behaving in its myriad roles over a twenty-four-hour period. You may also picture your emotions, particularly their manifestations in states of joy, anger, and sadness. Picture too the mind-stream with its continuing flow of ideas, images, concepts, and symbols.

The self is also a point of existence from which choice and control are exerted. The self is also a point of organization, directing and balancing the three elements of the personality—the mind, the emotions, and the physical body.

The self is at the core of every individual. It is its central position—above and separate from all the stresses (internal and external), tensions, drives, desires, relationships, and multiple distresses experienced by the personality—which enables the self to deal with the inner and outer worlds. Assagioli asserts: "We are dominated by everything with which our self becomes identified. We can dominate and control everything from which we disidentify our self.[7]

If a man of twenty-five years is identified with the goal of becoming a millionaire by age thirty, he is then unable to freely choose the course of action his life will take because that course of action has already been predetermined by his specific identification with becoming a millionaire. Everything he does will be subservient to the attainment of that goal. Thus he has no real choice in relation to most of his "chosen" activities.

Identification also profoundly affects the way we describe our existential position. If I say to myself, "John makes me angry," this means that I am identified with the idea that someone outside myself chooses my emotions for me. If, through being centered in the self, I can take responsibility for my own emotions by saying "Sometimes the things John does evoke my anger," I take a step to disidentify myself from the idea that an external situation controls my responses. I begin thereby to exert a degree of control over my situation through the disidentification process.

The expression of the qualities of the self occurs by means of the will, through the control of goals and attitudes, through direction of the process of incoming data as influenced by tension levels, and through choice and final decision-making, which are illuminated by the full awareness of external events, of the three elements of the personality, and of the self. Assagioli points out the existence not only of a personal self but of a higher self. The higher self deals with integration on a higher level, a "spiritual psychosynthesis."[8]

The discovery of the self and practical applications of training of the will will be discussed further in Chapter 22.

Chapter 12

THE FEEDBACK NATURE OF THE MESSAGE SYSTEM

A detailed study of the diagram showing the functional model of man reveals that there is, strictly speaking, no beginning or ending of the series of events occurring within the system. The previous chapters arbitrarily began with the three sources of input. It is apparent, however, that the bank of concepts, ideas, images, and symbols composing the memory is both an input and a way-station between the input system and the processing system.

Likewise, muscular behavior, while it is clearly an output of data processing, is also fed back as input, both directly by our own awareness of what is happening with the physical body, and also indirectly by participation of the physical body within the environment, influencing it and receiving influences from it. We also take in data from remote environments, as when we are viewing a television newscast or reading a magazine or novel. These stimuli or inputs can subsequently influence us, but they are remote in the sense that initially we are geographically separated from participation in the events we see or read about.

Likewise, emotions, internal sensations, and autonomic nervous functions—all of which comprise our internal awareness—while clearly an output as the result of data processing, are also an input, completing the feedback loop to the internal input events as stimuli.

This completes the description of the total feedback nature of the functional model for man. It might also be noted at this point that the feedback nature appears to be a largely self-regulating mechanism. The two chief points of entry from which, theoretically with this diagram, the system can be changed are, first, the environment and, second, the self through the formation of goals and attitudes set and maintained by the will.

Luria stresses the importance of environmental influences, particularly up to the age of five and a half, when internal speech begins to organize new links within the thought processes and to regulate behavior from elective connections. Following this, internal speech becomes a significant controlling element in behavior. Luria also states that active attention and willed action are learned processes.[1]

In considering the process of self-modification, it is important to be aware of retrospective instructions and positive or negative feedback. Behavior sequences are facilitated or inhibited as we look back on them by contingencies of reinforcement, and that assessment operates as a predictive influence on the next sequence of similar behavior.[2] In a human context, the instructions may be natural, artificial, conscious, or symbolic. An analogy in microbiology describes the internalizing process by which a symbolic system is taken in: no matter how inapparent the difference, the host, whether it has taken in a symbolic system or a virus, is never again exactly the same. Thus, the process of adaptation and self-modification continues with each instance where data is taken in, processed, and formulated into output.

Section III

DEALING WITH TENSION AND FACILITATING ADAPTABILITY

It is clear that excessive tension renders the human system prone to debilitating diseases and distress on every level—physical, emotional, and mental. Though the system instinctively begins working to bring tension to more manageable levels when stimuli threaten to disturb its equilibrium, its methods for doing so often have a negative character: decreased memory, screening out of unpleasant incoming data, withdrawal of affect, yielding under pressure to self-destructive habits and patterns of behavior—all are examples of temporary relief, as previously discussed.

At this point I wish to focus on the many positive ways in which we can actively take part in our own recovery from undue stress and tension. Medications and manipulation of the environment—change of spouse, job, or residence chief among them—are two popular means we resort to in order to cope with great tension, yet they fail ultimately because they do not attack the root causes of distress, which reside within us.

The only lasting benefits to the distressed system come from the cultivation of new patterns and activities that prevent the buildup of excessive tension in the first place: regular physical exercise, service to others through volunteer or professional work, and involvement in hobbies and artistic pursuits are excellent ways of facilitating adaptability. These are discussed in the ensuing chapters, along with the therapeutic techniques of conscious relaxation (meditation, autogenics, yoga, biofeedback) and creative visualization for the setting and actualizing of positive new goals. All will, I hope, show the reader that the answers for man are within, that a sane and a healthy existence is within his grasp if he will but exercise responsibility and choose the path toward it.

Chapter 13

THE USE OF MEDICATION

For patients with various distresses, the first level of treatment applied by the vast majority of practitioners of medicine in advanced Western countries is the use of pharmaceutical preparations. For nearly every distress experienced by man there is a pharmaceutical preparation for the relief of symptoms.

Thus, for ulcers and hyperacidity there are antacids; for excess chronic anxiety there are tranquilizers; for depression there are anti-depressants; for arthritis and inflammatory conditions there are anti-inflammatory agents; for rhythm disturbances of the heart there are antiarrhythmic drugs. For pain there are analgesic drugs; for infections or the presence of bacterial agents in the system there are antibiotics.

The use of pharmaceutical agents is justified by scientific understanding of the chemical events within the system when distress is experienced. The drug used for any particular distress is, thus, chemically tailored to interrupt the electrical and chemical events in the physical body which are leading to actual distress or to the feeling of distress.

Several problems are implicit in the use of medications. First, they do not always succeed in doing what they are supposed to do. Anti-pain, anti-hypertensive, and anti-inflammatory drugs frequently fail to adequately relieve pain, lower blood pressure, or stop inflammation. Knowledge of the infinite variety of chemical and electrical events within the body is limited, and consequently the physician's ability to influence those events with specific drugs is also limited. Medications deal with the fine chemical balances within the body only in a gross sort of way.

Second, drugs frequently adversely influence not only the chemical processes of the distress, but also other processes in the body which, prior to drug therapy, were functioning in a normal way. These are known as "side effects." Thus, the choice of giving a drug or not must be balanced with concern for the risks of the distress, on the one hand, the potential for drug control of the chemical reaction related to the distress, on the other hand, and finally with the potential for upsetting other normally functioning mechanisms.

A good example of the dilemma physicians face is the appearance of a patient with a severely sore throat. If the agent causing the sore throat turns out to be a strep bacterium, antibiotics may be of great help. However, antibiotics may also destroy normal bacteria in the system, leading to the overgrowth of yeast organisms in the bowel, vagina, or skin. I have had the experience of working with such patients, who later had yeast problems that caused them greater distress than the original distress of the sore throat.

The next hazard concerning the use of medications relates to the tendency for many patients to look for simple solutions. In giving antibiotics to a patient with chronic respiratory infections, the basic underlying problem of his low resistance to such infections is not being addressed. One of the common predisposing factors in respiratory infections is the smoking habit. Thus, the first method of treatment for a smoker with recurring respiratory infections ought to be involved with curtailing or eliminating his smoking habit so that the resistance of his respiratory tract can be enhanced. Similarly, in patients with chronic headache, the use of strong analgesics may not be as valid in the long run as the recognition of the stress and tension pattern leading to the headache in the first place.

The last hazard in the too frequent administration of medications is the tendency of organisms to accommodate to such medications. This is seen, for instance, in the tendency of bacterial organisms to develop mutant strains which are highly resistant to antibiotics. Two decades ago, after penicillin had become widely used, strains of resistant staphylococcal germs appeared. These resistant strains, in certain instances, defied all known antibiotics. Thus, a race has developed to find newer, more potent antibiotics which will keep up with the tendency for certain bacteria to adapt, modify themselves, and become resistant.

The host organism (the patient being treated) also adapts to the administration of medication. It is common with the use of pain medications, for instance, for a patient to experience substantial relief from an analgesic, only to find that within a period of days or weeks the same dose of medication does not completely relieve his pain which is present at the same intensity as earlier. Thus, with certain drugs, especially narcotics, habituation or addiction tends to occur, the patient wanting larger and larger doses of medication to keep up with his body's accommodation process. The patient and physician may therefore get into difficulty with unfeasibly high doses of ineffective medication.

It must ultimately be pointed out that pharmaceutical preparations, as effective as they are for certain conditions, rarely "cure" anything. For example, we think of antibiotics as curing pneumonia. In actuality, the curing is done by the body's own defense mechanisms which are given assistance when the antibiotic either kills or immobilizes the bacterium causing the pneumonia. Anti-seizure drugs do not "cure" epilepsy, nor do anti-inflammatory drugs "cure" arthritis. Medications are "crutches"—they are a helpful adjunct to help control a set of symptoms or a set of conditions until a degree of healing can be accomplished by the body itself. In some instances, the lack of knowledge about a particular condition means that we do not yet know how healing or a "cure" can be accomplished by the organism. Insulin-dependent diabetes is such an example. In other cases, new means by which the organism can heal itself are being discovered and are gradually being applied by health practitioners.

A crutch is appropriate when one has a broken leg, provided the leg bones have been set properly and are starting to heal. The crutch is used in anticipation of giving it up at an appropriate time—when healing has occurred. Thus, I prescribe most medications for temporary use, until the system itself has regained its balance and can sustain its own healing powers. Medications are the first line of help to patients in distress, but they need to be supplemented by the ameliorative techniques described in subsequent chapters which have greater potential for more permanent "cure".

Chapter 14

MANIPULATION OF THE ENVIRONMENT

Theoretically at least, one obvious way to decrease the amount of tension and distress at any given time is to decrease the amount of stress to which the organism is exposed.

"Alfred" is a junior executive with a duodenal ulcer. He carries a load of chronic excess tension and relates his stress to his job and his superior, who is autocratic, unfair, and fails to recognize Alfred's contributions and innovations on behalf of his company. Alfred senses that if only he did not have this kind of boss, his tension would be lessened. He does not have the option of getting rid of his boss. However, he does control one variable in his situation—he can decide whether or not he will continue to be employed in that position.

Once identified with the belief that his superior is the cause of his troubles, Alfred may then act to change his employment. He may take another job which is less favorable to him financially or from the standpoint of his career development. Or he may take a job which is less favorable from the standpoint of fitting his needs and personality.

What, then, is the long-term result of this kind of action? I would like to relate my own experience with patients manipulating their environment through such choices. Following a change in employment, there is usually a functional improvement with less tension and decreased distress. Unfortunately, this relief is often short-lived. Many patients ultimately find that their new employment situation has some great disadvantage fully as unsatisfactory as before.

I observe a similar phenomenon among my patients in regard to divorce. One partner may conclude that his or her spouse is the chief cause of his excessive tension and distress. The simple answer is divorce. All too often, however, a subsequent marriage entered into by the patient may also fail. Thus, the spouse faulted in the previous marriage turns out not to be the chief stress in the patient's functional equation after all.

Likewise, I observe patients trying to decrease what they believe is their major cause of tension by focusing on a disagreeable minister, a rebellious teenager, a recalcitrant board of directors, or an unfair competitor. In all of these circumstances, in which patients could not control the actions of someone outside themselves, and compensated for it by making some behavioral change themselves—resigning, moving, switching, or withdrawing—the ultimate results frequently did not reduce their distress as they had hoped.

In all such unsuccessful attempts at manipulating the environment, the problem revolves about the fact that the external factor cited by the subject is not the only significant stress involved. Persons in such circumstances abdicate their responsibility for recognizing the factors within themselves which are major contributing factors in their continuing distress. Thus, a reasonable choice of elements within our environment to which we can adapt must be combined with changes we are willing to make internally in order to successfully link stresses with satisfactory adaptation. In this way, we can ultimately control the amount of tension and distress that we experience.

Chapter 15

RELEASE OF TENSION THROUGH ACTIVITIES

A. PHYSICAL EXERCISE

Physical exercise provides three advantages for man: (1) the maintainance of good muscular tone to provide a reserve for activities we do not commonly engage in; (2) the maintainance of a healthy cardiovascular system through challenge to near-capacity on a regular basis; and (3) the sense of well-being which is due to the escape of excessive tensions through this means.

I am frequently amazed at how quickly muscular tone disappears and tissue atrophies when a body part is immobilized. If a patient with a forearm fracture is placed in a long arm cast from the fingers to the middle of the upper arm for a period of six weeks, the muscle mass of the part of the arm included in the cast loses about one-third of its volume during that time. The arm, when removed from the cast, is weak and appears "puny" when compared to the opposite limb, due merely to the fact that the muscles involved have not been challenged or permitted to move for six weeks.

The basic principle of challenge in regard to physical, mental, and emotional functioning holds that those parts of ourselves which we do not use we eventually lose.

143

A friend of mine who operates a surveying business pointed out to me not long ago that since the advent of hand-held calculators to speed up numerical transactions in the field, he has not figured in his head any basic arithmetic while working at his transit. On one occasion when his calculator ran out of battery power, he was forced to return to making mathematical calculations in his head, which he was scarcely able to do. He had lost the calculating ability during the many months he had not been using his mind for that job.

In the same way, those muscles in the body which we do not use become atrophied and weak. Persons often experience this when they make the first hike in the summer, work in the garden for the first time in the spring, or ski for the first time in the winter: if they have not been maintaining their body and musculature on a regular basis they will experience tremendous soreness the next day in those muscles which were challenged but were not ready for the challenge.

The benefit to the body's chemistry through vigorous exercise was pointed out in the 1975 report of the American Heart Association.[1] The fat and lipid content of the bloodstream, including cholesterol and triglycerides, is commonly accepted as a significant factor in the production of arteriosclerosis. The serum lipids in forty-one middle-aged male long-distance runners were found to be much more like those of younger women than those of sedentary middle-aged men.

Many in the running program had developed the habit only a few years before the blood studies were done, and were not life-long athletes. The A.H.A. report indicates that vigorous exercise may offer the advantage of actually slowing down the insidious underlying disease process that sets the stage for heart attacks in the first place.

The advantage of exercise to the heart and vascular system is now recognized by most physicians. Lawrence Morehouse points out in his book *Total Fitness* that the proper kind of exercise to challenge the cardiorespiratory system is steady, easy activity with a rhythmical, continuous character.[2] One steady-endurance exercise he promotes is running in place. Any other activity which mimics this—such as swimming laps in a pool, skipping rope, jogging, walking up a steep hill, hiking, basketball, tennis and other participatory sports, and riding real or exercise bicycles—offers the same kind of steady activity with a gradual warmup, resulting in elevating the pulse rate to a challenge point for the system.

Provided you do not have a specific health problem, an appropriate heartbeat following five minutes of exercise of this type can be calculated by subtracting your age from the number 220, then multiplying the remainder by .6. For example, the calculation for a fifty-year-old person would be $220-50 = 170$ X $.6 = 102$. Dr. Morehouse refers to this as the basic training pulse rate. There is a cardiovascular training level appropriate for each individual, below which the system is not stimulated sufficiently to produce any training effect.

Three signs indicating that a person has been engaging in exercise sufficient to produce a training effect on the cardiovascular system are: (1) increase in pulse rate (for most persons the level is between 100 and 150 beats per minute); (2) perspiring from most areas of the skin; and (3) breathlessness. Dr. Morehouse stresses that by engaging in a period of exercise of six minutes or less from two to three times a week, most persons can reach the significant indices of cardiovascular training. In general, it is wise for those not in good physical condition to be certain that they have no contraindication to vigorous exercise by a visit with their doctor. Once this is done, a period of challenging exercise two to seven times a week in which the heart rate increases to a level of between 100 and 150, breathlessness occurs, and more-than-normal perspiration occurs, is a significant step toward maintaining proper health.

An excellent self-administered standard test of general physical fitness is found in *Healing For Everyone* by Evarts Loomis and J. Sig Paulson.[3] Of the ten individual tests described in their book, which were modified from Thomas Cureton's *Physical Fitness and Dynamic Health,* one key test will be described here briefly.

Run in place for sixty seconds, lifting your feet at least four inches from the floor. Then take three deep breaths, and hold your breath for sixty seconds. If you are unable to accomplish this easily, your cardiorespiratory system would appear to be in need of training.

Several rules of thumb apply to cardiorespiratory training. The first is to avoid vigorous exercise after a meal of any size. While this precaution is not thought currently to be as great a problem as it was considered to be in the past, it is still valid. Second, when considering exercise approaching capacity, be aware that your capacity will vary from day to day and week to week. I advise patients never to utilize a stop watch, to compete with anyone else doing the same exercise, or even with their own previous record for a particular sequence of exercises. Third, be aware when training occurs and the heart and vascular system begin to become conditioned, that exercise of the same intensity will gradually provide less and less challenge. For example, a woman who is not in condition may choose to jump rope three times a week. Let us say that this woman finds that after one minute and fifty seconds of jumping rope she is aware that her pulse is between 100 and 150, she is breathless, and starting to perspire. Following the rules indicated above, it is time for her to stop or slow down. If she repeats this procedure week by week, she will find that in the second, third, and fourth weeks, if she stops at one minute and fifty seconds, she is less and less breathless and her pulse rate will not increase as much. These are signs that the training of the cardiovascular system is occurring. Therefore, she must gradually increase the time that she is skipping rope to two and a half, three, or perhaps four minutes at the same intensity of activity to maintain the challenge.

The third advantage of regular exercise is the effect it has on the sense of physical well-being and on the state of relaxation of the muscular system. In working with patients for many years and suggesting regular challenging exercise, I have yet to hear any individual tell me they felt worse while they were engaging in such a program. There is always a sense of aliveness in the body which accompanies the process in which the musculature, including the heart, "gets into shape." This vibrant sense may somehow be linked to an awareness of the presence of reserve capacity. I am aware of the change in appearance of many patients when they begin to engage in a program which challenges their physical capacity on a regular basis. They look more alive and there is a new spring in their step.

There is also a beneficial effect on the physiologic systems which manifest some of the distresses discussed earlier. Somehow, the channeling of excess tension into hard physical activity, however brief, tends to spare some of the physical systems which bear the brunt of that tension when it is not expressed through exercise. The state of muscular relaxation seems to be notably better in those who exercise regularly. It may be that somehow the muscles need to "learn" the contrast between the contracted state and the relaxed state, and exercise is one important step in that learning process. I have experienced in my own patients a tendency for those suffering from headache and backache to gain the ability to deal with these kinds of pain much more effectively once they are on a regular exercise program. A series of exercises aimed at increasing relaxation of specific body parts will be discussed in Chapter 16.

Several years ago, a scientific study followed twenty-three men with established primary ("essential") high blood pressure for a period of six months.[4] No changes in other avenues of treatment for their condition were made during those six months, in salt restriction, diet, weight reduction, or anti-hypertensive medications.

The men were put on a twice-weekly walk-jog-calisthenic graded-exercise program approaching their physical capacity, much the same as the exercise program I have already described. After six months, their blood pressures were compared with the figures from the beginning of the study. There was an average fall of thirteen points in the systolic (upper pressure reading) and twelve points in the lower (diastolic) reading of each participant. Thus, for example, one man with a blood pressure of 153 over 102, on the average, dropped his blood pressure in that six-month period to a level of 140 over 90, apparently due only to the exercise he engaged in. Control subjects who did not have high blood pressure showed an average drop of only six points in the diastolic reading.

Exercise may have a beneficial effect on patients with coronary artery disease and angina pectoris (chest pain in which the heart muscle is inadequately supplied with oxygen from the coronary arteries). Angina is frequently the first warning of coronary artery disease eventually leading to heart attacks.

In recent years, in several locations around the United States, exercise programs have been designed and implemented to give coronary disease patients the opportunity to improve their functioning heart status and to allow medical specialists to conduct research in the field. One of these programs is sponsored by CAPRI.[5] It is a regular, monitored, individually tailored exercise program for persons who have suffered heart attacks or for those with anginal heart disease.

B.   Task-Oriented Exercise

The above section on exercise will sound like drudgery to many readers. It need not be so, and in hopes of pointing out some of the other ways that exercise can be utilized, I bring up in this section exertion in work activities. Many persons, particularly men, are often employed in work that requires steady, muscular exercise such as lifting, carrying, hammering, or climbing brief distances. This form of exercise is excellent for maintaining the tone of the muscular parts involved—usually limbs, chest, trunk, and back. Frequently, however, there is not present the kind of challenging total exercise which stimulates the heart, lungs, and circulatory system to near-capacity activity.

Therefore, even for individuals who regularly do muscular work on their job, I recommend a form of cardiovascular exercise such as described in the previous section or some kind of athletic or constructive pursuit, including the following: splitting wood for five to fifteen minutes with an axe or wedge and mall; mowing a lawn with a reel-type push mower; playing a game of tennis or skiing nonstop from the top of the chair lift; running up one flight of stairs with a load of laundry; and riding a bicycle to the supermarket to pick up a small load of groceries.

The number of power-driven gadgets which now spare us from physical work is quite incredible. These range all the way from automobiles, motorcycles, and motor bikes to power winches, power mowers, skill saws, chain saws, hedge clippers, can openers, automatic door openers, and automatic tooth brushes.

Too frequently we are tempted to utilize such gadgets, which rob us of the opportunity for muscular challenge and exercise.

C. CREATIVE PURSUITS

The next type of activity helpful in reducing tension is that of creativity in art, sculpture, music, writing, drawing, painting, poetry, woodworking, the design and sewing of clothing, and many, many other possibilities. The expression of creative impulses in these ways provides an outlet for excessive tension, making it unnecessary for that energy to be channeled into the pathways which lead to physical, mental, and emotional distresses.

It is interesting to note that a number of great masters of literature and music have revealed that they had an inner urge to create that was so strong that frequently they could not rest until they had given it expression. This urge to creativity can actually be regarded as a stress which induces a sufficient amount of tension to push us into expressing our energy in whatever creative way we possess.

Many people who have countered my suggestions for expressing themselves in creative ways become very defensive and deny that they have any creative ability. In practical terms, in working with people who have this feeling about themselves, I have frequently discovered that if they are willing to be open to it, creative abilities do reside within them and await discovery. Persons who discover abilities to create through singing, playing instruments, sculpting, or dancing derive great satisfaction from such pursuits.

I am consistently impressed with both the amount of creative talent which persons will express once they are open to its discovery in their inner being and with the lowering of distress levels once a creative outlet and a focus for excessive tension are found.

The benefit of creative pursuits with regard to human happiness has been confirmed by the gradual establishment of the profession of occupational therapy. In many large hospitals, particularly those with mental health units, the occupational therapist plays an increasingly important role in helping people find creative ways to permit the energy of their excess tension be expressed.

D.   VOCATIONAL AND AVOCATIONAL PURSUITS

Other pursuits of an avocational nature can also transmute excessive tension from distress targets in the system. The extensive volunteer system in hospitals, churches, schools, counseling centers, and nursing homes serves this function, as do hobbies —stamp and coin collecting, weaving, reading, furniture refinishing, landscaping and gardening, studying geneology, to name just a few. One survey of retired persons has shown that maintaining activity and meaningful interests are significant factors in the continuance of good health.[6]

One's occupation or lifework may provide a significant outlet for excessive tension. The relatively high value placed on work in our society is enhanced if the subject himself genuinely enjoys his work, particularly if he sees it in terms of its contribution to the functioning of social, economic, and service institutions. In this case, it is much easier to transmute the energies and have them fully expressed in a vocation.

E.   PHYSICAL EXPRESSION OF THE EMOTIONS

Individuals who are chronically anxiety-prone, chronically sad and depressed, or chronically angry and resentful suffer from overdone emotions which frequently feed back into the system as additional stresses and provide the breeding ground for excessive tension. It is important for such persons to be able to find a socially acceptable activity which provides an outlet for these emotions.

Let me start with anger. Anger is a normal emotion experienced by nearly everyone at one time or another, and often related to the frustration of a perceived need. I frequently suggest to patients who experience excessive anger and outrage a good deal of the time that they find outlets such as shouting, pounding, thumping, slamming, or pummeling. Pounding may be carried out on beanbag chairs, mattresses, pillows, full laundry bags, and other inanimate objects which absorb the patient's energy without damaging or being damaged by him. Bioenergetic analysis, developed by Dr. Alexander Lowen as an extension of the therapeutic principles of Wilhelm Reich, employs just such techniques to elicit the physical expression of deep emotions.[7] Other so-called body therapies—primal therapy, for example—and psychodrama also encourage the release of emotion through such physical means.

I have seen many patients who clearly harbor resentment and anger which they have never been able to express, either toward someone still important in their lives or someone important in their past who might even be deceased. As long as the recollection of relationships with persons in the past engenders high levels of negative emotion, there are unresolved issues clogging up the input and processing channels of the organism, preventing input of a more productive kind of data. This will be discussed more fully in Chapter 19.

One good rule of thumb in a household where family members need to get along better with each other is to agree that it is acceptable to talk about one's anger, to shout, slam doors, pound on cabinets, and otherwise work out ways of expressing the anger, as long as those ways do not impugn the character of anyone else or question their motivations. This kind of an agreement within a family essentially says, "It is O.K. to have negative feelings", and "It is O.K. to express those feelings as long as there is no destruction of property or attacking the character of other members of the family."

Anxiety is a condition associated with many physical distresses and is experienced by a great portion of the population at one time or another. Anxiety is an emotional state of vague uneasiness which is akin to fear but not as clearly defined or as severe as the latter. Both are related to an injury or threat of injury as perceived by the individual.

Two helpful methods for releasing anxiety are, first, sharing the anxious feelings with other persons, particularly those who listen empathetically, and, second, learning appropriate breathing techniques to counteract the improper breathing found during anxiety states.

Gordon Deckert has described the type of breathing pattern associated with fear and anxiety in the following terms. The subject tends to breathe in the "upper" register of the breathing cycle, inhaling deeply, exhaling partially, and then again inhaling before the full amount of air can be expelled fully. This tends to cause more rapid breathing than normal, and gives the subject the feeling that he is "not getting enough air". A slightly gasping quality, and a wavering, thin pattern of speech, follow from this irregular pattern of exhalation.[8]

Anxiety, fear, and panic are increasing degrees of the same emotion. As with all emotions, each is at once an output (an expression of the system) and an input (a stress). In this respect, overdone emotions can easily produce a self-feeding cycle; once anxiety is triggered the subject becomes increasingly anxious about his anxiety and the cycle escalates to outright fear and possibly sheer panic.

Sadness is the emotion which eventually results when the subject is aware of a sense of real or threatened loss. The loss may be related to significant persons, property, position, or esteem. Usually, sadness is the most important element in depression.

Physical expression of sadness is accomplished through crying. All too often I see patients who believe that it is a sign of weakness to cry and who will go to almost any length to suppress crying by being busy, becoming angry, or engaging in self-destructive habits such as smoking, drinking, or overeating. This refusal to express sadness through crying is often the result of a childhood prohibition expressed by peers or family in such terms as, "Big girls and boys don't cry." This tends to make the youngster feel that there is something wrong with crying and, consequently, in adult life, the person goes to great lengths to avoid it.

The story of "L. D." illustrates the effects of sadness on the system, especially when no outlet has been provided for its expression. This woman was plagued with recurring nausea with occasional vomiting. Examination by X-ray showed no ulcer. The motility of the stomach was quite slow and there was delayed emptying of the barium at the outlet of the stomach at the time of the X-ray examination. She failed to improve from any medicinal approach I suggested, and only after taking a meticulous history was I finally able to relate the beginning of her nausea and vomiting to the death of her brother. Their relationship had been particularly close, but the patient had never actually psychologically acknowledged her brother's death, said her goodbyes to him, or expressed to anyone else her anxieties about what she would do without his presence in her life. On expressing these anxieties, and working through by role-playing the farewell to her brother, a great deal of crying occurred, which the woman had not permitted herself to do. Subsequently, the nausea and vomiting became much less frequent and very soon disappeared altogether.

Concerning the expression of emotions such as anxiety and fear or anger and sadness, I do not wish to leave the impression that it is wise to dwell on their expression. Finding effective outlets for them, however, tends to remove them from the feedback cycle and keep them from building up to a dysfunctional situation. Conversely, emotions which are present but denied and not expressed will inevitably appear in some other emotional way in the system, or affect the mental or physical apparatus in adverse ways. Therefore, once the excess emotion is present, it is a mark of progress to recognize it and find a suitable expression for it which will discharge its strength.

F.   Self-Expression through Writing

I have previously mentioned writing in describing worthwhile creative pursuits that effectively aid in the discharge of excess tension. I would like here to make a special note of the importance of writing in terms of personal growth. I urge persons in my counseling practice to write. This means writing down dream contents, random thoughts as they may occur during the work day, and thoughts which occur in periods of relaxation and passive contemplation. It is also helpful to keep a journal of reflections about one's growth process. This provides encouragement in terms of looking back and seeing where one has been and comparing it to the state to which one has progressed. Periodically, we tend to lose track of our own growth and progress unless it is in written form. Writing as a part of goal-setting exercises is also of great importance, and will be discussed further in Chapter 22.

In *The Art of Hanging Loose in an Uptight World,* Dr. Ken Olsen mentions a writing technique which I have found very helpful. He suggests that persons experiencing insomnia pay attention to what is happening with their thoughts. This, in essence, is part of the technique of disidentifying from the stream of thought and observing its content from the vantage point of the self (see Chapter 20). When the thought content is contacted, Olsen suggests that it then be written down in consecutive form on a sheet of paper or in a notebook. When the extent of the thoughts for that particular time have been transferred to paper, the paper can then be moved to another room, whereupon the person can return to his bed and give himself "permission" to fall asleep. Several patients of mine have benefited from this technique. I have also found that the thought content in this exercise tends to be highly repetitive and provides material which a counselor or therapist would find useful in terms of working with the subject on his individual growth.

G.   Use of Humor

I have talked in the preceding pages about various activities which encourage the release of energy accompanying excessive tension. Humor is another such activity. The ability to see humor in our situations is a valuable strength which all of us could cultivate. Tense moments are often broken by laughter. Frequently, it takes only the insight from someone slightly removed from a given situation to see humor in it. This is one of the qualities the self can bring to a situation: when consciousness is centered in the self and not identified with physical, mental, or emotional relationships or with any situation which appears to be threatening, the humorous element in it can be sensed from that position as observer.

Chapter 16

CONSCIOUS PASSIVE RELAXATION

A dictionary definition of "relax" is: (1) to make loose, (2) to rest, (3) to become less tense. In a very real sense, the state of relaxation is the opposite of the multiple states of distress which are triggered by excessive tension.

Sometimes patients come to me relating that they have seen another physician and no organic process has been found to explain their symptoms, and have been told various things from "There is nothing wrong" to "Just forget it and go about your business" or "Just take it easy and relax". There are several devastating errors in these kinds of statements. In the first case, when distressing symptoms are present, there is *always something wrong.* I believe a doctor should more accurately say, "I find nothing organically or structurally wrong to explain your symptoms." Indeed, a great deal of man's distresses do not result from organic disturbances in the body, but from functional disturbances in the organism, whether mental, emotional, physical, or spiritual.

To illustrate how great a distress can result from a functional problem, consider the pain present in a calf muscle when a "charlie horse" is present. This type of pain is very intense. There is nothing organically or structurally wrong with the muscle. If a biopsy were to be taken from such a muscle during the grip of a charlie horse, and the piece of muscle tissue submitted to a pathologist for examination, no abnormalities in that muscle biopsy would be visible under the microscope. Functionally, however, a great deal is wrong. The muscle fibers are overcontracting and far too great a percentage of them are working overtime. The result is inadequate blood supply, accumulation of excess lactic acid, and marked pain.

It is not feasible for most people to "forget" a distress and completely ignore it. Physiologically speaking, it is probably true that the awareness of distress, like an element of data, is imprinted in the memory permanently once it has passed the threshold. To go about our business may make us less aware of the distress, but such phenomena reenter the conscious mind when we are quiet and not focusing on external affairs, as in the moments before we go to sleep.

To "just take it easy and relax" in an effort to alleviate distress is easier said than done. Therefore, in the following paragraphs, I will present three different approaches to the learning of relaxation, with specific instructions and methods which can be followed in a conscious routine. The ultimate goal, of course, is for the relaxation to become an unconscious habit. For someone who does not know how to relax at will, the process of training the unconscious by the regular practice of a routine centered in consciousness is the easiest route to follow.

The first series of relaxation exercises deals with loosening up the various muscle parts. Loosening the neck and shoulder areas comes first and is done while seated, either in a chair or while cross-legged or standing. There are six cardinal directions in which the head and neck can move. These are forward to drop the chin on the chest; backward to arch the neck; bending to the left side; bending to the right side, in each case pointing the ear downward toward the shoulder; and rotating the head on its vertical axis first to the left and then back to the right.

These cardinal motions should be gone through slowly, allowing the head to flex forward and extend backward, then from side to side, and lastly turning from one side to the other, gradually in each direction reaching the point at which the tendons, ligaments, and muscles begin to feel tight. Later, when the muscles have begun to obtain good tone, one slight bounce can be done at the end of each range of motion.

The next exercise is an isometric procedure done by placing the palm of the hand against the side of the head and resisting the hand with the head and neck so that no motion occurs. As the push is accomplished, a tightening of the neck muscles on that side of the head will be felt. This is repeated two or three times and then the palm is moved to a different location over the skull. Altogether, eight different places around the head are utilized so that each section of the neck muscles gets a chance to contract and resist the hand against the head.

The next stage involves lifting the shoulders upward toward the ears, tightening shoulders and neck, holding for about three or four seconds, and then letting both shoulders drop suddenly while breathing out and saying "Relax" to oneself as the shoulders drop. This is repeated four or five times.

The next step is rotation of the shoulders, both together, to describe two parallel circles. The shoulders are raised as much as possible and then rotated forward as much as possible, then downward and backward, and finally back to a resting position. This is repeated several times in a forward direction, as just described, and then reversed so that the shoulders describe the same circles proceeding in a backward direction.

The last exercise for the head and neck involves extending the arms straight out from the body and parallel to the floor. The arms are stretched out as much as possible and a finger is used to describe a circle about six to eight inches in diameter, first by rotating the arms in a forward direction, then by repeating the procedure in a reverse direction. Imagine that the index finger is a piece of chalk which can barely touch a blackboard in either direction. Let the chalk describe a circle on the blackboards first in one direction and then in a reverse direction.

The second body area to be loosened includes the upper arms, forearms, and hands. The first step is to hold the arms one at a time, bent at a right angle, with the forearm parallel to the floor and the upper arm in a vertical position with the elbow against the body. At any chosen signal, the arm is completely relaxed and the forearm allowed to drop precipitously so that the entire arm assumes a vertical position with the hand at the side. When the arm is completely relaxed in this fashion, the forearm will come to rest with a slight bounce as the limitation of this straightening motion of the elbow reaches its fullest extent. This is repeated two or three times, first on one side and then on the other.

The next step is to lean slightly forward and to the right, letting the extended arm hang loosely from the shoulder. The arm is first swung in a small circle, as if it were a weight at the bottom of a chain. Then the hand is shaken vigorously back and forth in a motion similar to shaking water off a wet hand when no towel is available. The same shaking motion is then extended to the entire arm while rotating it slightly on the long axis as much as the shoulder permits. These motions are then repeated with the opposite hand.

The next phase involves loosening ankles and legs. In a standing position, first lift the right knee slightly, holding onto the top of a chair if necessary for balance. The right foot is then gently shaken in a forward-sideways-backward motion combined almost into a rotary pattern. At the same time, if the calf is relaxed, the large muscles of the lower leg will jiggle loosely. This exercise is repeated for the left ankle and left calf.

Next, to relax the thigh muscles, sit at the edge of a chair with the feet flat on the floor and the knees flexed ninety degrees. A series of shaking motions is done with both knees together, alternately adducting (drawing the knees toward one another) and abducting (drawing them away from one another). This shaking motion, as the thigh muscles are relaxed, results in a stimulating sort of jiggling of the quadriceps and hamstring muscles of the thigh.

The last step is to bring looseness to the entire trunk. From a standing position, let the head fall gently forward to a relaxed position of flexion. Permit the shoulders to fall forward and downward, then allow the trunk to flex at the waist, bending forward. Allow the trunk and arms to bend further forward, the arms hanging loosely in a comfortable position, the hands attaining a comfortable level between the knees and the floor. Then gently bounce at the end of these series of dropping motions.

During the above series of loosening exercises, it is important to maintain the mind-set of permitting the muscles to relax.

It is helpful to repeat the words "Relax" or "Let go" frequently during the motions described.

The second approach to relaxation is that of educating the muscles regarding contraction and relaxation. I am convinced that many persons who believe they are in a relaxed physical posture are not actually relaxed because they really do not know what relaxation is. This is only to say that awareness of our own tension and relaxation is profoundly influenced by our past conditioning.

Not infrequently I observe signs of excessive muscle contraction in a patient and I suggest that he or she may be tense. Most often, the patient tells me, "I am really quite relaxed". I think this is not conscious denial as much as it is a failure to be aware of what a really relaxed state is, having never had the experience of being in that state.

With this in mind, I would like to offer the following instructions which will permit the reader to begin to experience the extremes of contraction and relaxation more distinctly.

Do the following exercises lying on your back, face up, hands at your sides or gently folded over the abdomen. The feet should be uncrossed, with one or two pillows under the knees. Glasses, pencils, shoes, and anything that can fall out of the pockets should be removed beforehand. All this preparation done, close your eyes, and clear your mind of all extraneous thoughts.

First, pay attention to your breathing. Take two or three deep breaths, filling your lungs with as much air as you can, holding it briefly, and be aware of the state of muscle contractions across the back and chest while holding your breath. Now, relaxing all the chest muscles, allow the air to empty slowly from the lungs without doing any muscular work. As the air leaves the lungs, say to yourself, "Relax". Now, take a second breath, paying attention to the state of contraction by holding your breath briefly before exhaling. Then exhale, letting the air escape gently yet as fast as it wishes, as you relax all the chest muscles.

Now, turn your attention to the abdominal muscles, pulling them as tight as you possibly can, as if you are preparing to do a sit-up exercise. Hold the contraction for three or four seconds, very tightly, and then let go suddenly. Pay attention to the feeling as you let go. Then tighten the abdominal muscles once again, holding for three or four seconds, and then let go again, saying to yourself as you relax the muscles, "Let go". Repeat this one more time.

Next, pull in the buttock muscles as tight as you can, tightening all the pelvic muscles along with them. Hold them tight for three or four seconds and then rapidly let go of all the muscles at once, leaving them limp and loose. Say to yourself, "I am relaxed; I am comfortable; my muscles are heavy." Again contract the muscles in the buttocks as tight as you can for three or four seconds and then say, "Let go", and let them relax.

Turn your attention to the hands next. Clench both fists, all the fingers, and both wrists as tightly as you can and hold for three or four seconds. Then let the tightness go suddenly, completely relaxing both hands. Repeat this again, clenching the fists for four seconds and letting go into a state of relaxation. Next, clench both fists, forearms, and upper arms, contracting every muscle all at once for four seconds as tightly as you can and then suddenly relax, letting all the muscles go limp. Do this once more by clenching the fists, forearms, and upper arms— all the muscles that you can at once—and then suddenly letting go, letting the muscles flop, letting the elbows and hands drop to the floor, heavy and relaxed. Your arms and hands are now especially relaxed; the hands begin to feel warm and the arms feel heavy and limp. Now, stop again to pay attention to your breathing, taking in as much air as the lungs will hold, hesitating briefly, tightening the chest muscles and being aware of the tension, holding the breath for three seconds and then letting the breath go. Relax and let the chest muscles go limp, while allowing all the air to escape as quickly and comfortably as it wants to. As you exhale, say to yourself, "I am relaxed; I am comfortable; I am warm."

Pull your toes upward toward your head next and feel the tension in the calves and ankles. Tighten all the muscles in your feet all the way up into the calves and thighs, lifting the foot off the floor slightly and straightening the knee slightly, pulling everything taut for three seconds, then letting go swiftly and letting the leg go limp and heavy. Do this again, tightening all the muscles, pulling the foot up, pressing downward and upward at the same time, tensing all the muscles at once—foot, calf, and thigh. With the foot slightly off the floor, hold it tightly for three seconds, and then let go, letting the knee drop to the pillow. Repeat this twice with the other leg.

Then pay attention to the muscles of your shoulders, neck, face, eyes, and scalp. Press the shoulders upward toward the ears, tensing the muscles from the shoulders across and upward to the back of the neck, tightening the jaw and neck muscles beneath the chin and all the facial muscles around the eyes, forehead, and cheeks. Purse the lips and furrow the brow. Tighten all these muscles at once so that everything from the points of the shoulder up to the forehead is as tight as you can make it for three seconds. Then, relax. Let everything go all at once. Let the facial tension go, let the wrinkles disappear, let the muscles go limp. Repeat this for three seconds and then let go and relax.

Now you are ready to do everything all at once. Take as deep a breath as you can, tightening down the chest muscles while holding the breath, tightening the abdominal muscles, the buttocks, the fists, the arms, the legs and feet, the shoulders, neck and face all as hard as you can for three seconds. Then, suddenly breathing out, relax all at once, letting everything go limp as you exhale and say, "Relax". Repeat this a second time, tightening everything from the chest, abdomen, buttocks, legs, arms, shoulders, and face as hard as you can for three seconds and then suddenly relaxing. Give yourself permission to just lie in that comfortable position, relaxing for several minutes, letting all the muscles exist in a limp state, doing only the minimal amount of muscular work necessary to keep your breath going.

The above series of exercises can be very helpful in terms of merely practicing to be relaxed and also at times of mounting tension. It may also be used if you are having difficulty relaxing before bedtime.

The third approach to relaxation is done either in a seated position with the spine fairly straight, the shoulders relaxed, hands loosely in the lap, and both feet on the floor; or it may be done in a lying-down, face-up position, the knees slightly bent over a pillow and the hands loosely lying on the abdomen or at the sides. Permit your eyelids to close gently and then say to yourself, "I feel quite quiet and I am beginning to feel very relaxed. I am aware of an area of warmth the size of a dime on the top of my scalp. The area of warmth is beginning to spread out over all sides of my scalp. It is proceeding downward to my eyebrows, my ears, and the back of my head. As the warm feeling spreads, it brings with it a state of relaxation in the muscles of my forehead and neck. The wave of warmth descends over my face, down over the neck into the shoulders. The muscles of my face relax. The small muscles around my eyes relax and go limp. The muscles in my tongue allow it to fall loosely in the floor of my mouth. My jaw opens slightly as the jaw muscles relax. The contraction in my neck and shoulders is gone. The warmth flows down both arms. My upper arms, forearms, my hands, and my fingers are becoming warm. My shoulders, my arms, my hands, and my fingers are growing heavy, relaxed, and warm. My arms are becoming heavy, relaxed, and warm. The warm feeling spreads downward over my chest and upper back, downward, downward over my abdomen and low back, down to my pelvis and buttocks. My breathing becomes easy, gentle, and regular. The muscles of my abdomen relax and my back gives the full weight of my body to the chair or to the rug as I relax. The pelvic and buttock muscles relax and become heavy. The warmth spreads down, down my thighs, my knees, my calves, and my feet. I feel the warmth spreading into my toes. I feel my legs becoming heavy, relaxed, and warm. I give the full weight of my legs to the rug and the pillow. They are heavy and warm. Warmth flows to all parts of my body. All my muscles are becoming relaxed, warm, and comfortable. My mind is quiet. My emotions are calm. My mind is quiet, my emotions are calm, my body is relaxed. My skin is warm. I am alert. I am aware of my inner relaxation. I am aware of an inner stillness. I am quiet, comfortable, relaxed, calm, and warm."

Critics would say that the above is only a series of words and does not translate itself into actual states of relaxation. My experience has been otherwise. I personally find these relaxation exercises very helpful. Moreover, when I supervise exercises such as the last two I have described, clients and students in my classes report that they do indeed feel very relaxed and are able to begin using these phrases at home to introduce relaxation into their routines.

One way to check out the state of tension or contraction in the musculoskeletal system of your physical body is to "look in" on it from the position of an observer at some point when you are driving. Many people, when they perform this test, observe themselves grabbing the steering wheel in a very tense fashion, squeezing the wheel with their hands, and contracting the shoulder muscles and upper body as if to wrestle with the car. Once they have observed this, they can then voluntarily choose to grasp the steering wheel further down, only as tightly as is necessary to make the required motions, and to relax their shoulders and upper body, controlling the car in just as reliable a fashion as before yet without the intense overcontractions of the body parts involved.

Before leaving the subject of relaxation, an additional comment on breathing is in order. Breathing is the process of taking in air containing oxygen to supply the body with the essential component oxygen, used in many critical chemical processes sustaining life in the physical system. I previously mentioned that anxiety can be frequently confirmed from the pattern of breathing. An astute observer can also detect sadness and anger in the breathing pattern. Breathing may be divided into chest (costal) breathing and abdominal (diaphragmatic) breathing. In the normal state, approximately half the lung volume of air is exchanged with each method. With inspiration, the muscles of the chest lift the ribs upward and outward. This induces a very minimal vacuum in the pleural space between the chest wall and the lung. Because of this slight vacuum, the lungs then expand in order for the pleural lining of the lung to expand with the chest.

At the same time, in normal inspiration, the diaphragm muscle (a very thin sheet of muscle existing in the horizontal plane and shaped like two domes, one in either half of the body and separating the lungs in the chest above from the contents of the abdomen below) contracts, attempting to pull inward the lower margins of the ribs. The lower margins of the ribs, however, are being expanded or at least fixed by the motion of the chest muscles. The only direction that the diaphragm muscle can move, then, is to pull downward as its fibers shorten.

It is helpful to observe your own chest and abdominal-diaphragmatic breathing by looking in a mirror. Observe first the upward and outward movement of the chest on inspiration. Observe then its downward and inward movement on exhalation. Then, looking in the mirror somewhat sideways, observe whether the abdomen moves forward during inspiration. You can check this out by placing one hand over the back side of the flank and the other hand over the middle of the abdomen. If the space between your hands expands and the abdominal hand moves forward as you breathe in, then you are using your diaphragm. If there is no forward movement of the abdominal hand, the diaphragm is not contributing to the exchange of air and you need to learn to do so. Many persons with chronic obstructive lung disease, asthma, and emphysema have never learned to breathe properly with the diaphragm. In my experience, when the exchange is already compromised by disease, it usually gives a great feeling of relief for a patient to begin to increase his air exchange by using the diaphragmatic portion of his breathing apparatus.

One fast way of checking out diaphragmatic breathing is to be aware of your breathing pattern just before going to sleep. The body falls into a normal respiratory pattern utilizing a significant portion of the diaphragmatic breathing as sleep approaches. By placing one hand on the abdomen while lying on your back, an upward movement of the abdomen should be felt when the breath is being taken in. The hand should then fall during exhalation as the breath escapes from the lungs. If diaphragmatic motion is not present in either the mirror test or the pre-sleep test, it is helpful to obtain advice from a respiratory therapist or physician to learn how to breathe effectively so as to consciously expand the abdominal muscles during inspiration. In beginning to train the respiratory apparatus, the diaphragm will follow along as the abdominal muscles are thrust forward in inspiration. This begins as a conscious training effort and eventually will result in an unconscious habit of satisfactory breathing.

Many people can benefit from the techniques described above. There are others, however, who seem to need confirmation of their progress in learning to relax by some kind of measurable proof. In other words, many individuals may be aware of the positive feedback effects of techniques like the relaxation exercises I mentioned, while others may be less aware and will learn better when they can take some objective measurement of the positive feedback influence.

The science of electroencephalography, the recording and interpretation of the electrical patterns of brain wave activity, has grown since the 1920s, and the procedure is now commonplace in medicine. Certain brain problems can be localized and seizure tendencies predicted on the basis of interpretations of brain wave electrical activity. Biofeedback is the name given to the emerging science of measuring physiological functions and providing feedback of those measurements to subjects for the benefit of their education and training in self-awareness.

Brain wave activity has been divided into four levels, based upon the electrical frequency in cycles per second, associated with output from certain anatomical brain sources and with certain states of consciousness. Delta wave activity, one-half to four cycles per second, originating in the central and parietal (above the ear) regions, is produced during deep sleep. Theta activity, four to eight cycles per second and also originating in the central and parietal brain, is present in light sleep and in deep states of reverie. Alpha wave activity, eight to thirteen cycles per second, originating from the occipital (posterior) brain, is present in a state of calm and relaxed wakefulness, when the subject imagines pleasure, security, warmth, or lets the eyes go out of focus. Beta wave activity, thirteen to thirty cycles per second, originating from the cerebral cortex, is found in states of normal, fully conscious activities and rational thinking. Experiencing twinges of emotion seems to cause the Alpha wave activity to yield to Beta activity.[1]

In the past ten years, a variety of electrical devices have been designed and perfected to give visual or auditory feedback of the state of electrical activity of the brain.

Much data has been accumulated by investigators working with Alpha feedback electroencephalograph machines, which give audible signals distinguishing Alpha, Beta, and Theta waves. It has become apparent that with some degree of training the desirable Alpha state can be increased in most subjects. Ten percent of subjects, for reasons not clear, cannot produce Alpha wave activity at all.

Two other types of electrical devices designed to study biofeedback are those measuring skin temperature (temperature level is indicated on an indicator dial) and those measuring relaxation or contraction of the muscles.

Dr. Elmer Green, of the Menninger Clinic, is one experimenter who has had a significant amount of experience in the use of thermal feedback devices for training in control of bodily functions. Dr. Green combines biofeedback training with autogenic phrases and principles of autogenic therapy patterned after Schultz and Luthe, who found that the initially important principle was that when the subject actively tried to raise the temperature of his skin, it invariably went down.[2] When, however, he relaxed, closed his eyes, and listened to phrases utilizing words such as "quiet," "relaxed," "heavy," "comfortable," "warm," "serene," and "still," his skin temperature was much more likely to rise. Green and his associates also found that subjects began to invent their own visualizations when they discovered that certain phrases were personally helpful.[3]

The principles of biofeedback are, first, that every change in the physiological (body function) state is accompanied by an appropriate change in the mental and emotional states, conscious or unconscious (likewise, every change in mental and emotional states is accompanied by an appropriate change in the physiological state);[4] and second, that any function which can be monitored and the results fed back to the subject can be voluntarily controlled by that subject.[5]

With training, most subjects are able to correlate awareness of their internal state with physiological changes in function measured on the biofeedback monitor. Awareness of the psychological state is usually experienced in a series of images or symbols. By learning to invoke those subjective images and thoughts, the subject can make the associated physiological changes occur.

With biofeedback learning the relaxed state can be achieved, with measurably increased skin temperature, increased muscular relaxation, increased Alpha brain wave production, decreased pulse rate, decreased respiratory rate, decreased blood pressure, increased galvanic skin response, and decreased lactic acid level.[6] Work in decreasing blood pressure by utilizing biofeedback is reported by Benson;[7] heart rhythm control by Weiss and Engel;[8] decreased migraine and muscle contraction headaches by Sargent and others;[9] pain diminution by Gannon and Sternbach;[10] and anxiety reduction by Haugen and his colleagues.[11] Cardiac rhythm disturbances, Raynaud's phenomenon, hypertension, insomnia, and phobias have also been reduced through biofeedback training. The greatest success has been achieved with muscle contraction and migraine headaches, chronic anxiety states, insomnia, and phobias. More moderate success is reported with high blood pressure.[12]

Similar benefits are possible with the use of electromyograph (EMG feedback device), in which individuals learn through a period of training to relax the muscles in the area where electrodes are attached. By observing a dial or hearing a sound which tell him whether his muscles are relaxed or not, the subject learns to identify with a certain internal state associated with relaxed muscles.

Thus, with all three methods mentioned here, the biofeedback subject learns to identify and is then trained to produce the subjective state that is associated with the production of Alpha brain wave activity, rise in skin temperature, and the relaxation of skeletal muscles.

Dr. Norman Shealy has had extensive experience in the field of pain and methods for coping with it. One of the most successful has been the combination of autogenic training and biofeedback. Dr. Shealy found that his patients could successfully deal with their pain if they learned to purposefully put themselves into Alpha or Theta states and remain there.[13] Eighty percent of patients experiencing headache pain from muscle contraction or migraine sources are able with temperature biofeedback to learn to control their pain. Biofeedback training has also been used successfully for such diverse distresses as weakness and fatigue, chronic backache, glaucoma, and hyperventilation.

Stress is an alerting mechanism which accelerates the brain's activities into the Beta state. Voluntarily putting the brain activity into Alpha or Theta states, as Shealy describes, automatically reduces the effects of stress, whatever they are. Stress often manifests itself as pain, and pain and anxiety are

frequently linked: a high level of anxiety can lower one's tolerance for pain. Pain, in turn, aggravates the emotional anxiety
state. This constant feedback experience of a physical distress
aggravating an emotional distress and vice-versa is frequently
interrupted only by some cataclysm within the system, or by a
decision by the self to take charge of the body, mind, and emotions and to start sending positive messages.

Biofeedback and autogenic training both function effectively to reduce the negative effects of stress and excessive tension by training the mental faculty to balance physical and
emotional functions. The training effects follow the pathways
outlined in the functional model diagram provided in Section II.

For years it was accepted in medical and scientific circles in
the West that hypothalamic functions were exclusively autono-
mous. The experience of many investigators in the last fifteen
years, however, indicates that through volition and proper training, much of those functions could be varied and brought under
some degree of control. When an individual decides to take
charge and issue positive messages utilizing this control, decreased distress and increased health result.

Chapter 17

MEDITATION

In the last five years in the United States, the practice of meditation has become common. Transcendental meditation is a rapidly spreading movement now involving tens of thousands of persons.

Meditation is not easily defined. It is helpful to begin by mentioning some of the associated descriptive words which apply to it. Above all, meditation is associated with relaxation. All meditative techniques with which I am familiar have as one of their guiding principles the assumption of a relaxed posture and/or state of mind to begin with. The second factor common to meditative techniques is concentration. Transcendental meditation involves concentration on a mantra. Other forms involve concentration on a seed thought, a word, a picture, a series of phrases, a goal or objective, or a conundrum or riddle. Concentration is especially apparent in the practice of certain forms of yoga. The intense concentration of certain masters of yoga has been demonstrated in experimental laboratory tests by the inability of others to distract them from their meditation by banging gongs, flashing lights, or even holding hot test tubes against their skin.[1]

The next element common to all forms of meditation is that it is involved with or leads to an altered state of consciousness. It is one of the various states of consciousness enumerated by Garfield and Pelletier in *Consciousness East and West.* This state makes possible an inward-directed sort of journey in which the meditator frequently contacts a deeper or "higher" part of himself, often sensing that he has reached the ultimate reality transcending his normal experience.

For many, this journey is a mystical one, as described by Wapnick.[2] The first element in it can be termed the "awakening of the self" which is involved in the realization of a strikingly new and different level of existence beyond normal sensation— a higher and more desirable level. This awakening is followed by a deepening consciousness that the former patterns of living are no longer satisfactory. The third stage is characterized by a joyous apprehension of what the meditator experiences to be a more absolute reality. There is a sense of separateness and at the same time an awareness of relationship with the ultimate. The fourth stage is that of a sense of aloneness and alienation from previous experiences. The next stage is the culmination of total absorption in an asocial world described as a state of pure consciousness in which the individual experiences "no thing." The final stage for most mystics is the return to the requirements of the social situation in which he exists, reinvolvement with the world, with the freedom to live within it—without, however, society's customs and institutions providing obstacles to his self-fulfillment.

Regardless of the level of involvement, anyone practicing meditation will experience increased inner peacefulness, a sense of calm, and a sense of organization and control from a point of consciousness continually coming closer to that definition of the inner self and ultimately the higher self.

Any meditative approach has as part of its aim the attainment of feelings, motives, and values that were previously held out of awareness. The freeing of one's self from distracting stimuli to concentrate more fully on subtle stimuli unconsciously shaping one's perceptions and behavior is part of any meditative process.[3] Deikman discusses the reinvestment of attention in unconscious processes of perception and behavior as leading to the state of awareness advocated in most approaches to meditation.[4]

Meditation-induced transcendent experiences, as described by Pahnke and Richards, commonly include a feeling of unity, states of insight into truth, transcendence of space and time, a sense of sacredness characterized by awe, deeply felt positive emotion, paradoxical sensations such as being reborn through death, difficulty in verbalizing the experience, a feeling of transiency, and positive changes in attitude and/or behavior.[5]

Meditation can be reflective, receptive, or creative. These distinctions elaborated are by Assagioli.[6] The working of the mind normally proceeds spontaneously under action of stimuli and demands of various kinds. The mind, untrained, operates independently of the will, and is really an instrument to be made use of by the will. A certain psychological distance or "nonattachment" is needed to begin to be able to direct the mind.

Assagioli mentions the importance of concentration and clarity regarding any chosen theme for reflective meditation, watchfulness for deviation from the chosen theme of reflection, and persistence in continuing to look at the theme from an ongoing parade of unsuspected angles revealing a wealth of development in it. Themes mentioned for reflective meditation are desirable psychological and spiritual qualities—for example, joy, faith, courage, and serenity. The object of contemplation may also be a "seed thought" whose meaning is either simple or paradoxical, such as the koans of Zen Buddhism. An example of a koan might be "to make haste slowly". Visual symbols may also be chosen. The last subject Assagioli mentions as suitable for reflection in meditation is the self-enhancing understanding, interpretation, and evaluation of what is discovered in one's self.

Assagioli also discusses receptive meditation, beginning with silence and the attitude of patience. The goal is illumination—a high form of inner vision involving the revelation of degrees of ultimate truth found in all life. Additional characteristics of a state of receptive meditation are the awareness of intuition within oneself or a comprehension of the nature and essence of reality; the receipt of a message heavily laden with meaning; a special awareness of contact with the self; or, lastly, the possible stimulus to action to engage in a particular activity or task.

A third type of meditation is described by Assagioli as "creative". This is a means of modifying, transforming, and regenerating the self and the personality. In this form of meditation the imagination is used to suggest the model which we would like to assume or meet; this is followed by vivifying the ideal with warm feeling and propulsive desire.

Dr. Herbert Benson, in *The Relaxation Response*, describes the state of relaxation and the techniques for eliciting the "relaxation response."[7] These include meditation, autogenic training, progressive relaxation, and hypnosis. The measurements of physiological changes evidencing an increased state of relaxation include decreased oxygen consumption, decreased respiratory rate, decreased heart rate, increased Alpha brain wave production, decreased blood pressure in persons with hypertension, decreased muscle tension, increased skin temperature, and increased skin galvanometric resistance.

There is in scientific literature evidence that portions of the hypothalamus, when stimulated in animals, elicit the fight-or-flight response. There is likewise evidence that the hypothalamus contains a center which, when stimulated, induces opposite responses with physiological changes typical of relaxation, including those just described for human beings.[8]

An excellent summary of the physiological effects of meditative states is provided in *Consciousness East and West*, by Pelletier and Garfield.[9] Wallace, in one of the most extensive summaries of experimentation, found that brain wave patterns during meditation indicated wakefulness combined with a state of restful alertness.[10] He also found that metabolic rate (rate of turnover of chemicals within the body) was generally reduced to a level below that of deepest sleep. Total oxygen consumption decreased twenty percent below that for a night's sleep; cardiac output (heart pumping volume) showed a decrease of twenty-five percent from normal wakefulness, compared with a twenty percent decrease below normal wakefulness during deep sleep. Galvanic skin resistance (this decreases with stress) increased two- to eight-fold during a brief meditation compared with a two-fold increase after a night's sleep. The concentration of lactate ion (which accounts for pain, fatigue, and in great measure for anxiety) decreased over thirty percent during meditation; skin temperature increased 1.2° centigrade during meditation, compared with no increase in non-meditators sitting with their eyes closed.

Another investigator, Hartman, has shown that the dreaming state is necessary to prevent mental deterioration and psychotic-like behavior and is accomplished by the production of certain chemicals during that state.[11] Further, the obstruction of the more sensitive inner layers of the nervous system by deep-rooted stresses accumulated over one's lifetime may be responsible for the fact that only a small percentage of our mental potential (two to fifteen percent) is usually available. It may be that these stresses are relieved only during periods of profound rest, as in deep meditation, when even deep sleep has been insufficient to reduce them.

The total pattern of physiological response occurring in meditation suggests to Wallace and Benson that this constitutes an integrated response or reflex mediated by the central nervous system.[12] They consider this response to be clearly the opposite of the fight-or-flight response, which is involved with a hypermetabolic state (increased metabolic state), increases blood pressure, heart rate, and oxygen consumption. The relaxation occurring with meditation produces precisely the opposite effects.

In one study, meditators and non-meditators were subjected to high amplitude noises. It took non-meditators thirty to thirty-five repetitions to become habituated to the stress of the noise, whereas meditators required only ten to fifteen repetitions.[13] The conclusion was that meditation has a cumulative beneficial effect in regard to handling stress.

It may be that for most persons starting meditation with some instruction is the best course. It is, however, not impossible to begin on your own, as I shall now try to describe.

First, it is usually best to find a quiet place where you will not be disturbed and can maintain a physical position in which relaxation is possible without falling asleep. The lotus or semi-lotus positions with the legs crossed, seated on the floor, may be comfortable for some. Others will want to sit on a firm chair, holding the spine erect, and with the feet placed a few inches apart flat on the floor. The head should remain erect and preferably the eyes should be closed.

Next, it is important to consciously relax the neck, back, shoulders, and abdomen as much as possible at the outset. Focus on your breathing. While taking two or three deep breaths with the chest and abdominal muscles, I find it helpful in my own meditation to think the words "Relax" or "Let go" as I breathe out. As relaxation occurs, I think in turn of relaxing my physical body, calming my emotions, and finally stilling my mind. Then I am ready to turn my thoughts to the theme of my meditation. As previously mentioned, this may be a desirable psychological or spiritual quality, such as serenity, joy, peace, or courage. It may also be a "seed thought" such as "I seek peaceful relationships." In the case of transcendental meditation, it may be a mantra.

As awareness reveals from time to time that consciousness has strayed from consideration of the meditation's theme, it is important to gently bring the thought back to the subject, returning as often as is necessary for about ten to fifteen minutes of total meditation. Whatever happens in this period of time can be observed from the position of the meditator and recorded for later use. This brief outline, I trust, may be helpful for those who want to begin the process of meditation on their own.

Chapter 18

FULFILLING RECOGNITION NEEDS

As stated earlier, the necessity for physical stroking or repetitious bodily contact is essential for survival of the human infant. The condition known as marasmus was formerly observed in homes for dependent children where, due to insufficient understanding and assistance, there was deprivation of this kind of contact. In most of these cases where children died, no physical or organic cause was ever found to explain the deaths.

The need for physical stroking continues through life. The contact of the tactile portions of the skin of one human being with the corresponding portions of the skin of another person is a sign of relationship, and to an infant it is a sign of being recognized.

Experimentally, the significance of being held in infancy has been demonstrated in animals. In one controlled test, young rats held daily for three minutes compared with control rats not picked up showed longer and greater antibody responses following stress challenges than the controls.[1]

I am consistently impressed with the lack of happiness in homes where parents do not physically demonstrate affection for each other or for their children. Lack of affection on the physical level in childhood results in an inability to so express recognition in adulthood, and causes persistent problems.

In many of the classes I have taught on stress, the groups always seem to take a sudden and distinct turn toward greater warmth and coalescence when I introduce the opportunity for members of the group to give each other a back massage and in this way make positive physical contact.

Before proceeding further, let me clarify what I mean by a stroke. A stroke is a unit of·interpersonal recognition. As such, it can be either positive or negative. In terms of early infancy, it has been noted that stimulation from strokes seems to be of primary importance. The best situation would seem to be positive recognition, the next best, negative recognition, and the worst situation, no recognition at all. Positive strokes are complimentary expressions of recognition. As infants develop, strokes cease to be completely physical as they take on symbolic form. Thus, words of speech, the sound of expressions, gestures of various kinds become as meaningful as physical touching itself.

Positive recognition helps a person to develop along an emotionally healthy route, with a sense of being O.K.[2] It leaves the receiver feeling good, alive, alert, and significant. It endorses his sense of self-esteem and stimulates his sense of being able to respond positively. Thus, positive strokes may be expressed with phrases such as, "I'm really happy that you're my daughter," "I'm really glad to have had you as an employee," "I appreciate your work," or "Your driving is excellent." They may also take the form of paying attention. We all know how important it is to have the feeling that someone is really listening to us. Therapists, if they are successful, learn very early on that listening is a skill which they must develop with great care. Not only must they listen, but they must be able to communicate to their patients the fact that they are indeed listening and also understand what the patient is saying.

Genuinely positive strokes are authentic, consistent with the facts at hand, and are expressed without irony or sarcasm. A father surveying a broken window and observing his son with baseball bat in hand may say to him: "You really appreciate our house." This is not a straight message, nor is it authentic. The non-verbal communication of negativity outweighs the positive words which are actually spoken. The false or overdone compliment is an other example of a negative non-verbal stroke combined with a seemingly positive verbal statement. Such expressions do not build good relationships and do not meet the emotional needs of the persons involved.

There are certain rules for the expression of positive recognition which can be studied to great advantage by anyone wishing to understand his own level of tension and what to do about it.[3] The first rule is the acceptance of positive recognition from others. A reader may scoff at this point and say that he always accepts positive recognition from others. On careful inspection, however, many persons can analyze their own reactions and see that they often discount positive strokes offered them.

I heard one woman friend complimented on her leadership in planning and running a P.T.A. carnival: "Pat, I really appreciate the efficient way you organized the carnival; it's coming off beautifully!" My friend replied, "Yes, but I really didn't do too much; the hard work was all done by my committee chairmen." It may well be true that her committee chairmen did a good deal of the work, but think what this message is doing to her own system. First, it means that she is rejecting the sincere, well-intentioned compliment of a friend. This does not foster the relationship between the two. It says to the friend, "You really don't know the truth of the matter, and I don't believe in your ability to comment on it properly."

This type of discounting response ("Yes, but ... ") is a denial and a rejection of the positive aspect of the compliment offered. It arises from a negative attitude toward one's self and tends to pass along to the internal computer the information that "I am really not worth being complimented." The negative attitude tends to trigger from memory other associated negative data. The feedback system then returns this data in the form of tension, resulting from mixed feelings about our own esteem. The tension may then serve to further inhibit the input of valuable data which otherwise might be perceived.

How much better if my friend had said, "Thank you. I appreciate your noticing all the hard work that was done. My committee chairmen really worked hard on it, too." This reflects a positive response toward the complimenter's feelings and her

ability to judge conditions as she sees them. It also has a profoundly different effect on the internal functioning of my friend,
as it introduces a positive response, thus tending to elicit further
positive responses from memory and clear-cut feelings of accomplishment. This positive feedback decreases the system's
tension, permitting the inhibitory system to open up to a wide
range of further data which may prove valuable.

Three types of statements are offered in terms of strokes.
The first is an expression of what the subject thinks, feels, believes, or does. In terms of the normal exchange of information
between people, if we are to act in a complimentary fashion, we
must grant the right of each person to express how he feels,
thinks, and believes. We are then free to agree or disagree and
dicuss it further. This communication form is called an "I-mes-
sage".[4] Examples are, "I like my job," "I feel humiliated," or "I
object to your statement."

The second form of expression from a subject is the "you-
message". When I use a you-message instead of stating what I
feel, think, or believe, I am making a conclusive statement about
someone else's action or being. If I say to Howard, "You will
never make a home run swinging at the ball that way," I am
making a conclusive statement about Howard's behavior. Unless
Howard is a very mature, open person, his first reaction is liable
to be, "Don't tell me about my mistakes; I know them well
enough." Thus, this kind of statement frequently does not build
a positive relationship between the people involved.

Even when the "you-message" is complimentary, it may not
build a relationship. If Dad tells Douglas, "You looked real good
in the ball game tonight," one might think an enhanced relationship would result. If Douglas, however, does not believe that he
did well in the ball game, Dad's conclusion may cause Douglas
to distrust his father's motives in making that statement. He may
conclude to himself, "Dad's just trying to make me feel good,
and doesn't really believe what he is saying."

The third form of expression a stroker may use is that of the
"oracle message." You may remember that the oracle was, in
ancient Greece, a location where a voice gave answers to note-
worthy problems. A typical oracle message is, "It certainly is
stuffy in here." The problem with this type of message is that not

everyone may believe it, and the statement itself may be untrue. It states that the sender of the message believes he is acquainted with the "real" truth, and it implies that there may not be much room for compromise or an opposing opinion. Oracle messages tend also, therefore, not to build positive relationships and require skilled defensive responses.

The cardinal rule in positive recognition is that of first learning to give oneself positive strokes. Depending on our conditioning, we may have the unfortunate tendency to be aware of our shortcomings all too readily. I see many patients who are struggling with an internal perfectionist and who when a particular goal of theirs falls slightly short of their standards tend to emphasize their minimal shortcoming while failing to offer themselves a positive stroke for their major accomplishments.

I have been in households which to me looked meticulously kept, only to discover later that the homemaker in charge felt that her housekeeping efforts were never totally adequate. In this circumstance, she offered herself negative strokes for not being more perfect, rather than positive strokes for her accomplishments. Her perfectionism and internal demands for high accomplishment, coupled with the inability to give herself positive strokes, inevitably created much tension which inevitably further compounded her distress.

I sometimes ask people to list their accomplishments in a journal. By adopting this method, many individuals quickly become aware of a large variety of qualities or activities for which they can give themselves positive recognition and which they had previously discounted or totally disregarded for a host of reasons.

It is important to learn to give positive strokes to others when the opportunity presents itself. Persons who have grown up in a household where their models gave a great deal of positive recognition develop this talent naturally and are conditioned to the experience. Others have had less good fortune and must work at becoming aware of the opportunities to give good strokes and then acting on these opportunities.

When I encountered my own tendency to not offer others good strokes, it took considerable planning to develop the habit. I realized that too often such opportunities came and went before I acted on them. It was therefore necessary first to visualize opportunities before they actually occurred. Gradually, as I continued to practice the habit, I began to remember sooner and sooner when an opportunity was present. I would, later on, catch myself in the middle of an exchange with someone, change the expression of my conversation, and offer a positive stroke in mid-experience. With even more practice, I began to be aware of the opportunity for positive stroking before an event had taken place, and I could plan to act on it immediately. This conscious awareness gave way to habit and I now find myself offering recognition without necessarily consciously analyzing events as they are happening to look for the opportunity. Instead, the positive strokes proceed out of the unconscious habit, in many instances automatically.

Positive stroking of others develops positive relationships and also has strong feedback to stroking of oneself. To be able by habit or by conscious awareness to offer recognition to others is indirectly a way of giving positive strokes to oneself.

In learning the rules of stroking, one must also learn to give oneself permission to reject negative strokes from others. To be able to hear the criticism of others and accept it on a par with other information we have requires a relatively low tension level to start with. If my own tension level is high, I tend to reject criticism from others and to make up reasons for not believing it. Accepting criticism from others when we already are experiencing a high level of tension within ourselves breeds further tension because it threatens our own self-esteem. It is particularly devastating if a person is not used to granting himself the realistic right to carefully weigh strokes from others, deciding which are positive or negative, and then feeling comfortable enough to reject those which seem invalid. Thus, many people gather in negative strokes by the armload, as in the game "Kick Me". Eric Berne has outlined this and many other destructive games which all of us use at one time or another—games based upon being able to hear people offering us negative, unwanted strokes, accepting them, and suffering with the results.[5]

The last rule of recognition to learn is to ask for positive strokes when they are needed. When I mention this to patients, they voice the almost universal objection that they do not feel comfortable asking for a positive stroke, claiming that if they have to ask for it, it is probably not genuine.

Much the opposite is true. I estimate that when an individual has a need for a positive stroke and is willing to take the risk of asking for it, about ninety percent of the time the person to whom the need is expressed normally will give that positive stroke, and has in fact much of the time been wanting to give it without knowing how to go about it. Even in the ten percent of the time when the request for a positive stroke is rejected, some benefit is derived from the asking; frequently the rejection begins to clarify some of the issues causing friction between the persons involved.

Taking the risk to express a need and ask for a positive stroke to meet that need is considered by many people in our society as a sign of weakness. We talk about "negotiating from a position of strength" or say to a child, "Don't be a weakling", thereby expressing the attitude that vulnerability must be avoided at all costs.

I see many patients who postpone coming to my office because they feel that to admit that they are in distress is a sign of weakness. Often they have struggled for days, weeks, or even months to try to deny that they need help. Frequently, the first positive move that they have made in a long time is to call, after much agonizing, to make an appointment with me.

Let me return to the ten percent figure which I estimate represents those situations in which an expressed need for positive stroking is met with rejection. When a patient of mine tries out this direct approach with someone and finds his positive stroke not returned, a common response to the experience is "I was afraid of that." Almost without exception, however, the awareness that the person with whom they were dealing could not or would not return a positive stroke is the first step a patient takes in facing some realistic points of conflict that had been denied for too long, draining away tremendous amounts of energy in the process. Once these kinds of deep-seated issues are dealt with, the patient begins to free himself for real growth.

Turning these five rules for positive recognition around, one can construct a highly successful formula for being depressed by doing just the opposite: not accepting positive recognition from others, never giving oneself or others positive recognition, always feeling obligated to accept negative recognition from others, and never asking for positive recognition when they are needed. When dealing with patients who do not give positive recognition and who do not easily accept positive recognition (frequently those who are depressed), I often elicit laughter when pointing out that these five rules, reversed, are the perfect formula for being depressed. Many times, my depressed patients have been faithfully carrying out all five negatively stated rules.

Chapter 19

WORKING THROUGH EMOTIONAL
AND MENTAL BLOCKS

In working with patients who experience physical, emotional, or mental distress in unfairly great quantities, I frequently encounter blocks within them preventing them from moving toward positive growth. When the blocks are of long-standing duration and of substantial strength, it frequently requires professional help to dissolve them.

A patient came to me in the 1960s with symptoms of abdominal pain. Within a few moments of questioning, I suspected an ulcer. I arranged for him to have an X-ray, which indeed demonstrated an ulcer. I then prescribed antacids and medications to decrease the motility and acid secretion in the stomach, and told him to stay away from acid-stimulating foods and to "relax". Predictably, he adhered to this plan and reported to me in subsequent visits that his pain was gone and that his abdomen felt fine. I admonished him to continue the same regime for three months and at that point told him I was confident his ulcer had healed.

When he returned in six months and described an abdominal pain sounding suspiciously like the previous episode, with much less fanfare I arranged for him to have another X-ray, which again demonstrated an ulcer. I mentioned that perhaps there was some tension in his home situation, job climate, or lifestyle that was causing him distress. Vigorously denying all three, he again followed my prescribed regime and soon reported that his stomach was improved.

The patient continued to have low-grade symptoms of mild pain and indigestion. In my discussions with him, I continued to emphasize the matter of stress and tension. Again, he assured me that everything was fine at home, everything was O.K. at work, and that he was not aware of being under any excessive tension at all. As I began to delve into his life history, I discovered that he had moved from Alabama approximately one year prior to his first visit with me. His employer had given him the choice of either resigning from the company or moving to the home plant in Seattle. My patient chose the latter, settling in a suburban area with a nice home, pleasant neighborhood, and the amenities one might expect are available to a middle-class engineer. In looking for clues to the onset of his ulcer, I discovered further that three or four months before he first sought my help new owners had moved in next door. They were black. I then asked my patient about his childhood and found that he had been raised in Alabama in a fairly small town where the black population was held in great contempt by whites.

Having been thoroughly conditioned by the social values of his own white community, he denied that he had any prejudice toward black people. He then began to talk about how he felt when a black executive with a wife and two children moved into the house next door. They were excellent neighbors, mowed their lawn, had no wild parties at night, went to church on Sunday, and did all the other things that suburban Seattlites seemed to do. Further pursuing my patient's feelings during this time, we finally uncovered the fact that he began to feel vaguely uneasy, and was having difficulty getting to sleep even after a tiring day. It was just about this time too that he began to have the abdominal pain which eventually led him to see me, leading to the discovery of an ulcer.

I had no scientific proof in any sense that my patient's past prejudices against blacks was coming into conflict with new data about his excellent black neighbors. As we discussed the matter, however, he did become much more aware of his anxieties during that period. Once we had decided together that this conflict of conditioning from the past versus data from the present had something to do with his ulcer, he felt considerably relieved and told me it was very gratifying to be able to uncover this.

The patient did not return with any further ulcer symptoms. Although I subsequently lost track of him, he was free of all ulcer symptoms for several years, as long as I knew him.

Another patient, "E. B.", illustrates the necessity of coming to grips with a stress-producing complex of symptoms in order to overcome blocks existing in the present but related to the past.

E. B. came to me complaining of diarrhea, an occasional problem in the past but never one of great enough severity to require medical treatment. Her symptoms had been present for about two weeks and I assumed that some microorganism was responsible and treated her symptomatically, expecting her distress to disappear. When it did not, she returned and I undertook a complete examination of the gastrointestinal tract. All of the X-rays and other examinations proved relatively normal, showing no organic or structural pathology sufficient to produce her symptoms.

I told the patient that I thought excessive tension was playing a role in producing her symptoms. This she vehemently denied, stating that all was well at home, that she was quite comfortable with her social life, and that indeed she had no problems of any kind. I continued to offer her symptomatic treatment with medications, which remained partially successful. Approximately two months later she returned with the same complaints. The diarrhea was persistent, and there was no pattern of response to any particular food to make me suspicious of an allergic reaction. This time, she agreed to some extent that stress might be a factor in her illness.

We observed that about two months prior to the onset of her symptoms her mother had died. Her mother, who was elderly and had lived a long and productive life, had been ill for some time and her death was not unexpected. She had been in a nursing home for a number of months, for which my patient had some guilt feelings, believing that she should perhaps have cared for her mother in her own home. This guilt did not appear to be particularly strong, however, and I then inquired as to whether she had in a psychological and emotional sense said goodbye to her mother. She indicated that she had done this and her explanation seemed sufficient. She briefly mentioned something, however, in regard to the settlement of her mother's estate with what seemed to me to be an undeserved amount of emotion. I inquired further and found that she had been appointed the executor of the estate. In that role, she had found her sisters very uncooperative in obtaining all of the final bills, in accounting for the funds that had been used in caring for her mother, and in supplying necessary information in the many legal ways required for settlement of an estate.

At one point, her sisters had come to visit her in some apparent attempt to resolve these issues and my patient was so resentful that, on seeing them coming, she retired from the living room and would not talk to them, leaving her husband to be their host until they left. It was obvious that she continued to harbor great resentment toward her sisters.

During the entire time that she was telling me this, a considerable amount of emotion was present. She was visibly angry and on the verge of tears several times. I told her that I thought the diarrhea was related to the buildup of this kind of resentment and that it would remain until she had resolved this resentment within herself. I suggested that she express this verbally, speaking to an empty chair as if her sisters were present, in an attempt to express her emotions and get them out in the open and out of her system. She was unwilling to do this and was still not convinced that her symptoms were psychosomatic.

About a month and a half later, she returned to my office, still complaining of diarrhea. This time I felt sure it was psychosomatic. Since she had not been able to adequately express her angry feelings verbally as I had suggested, I advised her this time to take her pen in hand and write a letter to her sisters expressing all the resentments that she could think of which she had harbored over past and present issues. In addition, I suggested that she also list, wherever she felt it was appropriate, anything for which she appreciated her sisters. Initially, she said that there would be nothing favorable she could list, but I suggested that she think about this point. I then cautioned that, having completed the letter, she should do anything she wished with it *except* send it to her sisters.

She subsequently returned to report that her diarrhea was better; she had written things out as I had suggested. Ultimately, she also wrote a letter of reconciliation with her sisters which she did actually send them, thereby reestablishing their relationship. After this, the diarrhea subsided and remained under control with no further evidence of distress from this source of tension.

Another patient of mine found it necessary to work through emotional situations that were feeding back excessive tension and causing her intractable headaches. "H. M." was also depressed and overweight from eating unrelated to hunger. After appropriate neurological examinations and X-ray studies showed no evidence of organic disease, I discussed with her my opinion that excessive tension was probably causing her headaches.

Initially, I offered her medications to provide her with temporary relief. The relief was never complete, however, and as I changed medications and increased the dosage, I began to realize that no medication, not even narcotic derivatives, would completely relieve her symptoms. Gradually she became agreeable to the idea of seeing a counselor on a consistent basis to work on her problems.

Ultimately, it became apparent from the pattern of her headaches and from the psychological material she was working with that the headaches were linked to frustration and anger over unmet expectations from those around her. This was traced to her childhood, when her father was absent from the household because of his work for a number of years and later left the household completely. Her mother had gone to work during the day and was never home when she returned from school. Her mother was also frequently absent from the household during the evenings. H. M. had considerable anger toward an older and younger brother whom she felt ought to have helped her take care of the household. She also felt that her mother ought to have managed things so as to take care of the family more adequately.

The patient's frustration had become a pattern over the years, arising whenever other people did not meet the expectations that she had regarding things she felt ought to be done. She has gradually learned to reduce her unrealistic expectations of those around her as well as unrealistic expectations of herself. She has also come to realize that her mother really did do the best that she could have considering the difficult circumstances in which the family was placed after her father's desertion. Her headaches have now largely disappeared, returning only when her behavior lapses into the old pattern of frustration and anger over unmet, unrealistic expectations of herself and others.

Chapter 20

CULTIVATION OF POSITIVE ATTITUDES

As a physician, I firmly believe that the education of patients should emphasize the alteration of negative attitudes and the development of a lifestyle in which activities can be pursued with the least possible physical, emotional, and mental distress. Negative attitudes provide fuel for destructive emotions, since they tend to retrieve and be associated with negative recall data from memory storage. Dr. Harold Wolff asserts: "Of crucial importance is the need for every patient to understand with full appreciation the truly poisonous and destructive nature of hate, resentment, jealousy, frustration, envy and fear."[1]

If attitudes are negative and poisonous, the substitution of a positive attitude system would seem to be desirable to promote better health and less distress. Therefore, it is important at this point to identify the underlying attitudes which seem to be basic to the determination of the data matching and retrieval process.

At the heart of this attitude control is the continuum of hostility and love—the opposed attitudes underlying the determination of all other mind-sets. The greater the degree of hostility, the less love; the greater the degree of love, the less hostility. Love, as previously mentioned, can best be defined in terms of the word-picture "unconditional positive regard". Hostility is best understood as "negative regard".

Attitudes are mind-sets relative to ourselves, other persons, groups, or situations. Like all of our traits, present attitudes are dependent upon genetic legacy, past conditioning, and present state of awareness. In my experience, many persons experiencing significant emotional, physical, or mental distress harbor excessive hostility.

Persons filled with hostility tend to live in the negative feedback world of anger, sarcasm, envy, resentment, and frustration engendering negative reactions from others and ultimately from themselves. This in turn leads to increased tension and a further downward spiraling of the reaction cycle.

Love, by contrast, enables one to look at oneself and others with heightened self-esteem. The Greek word *agape* comes close to the meaning I ascribe here to the word "love"—that of unconditional positive regard. Biblical and early Christian sources also saw love in terms of a positive expression for all—family, friends, neighbors, and acquaintances.

Love as I use the word does not mean sexual desire. The unconditional positive regard of which I speak will frequently be found to be an important part of a stable and satisfying sexual relationship, but its scope does not necessarily include a sexual definition. Possession or control of things or persons is not love as I define it. In fact, the expression of unconditional positive regard oftens renders unnecessary the "possession" of a particular object or personal relationship. Nor is love respect, which involves a demand that someone live up to certain conditions which I place on him.[2]

Having mentioned some things that love is *not,* let me now list in positive terms some of its attributes. Love as unconditional positive regard makes it possible to be aware of the best parts within ourselves. Many persons with a legacy of bad memories concerning their perceived weak points and failings, come to have a hostile attitude toward themselves. They are caught in a feedback loop which elicits from memory mainly negative data about themselves. An attitude of unconditional positive regard brings with it heightened self-esteem, which is nearly universally accepted as one of the critical stepping-stones to a healthy, happy, and productive life.

Many times I have asked patients to list their good points. Amazingly, this is a difficult task for those who are lacking in basic self-esteem. Moreover, our strict Puritan heritage seems to have trained us to fear that we will become self-centered, conceited braggarts if we recognize the positive aspects of our own accomplishments, being, and behavior. On the contrary, I believe that pathology arises from being far too aware of our negative points and failures.

Positive regard for ourselves and others likewise opens up a host of new data-gathering services. It is the unconditional and undemanding nature of positive regard which allows us to see the best side of our neighbors, friends, and relatives. Frequently there is much positive data about other persons to which we will be blinded unless we can begin to retrieve certain bits of data blocked by negative or conditional regard.

For example, my expectation is that my children will do very well in school. If they do not live up to this demand, I begin to have negative thoughts and feelings of disappointment. This means that I have not been looking at my children in a genuinely loving way. Positive regard, in spite of their less-than-perfect performances, enables me to see the best in them, including the fact that failure is a part of learning.

Not too long after I began my private practice, a patient in my examining room told me, before I had a chance to ask him any questions or make any examination, "I have a sore throat, Doctor, and all I need is some penicillin." That statement immediately set me on the defensive because I felt somewhat angry that this patient was assuming that he knew more about his condition than I. After all, I was the physician with the training! After a number of experiences like this, my attitude changed somewhat and permitted me to ask myself the question in that situation, "Is there any valid reason why this patient is not correct?" This is a much more positive attitude compared to my previous hostile attitude and enabled me to ask that matter of fact question. Over the years, on recognizing the fact that many patients do know a great deal about their own needs, I have found that, indeed, some were correct and they did need penicillin. Had I not had an attitude of positive regard, I would not have been able to weigh properly whether a particular patient at a given time really did need penicillin and this would have affected my best judgment.

Patients frequently ask, "If I always maintain an attitude of unconditional positive regard for others, won't they just step on me like a doormat?" It is a common misconception that seeing other persons in a positive light means always saying "yes" to them, always being responsible for meeting their needs and putting their comfort first.

If I tell my son it is not O.K. with me to have his friend stay overnight on Sunday, I give my decision with positive regard for us both; that is, I do not demand that he *like* my decision or even that he like *me* at the time. I do not demand that he accept the decision without complaining; I do not demand of myself that I inform him of my decision in a "painless" way—which is realistically not possible. Instead, I state my decision with gentleness yet firmness, and picture the positive benefits we will both derive from the reasonable limits I have set—limits that will help my son to prepare adequately for school on Monday morning.

The next positive attitude to consider is that of forgiveness. The old adage "Forgive and forget" is not easily implemented in our daily lives. Many experimental psychologists believe that data, once received through the input system, is stored in memory within the realms of the conscious or unconscious, and is subject to recall under the proper circumstances—for example, under hypnosis, suggestion therapy, and the administration of sodium pentothal. It is not possible to simply "forget" past events; it takes continuing energy and a certain amount of continuing input to keep such events suppressed or repressed out of consciousness. We are thereby less free to use that energy for more creative purposes.

As for forgiveness, I do not mean excusing or pardoning behavior or attitudes I do not condone. If an event occurs in my neighborhood which offends me and I determine that I will not "forgive" the person involved, I must be aware that I have placed a demand or a condition that that person should have behaved in a way more acceptable to me. When he did not meet my demand, my positive regard for him was diminshed or abolished. I am suggesting a more appropriate "forgiveness" consists of my canceling the demand that the person behave as I wish him to. The cancellation of that demand then reestablishes my flow of positive regard toward him. I may continue to expect that he will behave in a reasonable fashion, yet there is no evidence that my demand or expectation that he behave in a particular fashion will teach him any more certainly or quickly to behave in that way. In fact, there is evidence that he may learn more rapidly to alter his offensive behavior if I continue to permit my positive regard to flow to him.

Forgiveness, then, is an important adjunct to love as unconditional positive regard. I might add that both attitudes need to be applied to oneself with as equal vigor as they must be to others. Failure or nonachievement of a goal may lead to diminished self-esteem for which I may punish my mind, my emotions, or my body. If this happens, the only means to reestablish the flow of positive regard to myself is by canceling the expectations and the demands which, because I failed to meet them, led to diminished self-love in the first place.

Many times I have had patients tell me in very emotional tones, "I'll never forgive _____ for that." My observation is that that person is usually experiencing some form of acute or chronic physical, mental, or emotional distress. The previously mentioned case of "E. B.", who was finally persuaded it was necessary to forgive her sisters, indicates that appropriate forgiveness helped to reestablish the equilibrium of her body functions.

It is frequently suggested to me when I stress the concept of forgiveness that this surely makes us prey to aggressive persons, who will "take advantage" of us. My experience is quite the opposite.

I would like to relate the story of "Irma", a patient who was chronically ill with asthma to the point that it limited her activities and was a great burden on her family. She became more and more dependent on becoming ill and requiring assistance from her family—and frequently from me—during times of stress. During the years that she was in my care, she was largely able to control her symptoms when she took small but persistent amounts of medication on schedule. I gradually began to suspect that she consciously or unconsciously was able to precipitate a worsening of her condition by failing to take her medications. When I confronted her with my feelings of frustration at the pattern which I observed I elicited much hostility on her part, and there was no improvement in her general function or willingness to take her medication. I later determined that I was not willing to continue treating her without her cooperation. I again confronted her on the issue of medication, yet— recalling her childhood history and adult conditioning and her present state of awareness—I determined that I would not abandon my positive regard toward her, whether or not we arrived at some accommodation which would permit me to continue to treat her.

Confronting her, then, in a very matter-of-fact and calm way, I stated what my observations had been and that I was unwilling to continue treating her so long as she precipitated her attacks by interrupting her medication schedules. I placed upon her the expectation that she would increase her own awareness of the pattern by which she became ill, yet not demanding this, since my positive regard still flowed very much toward her.

In confronting myself, I also realized that I was demanding of myself that I be responsible for her correcting the self-destructive pattern of not taking her medication. That demand on myself, which could be fulfilled only by the proper response on her part, was impossible for me to control; therefore, the amount of tension that I experienced in trying to change her behavior absorbed a great deal of my attention and energy, detracting from my ability to see her problem in larger terms.

It has been a painful lesson for me to finally arrive at the conclusion that, as a person involved in healing, I cannot be "responsible" for the actions of others since each person is ultimately in charge of himself. There is no way that I can "make" any patient take positive steps with regard to his health unless his awareness at the time permits him to choose to take those steps himself. I can, however, be responsible for helping to create the climate in which his awareness will gradually expand, permitting him to be aware of his own needs and of the choices he can make in order to fulfill them.

Returning to the example of my patient with asthma, I can report that when I confronted her, maintaining positive regard for her, her awareness did begin to change as she recognized that her unconscious pattern of becoming ill was part of some need to control situations and to satisfy unmet internal needs which she had never faced. This new awareness greatly reduced the impact of her unsatisfactory way of coping with her problems.

The third attitude contributing to the development of positive regard is that of accurate empathy, permitting us to perceive the needs and desires of others as they themselves define them. More often than not when we think about the needs of others, it is in terms of what *we* think they need. Thus, our interpretation of their needs gets in the way of seeing others' needs as they actually see them. It may well be that those needs are in our opinion less than ideal, yet we should be able to empathize with how the other person views his or her own needs at a particular time.

Often I find myself phrasing the needs of others in terms of what I think they should be aware of and should be sensing in regard to their own needs. I remember reflecting some years ago about a patient whom I saw in an emergency room because of great abdominal pain. After examining the patient, I proceeded to arrange for some very simple tests in order to make my diagnosis. The most important thing for the patient, from my standpoint, was that diagnosis. Looking back, I am aware that I was projecting onto the patient my own need to establish a diagnosis. An attitude of accurate empathy would have enabled me to be aware of the fact that the patient's need was for relief of excruciating pain. When the patient herself finally convinced me of this need, I gave her a pain-killing medication while awaiting the results of the tests I had ordered.

Accurate empathy enables me to sense another's need as he sees it. There may be situations, however, when I am unable or choose not to meet that need, even though I understand it. An alcoholic patient of mine, attempting to stop drinking, may for the moment sense his own overwhelming need to have another drink. It is helpful for me, by maintaining an attitude of accurate empathy, to understand that great sense of need, but it is nevertheless in my better judgment to choose not to meet that need by offering him another drink.

The fourth positive attitude is that of acceptance of the truth. Some persons experience a great deal of tension when they enlarge their awareness to perceive error. Their tension level is so great that the system, in order to remain intact, must obliterate any perception of error. In the extreme, this is the basis of serious paranoid behavior.

Learning occurs through both positive and negative feedback situations. Learning by positive modeling is successful if we achieve what we perceive to be the thoughts, feelings, and behavior of the person we are imitating. Learning also occurs through awareness of error. On making an error, we experience a certain amount of distress. This distress gives negative feedback; we experience a heightened amount of tension and can take steps from then on to learn from the experience and to correct the process so as not to repeat the error.

Many psychologists feel that correcting errors and learning through mistakes is the chief way in which a great number of people learn. Persons with sound personalities are willing to have their mistakes pointed out and learn through their errors. To be unwilling to learn from our mistakes or to be told about them means that the inhibitory system is trained to screen out all evidence of mistakes, as a result of which very little learning can occur. An open attitude relates to the attitude of forgiveness. Before forgiveness or cancellation of unreasonable demands can be invoked to restore positive regard to oneself or others, acceptance of the truth is necessary, even if it means awareness of one's own error.

Diana, a young wife with three children, came to me because of what seemed to be typical muscle contraction headaches. A short neurological examination and a few simple tests confirmed no evidence of other causes of headache. In a discussion with her about the sources of her tension, which I explained to her I felt were related to her headaches, it soon became apparent that she was very angry about her husband's drinking problem. In fact, she made this correlation herself and felt that her husband's bouts of heavy drinking, during which there was great upset and fear in the entire family, were responsible for her headaches. She was very resentful about his behavior. In fact, she was demanding that he change his behavior. Since his behavior was out of her control and since she was not able to fulfill this demand, she was experiencing a great deal of tension, which translated itself into excessive muscular contractions in the neck leading to headache. Diana rejected all suggestions that she had any responsibility for producing her headaches and chose instead to lay complete blame for them on her husband's drinking.

Some time later when her headaches had failed to improve, she gradually expanded her awareness and was able to cancel the demand that her husband stop drinking in order to give her relief from her headaches. Along with this, she became aware that his drinking had tended to obliterate her awareness of his positive attributes. As a result, she was able to confront her husband with positive regard, having determined that if he was unwilling to face his problems, she would be willing to initiate separation and divorce proceedings. She finally determined that either outcome—her husband's willingness to look realistically at his drinking problems or separation and eventual divorce—would be acceptable to her. Fortunately, in this case, confrontation with caring resulted in her husband's willingness to seek help, ultimately resulting in a greater family cohesiveness.

The last basic positive attitude is that of disidentification. As Assagioli has pointed out, we are dominated by everything with which we become identified and can dominate and control only those things from which we disidentify ourselves.[3]

We can frequently tune in to our internal speech and find ourselves identifying with certain conditions or certain parts of our personality. I may find, for instance, that a particular political personality offends me and I am conditioned to respond to him with a part of myself which becomes angry with him. The angry part, for as long as I am identified with it, will control my behavior. I may also become identified with a specific goal. I recall once being so identified with trimming a laurel hedge in my yard that I became completely wrapped up in wanting to finish the project, to the extent that I forgot about lunch and inhibited awareness of soreness in my elbows due to the excess physical activity I was involved in. Ultimately, I suffered the distress of great hunger pangs that finally broke through my identification with the project. During the time I was engrossed in the project, my absorption in it controlled my choices and dictated my behavior in undesirable ways.

There are certainly times when identification with a goal, a need, a service, or a desire is appropriate. We accomplish many good things because of the emotional enthusiasm aroused in our identification with such projects or goals. The point I wish to make is that we need to be aware of our central and centered ability to choose when that identification will be made. In order to be free to choose between various alternatives—whether or not to identify with a particular goal or project—we must be disidentified from them and identified with the self, which operates from a position of nonattachment, until such time as a choice is made to activate an identification.

From the self, then, it is possible, for instance, to be aware of anger and to control its appropriate expression without, however, being identified with it. Thus, instead of identifying with anger by saying, "I am angry", we can put some distance between ourselves and the identification of that emotion and state that "part of me is temporarily experiencing anger" or that "a wave of anger is attempting to submerge me." The self thereby surveys the entire scope of the personality at once, relegating the feeling of anger to a temporary situation and to only one part of the total personality.

Increasing awareness of the self and disidentification from parts of the personality, from the contents of consciousness, and from the mesh of conflicts and tensions within us allows for a more complete and objective observation of our relationships and attitudes. This permits an increasing amount of control over the personality, and the funneling of energy toward meeting goals which the self freely chooses.

The analogy of a Russian troika has been used to describe this relationship. The three-horse sleigh is controlled by a driver who holds the reins to each of three sources of energy which pull him and the sleigh. The three horses may be compared to the physical body, the intellect, and the emotions. They may work together or at odds. One may be stronger than the other two, yet each has its own characteristics to contribute to the whole.

In order for the sleigh to make progress, the driver must be willing to work with each animal, getting them to cooperate with each other; he must assume control of the situation and make choices about the direction and the intensity of activity needed to achieve his own purpose. He must not identify with one animal over the others, but must when it is appropriate make his identification temporarily with the needs of one horse as compared to the others. He exerts his will in making these choices and achieves his purpose—moving the troika—through the effect that his will has on the goals and attitudes of the animals.

Similarly, the driver of a dog sled knows each of his dogs contributes something to the forward progress of both driver and sled. The dogs have distinctly different personalities, differing strengths, different appearances, different emotional temperaments, different needs, and different relationships to the driver. Over a long period of time, he works with his dogs to achieve a harmony of the whole, to meet each of their needs, and to promote a satisfactory working relationship with each, working out assent to common goals and forward progress of the whole with a minimum expenditure of energy.

Only when he has a thorough acquaintance with each animal, realizing the strengths and weaknesses of each, can he set the climate in which all are willing to contribute their energy to the common goal of moving the sled.

Assagioli points out his own experience and that of others in working with subpersonalities—divisions of the total personality, each having a typical way of believing, thinking, feeling, and behaving, and each projecting a predominant theme or script.[4] Our life activities are expressed through these multiple personalities. Like the horses in the troika, our subpersonalities must be well synthesized. In the case of psychotic illness, subpersonalities may be so split off from one another that they cannot relate to each other or be controlled by the self. *The Three Faces of Eve* details three such distinct subpersonalities of one woman, who was incapable of bringing them under harmonious control.[5] With heightened self-awareness it is possible to forge a sense of common purpose and mutuality among those personalities.

Chapter 21

THE SETTING OF GOALS

There is considerable evidence that all behavior is goal-oriented. The goals that behavior seeks to meet may be consciously formed or may exist at various levels within the unconscious.

The establishment of goals and attitudes by the will is one of the two entry points into the feedback system of human function (see the diagram of a functional model of man). The six functional stages of the will mentioned by Assagioli can be listed as follows: (1) the establishment of a goal, including imagination, motivation, and valuation; (2) deliberation and selection from a variety of possible goals; (3) decision, meaning the conclusion of the selection process and the setting aside of other potential goals not selected; (4) affirmation—activating energy to foster the reaching of the selected goal; (5) planning and programming the means by which the goal will be achieved; and (6) direction of the execution toward fulfillment. The will calls upon strength to act directly and upon skill in making use of all available psychological and bodily functions to act indirectly toward achievement of the goal.[1]

Several observations need to be made at this point regarding will and the setting of goals. Habitual behavior and habitual responses are those responses which have, from long exposure to conditioning factors and repetition, become more or less automatic when a particular stimulus is evoked. Any given pattern currently identified as a habit (because the series of electrical and chemical events within the system are under the control of the unconscious) was, at one point near its origin, not a habit but a series of consciously directed, laborious steps which, only through the process of learning, became simplified and eventually delegated to the unconscious. Once a child has learned to walk, that activity can be termed an unconscious habit.

We are not aware of the origin of many of our habits; we are also not aware of the origin of many of our goals.[2] Thus, a goal still very much operative from the level of the unconscious may be still operating within us in a destructive way, completely without our conscious awareness. Thus, the self-destructive habits of smoking and drinking have their origin and original motivation in long-forgotten needs dating from childhood or the teenage years.

The next observation regarding the will and goal-setting is that the establishment of any goal implies a conflict with an existing habit or situation. To establish a goal, for instance, of arising at 6:30 a.m. each day means that for that person, the hour of arising has usually been later than 6:30. Thus, a conflictful situation is immediately established when the new goal is adopted. Tension results because of conflicting bits of data on the same subject existing within the system simultaneously. Merely to command the behavior to follow an activity in opposition to an existing situation or habit results in a high degree of failure. I have seen many patients who expressed a very strong "will" to stop smoking by pounding on the table with a fist and affirming that they were going to quit. About ninety-five percent of them, however, eventually drift back to smoking.

We can affirm, then, that the proper function of the will does not include the control of behavior. Rather it is the setting and maintaining of goals and attitudes. Thus, only indirectly does the will control behavior—through the influence of attitudes and goals on the receipt of data and its processing.

Goals must be framed in a positive reference. Several years ago, a patient of mine informed me that on my advice he had set for himself a goal to quit smoking. I did not quibble with that wording, as I did not yet understand the negative input that was at work within him. I now understand that his failure to succeed was, at least in part, linked to the fact that every time he repeated his goal to himself, he stated it in terms of, "I am *not* going to smoke". To *not* think about doing something does not seem to be a property or demonstrated function of the human mind.

Let me ask you, for example, to *not* think about the White House in Washington, D.C. I would guess that that command has probably now caused you to think about the White House. Therefore, a goal of *not* smoking is not a goal at all. Each repetition of that goal is a reminder of the smoking and is only an expression of a strong-willed determination to quit.

A more appropriate statement for my patient might have been, "I choose to breathe freely". This remark embodies an awareness of choice in the matter and the phrasing of his goal in a positive way, which permits his mind to picture a concrete achievement.

One of the incessant drives of the human organism is to keep tension within manageable limits. Whenever a new goal is chosen by the self, the level of tension is increased. The system then struggles with this tension, finding a way to reduce it, either by regression to the old habit and goal, or by abandoning the old goal and achieving the new one, thus reducing conflict and tension. In comparing a number of goals, the one most easily achieved is the one which permits the greatest decrease in tension when achieved. It may be necessary to initially choose a goal which introduces an amount of excess tension sufficient to generate action but not of such overwhelming proportions that immediate regression to a previous habit is inevitable.

Training of the will's goal-setting activities is learned like any other behavior which has been established by psychological principles. Once the will begins to function in this fashion, goals can be set and worked on at increasing levels of complexity. The more reasons a person perceives for attaining a goal, the greater the degree of motivation or level of tension.[3] Thus, it is helpful when selecting a goal to express it in writing in a positive way and to list all the possible advantages to the individual which result from attaining that goal. Balancing the list of advantages should also be a list of the disadvantages that come with failure to achieve the goal. These written lists should be reviewed frequently, and at least twice daily. The more often reminders of the goal and its advantages are encountered, the more positive input there will be. Words, phrases, or pictures symbolizing a particular goal serve to reinforce the positive stimulus. The forces of the unconscious will be continually at work supporting the old goal and habit, and so conscious repetition must be done in a methodical, calculated way.

Positive visual input to the mind's processing can be made by visualizing the symbols of the goal, visualizing the goal successfully completed, and scanning the written list of the goal's advantages and disadvantages; auditory input includes repeated reading aloud of the list and listening to a tape recording made of the goal process. Rewriting or typing the list several times (for eye-hand coordination) and memorizing it to begin to commit it to habit—these too enhance the chances of success in attaining the goal. Finally, the first small increments of success act as one of the strongest stimuli in causing the goal to become permanently integrated within the mind and to eventually being met as it proceeds from a conscious to an unconscious attitude.

The best time to begin working on a specific goal is when other tensions are at a low ebb. When tension is already at a high point, a new goal adds further tension. Since the selection process within the system seems naturally to turn only to the most pressing issues, goals which induce lesser amounts of tension and are elective rather than imperative are abandoned, since there is little energy left to work on them.

I should also like to emphasize the fact that a goal must be consistent with basic underlying attitudes. For instance, when an attitude of unconditional positive regard for a person is present, the introduction of some negative goal in regard to that person will be very difficult, if not impossible, to achieve because of the tension engendered by the conflict between the underlying positive attitude and the destructive goal. The destructive goal cannot take hold if the positive attitude is firmly grounded and habitual.

A woman of forty-eight came to me with widespread complaints, including stomach pain, low back pain, exhaustion, insomnia, and weight gain. No organic or structural causes for her symptoms were apparent after physical examination and laboratory tests. Our discussions brought out the fact that she had begun to resent her home situation.

Two young children had come into the custody of herself and her husband because of the incapacitation of their parents, who were her husband's cousins. My patient felt burdened by this unexpected responsibility. She began unconsciously to blame her husband for their situation, though she denied this at a conscious level. She began to take revenge on her husband. Her behavior, resulting from unconsciously set goals, took the form of being too tired for sexual relations, voicing especially loud complaints about her pain when her husband was present, and gaining weight in spite of knowing that he valued her being thin. Besides all the obvious conflicts in this story, one additional conflict became apparent: the unconscious goal of revenge was in conflict with her basic attitude toward her husband which, in the last analysis, was quite sound unconditional positive regard.

As she gained insight into her conflicts, she was able to set aside her negative goals, gradually bringing into play new goals consistent with her underlying positive attitudes. Her pain, exhaustion, insomnia, and weight gain gradually disappeared.

If you are motivated to enhance your own goal-setting apparatus, I suggest selecting simple goals to start. They may even be "useless" exercises, such as sitting quietly in a chair for five minutes or standing in one place comfortably for five minutes. Positive reinforcement for achievement of such simple goals energizes the goal-setting apparatus.

Proceed with selection of a more complex goal, assessing its possible value for you. Decide on a single goal by setting aside other potential goals and focus on the one chosen. Affirm your motivation and intent to activate the energy to achieve your goal. Except for the most simple goals, each of the above stages may take several days or weeks to implement.

The planning stage involves consideration of how the goal may be achieved. Detailed evaluation of the steps involved is frequently necessary. In this stage, further energy is attracted by periods of relaxation (see Chapter 16) in which the goal is visualized. The detailed approach by which it will be accomplished is visualized step-by-step as if it is actually being reached. The visualization may terminate with the final accomplishment of the goal. These daily visualizations are important before execution of the plan is actually undertaken, and constitute a preparation period of about three weeks. The execution stage is then undertaken; MacDougald's *Emotional Maturity Instruction* outlines an excellent approach.[4]

Any goals beyond the most simple should be written down. The goal should be stated in positive terms and include the word "comfortably"—for example, "I will comfortably give each of my employees a positive stroke every day." The advantages of achieving and disadvantages of not achieving the goal should then be listed. These are frequently mirror opposites, and it is helpful to see them on the written page.

Repetition is important: read the written page, listen to it on a tape recorder, rewrite or type it, read it out loud, and "see it" in the mind's eye several times a day, especially before sleep. Do not set a time limit on the achievement of the goal, since this may set you up for failure. Patience and persistence, which grow out of unconditional positive regard for oneself, need to be summoned as the goal slowly reaches accomplishment. In fact, you may benefit merely from visualizing yourself being persistent and patient! The first small increments of success are reminders that "Nothing succeeds like success."

Chapter 22

CREATIVE VISUALIZATION FOR GOAL REINFORCEMENT AND FUNCTIONAL CHANGES

The thought process involved in visualizations, images, and words precedes activity. Internal speech, as already mentioned, plays a controlling role in terms of the processing of data taking place prior to formulation of output. Images of ourselves, our goals, and of our success or failure in attaining them are held in memory and are called upon for activation of data processing on a particular subject, also prior to activation of output. Changes are made in attitudes, goals, acceptance of new data, and processing of data in order to make a change which will bring greater satisfaction and less tension.

In thinking about a particular aspect of his life, a person who is relatively satisfied that he is meeting internal expectations will experience more positive visualization than negative. In such a situation, there is little excess tension. If a person examines an area of his life and is not satisfied with it, he will generally summon up more negative visualizations and will tend to experience excessive tension.[1] The tension stems from the wide contrast between the way things actually are and how we would like them to be. Excessive tension may also stem from a wide disparity between how we would like someone else to be, contrasted with what realistically we see them to be.

The self-directing learning process receiving a stream of positive and negative feedback relative to visualized goals is termed cybernetics. An adult reaching for a glass of milk while seated at a meal first pictures the accomplished act at a conscious and unconscious level in his mind. The data is processed, and a combination of thousands of individual muscle fiber contractions (complete with millisecond-by-millisecond feedback) guides the arm surely and smoothly to the container where the fingers complete the action of picking up the glass of milk.

Contrast this by observing a four-month-old infant who is learning to grasp his own bottle of milk. His mind pictures the goal in a primitive way, but there are at least two differences from the adult. Many of the motor neuron cells in the brain which transmit the electrical and chemical messages in the adult are not yet developed in the infant. In fact, there are those who believe the challenge of making such attempts in childhood is linked with the development of these brain cells. Moreover, the brain cells which do serve the infant have not had the experience and feedback reinforcement of reaching the goal. Therefore, the motions of the infant's hand will be tenuous, and the feedback mechanism will result in gross over-corrections as the arm zigzags toward the bottle. As days pass, learning occurs, largely reinforced by the positive feedback of reaching the goal, and so the motion becomes smoother and smoother. From a mental standpoint, it becomes less and less consciously directed and more habitually controlled, within the realm of the unconscious.

Dr. Maxwell Maltz points out the existence of a goal-striving "servo-mechanism" consisting of the brain and nervous system.[2] This mechanism is impersonal or detached and functions automatically to carry out the goals set for it. Success goals tend to breed success and negative goals tend to breed failure. The servo-mechanism works only upon information and data which it receives. If the visualizations available for a particular individual have never included those of a positive self-image or high self-esteem, then those images are denied the computer. Therapy and counseling are directed at the creation and support of a positive self-image through increased awareness if such images are initially lacking.

The concept of the importance of thought and visualization in the scheme of human existence is not new. Patanjali, the codifier of ancient Indian thought, mentions the principle that "energy follows thought." All of the subsequent energies of mind processing and output in terms of muscular activity, emotions, and internal functions follow the thought process involving the elicitation of images and visualizations.[3]

As I have become aware of the importance of the image and visualization structure initiating goal-setting and goal-reaching activity, I am more and more impressed by the common tendency of persons who experience physical, mental, and emotional distress to picture negative images, including failure and disease. Unfortunately, the health care system in the United States reinforces this negative concept. Thus, most persons seeing physicians come because of disease, sickness, or symptoms which they interpret as representing sickness. Very few come to learn how to be healthy.

The Samuels', in *Seeing With the Mind's Eye,* state their conviction that it is an underlying yearning of all persons to feel good, to experience a sense of well-being, and to feel at peace with themselves and the universe. This corresponds to my previous description of the human organism's incessant drive to keep tension within manageable limits.

Information necessary for growth and fulfillment comes through the part of the unconscious which Assagioli terms the "superconscious" or the "higher unconscious".[4] From this realm come higher intuitions and inspirations; creative artistic, philosophical, and scientific impulses; urges to humanitarian action; higher awarenesses of altruistic love and sources of genius; high contemplation, illumination, and ecstasy. A chief goal of meditation, discussed in a previous chapter, is to get in touch with this higher unconscious.

The quality of our lives is changed by repetitively invoking positive visualizations and by creating and maintaining other positive visualizations relative to areas of dissatisfaction. The images we use seem to be the most consistent when we are in a state of relaxation and openness.[5]

Maltz describes an experiment in which three groups of students were involved in shooting basketball free throws. The first group practiced daily for twenty minutes, their scores being added up on the first and twentieth day. The second group was scored on the first and twentieth day, having had no practice in between. The third group was scored on the first and last days, and in the intervening twenty days spent twenty minutes each day imagining that they were shooting the ball and that it was going through the basket. The first group, practicing twenty minutes per day, improved twenty-four percent. The second group, with no practice, showed no improvement. The third group, practicing only in their imagination, improved twenty-three percent![6] This experiment proves that the entire system responds automatically to both real and imagined experience, regardless of whether it is supplied as input from external experience or from internal sources.[7]

In recent years athletes engaged in individual competitive sports as well as whole athletic teams have begun to realize the potential benefits of visualization. Football players, teams of oarsmen, boxers, and track competitors in many instances have enhanced their performance through visualization of their own creation or guided by a creative therapist.

There is little doubt that positive visualizations enhance our chances for success and that negative visualizations lessen them. Maltz describes Conrad Hilton, founder of the worldwide chain of hotels, as visualizing himself successfully operating a hotel years before he ever bought one.[8]

One patient of mine offers a good illustration of negative visualization. "Ethel," whom I was counseling for a number of chronic problems, told me during one particular visit that she was panic-stricken over the imminent wedding of her son. On questioning her, I realized she had been programming herself to panic by visualizing nearly everything that could go wrong with the ceremony.

I took her on a fantasy trip to the day of the wedding, reviewing everything in as great a detail as I could, from the time she got up that day to the return home with her husband after the ceremony. In fantasy, I had her visualize herself remembering the names of guests in the reception line better than she had ever done before. I then asked her to repeat this entire visualization several times a day prior to the wedding. This she did. In fact, she later told me had done it forty times by the day of the ceremony. The wedding went off without a hitch, and with great calm on her part. In a vast majority of cases, fear of an inpending event will gradually diminish with each subsequent positive visualization and be supplanted by a feeling of experience and confidence.

Carl Simonton, a radiation therapist, has made observations over the last ten years on a group of cancer patients who have done far better than would have seemed possible based on the stage of their cancer at the time of discovery and on a group who have undergone spontaneous remission not accountable in terms of their medical treatment. He noted that many who improved against these odds had a consistently positive attitude toward the possibility of their own recovery.[9] He felt, therefore, that a positive attitude might be taught to others. He developed a technique consisting, first, of inducing a state of relaxation; second, of visualizing a peaceful scene in nature; and, third, of asking the patient to visualize the cancer with as much anatomical and functional detail as he is able to summon up, and then to visualize billions of his own white corpuscles recognizing, destroying, and carrying off the malignant cells. Last, he asks the patient to visualize himself as whole and well.[10]

Simonton has also organized his patients in supportive therapy groups geared toward helping each other discover their negative attitudes and replacing them with positive ones. He has concluded that those patients enthusiastically following the instructions listed above show dramatic improvement. Likewise, his statistics indicate that persons who showed mild or no relief from cancer symptoms were uncooperative and never or rarely followed instructions.

Dr. J. H. Schultz, a German psychiatrist and neurologist of the 1930s, developed a series of six one-minute exercises which he termed autogenic therapy (see Chapter 16). The visualizations in these exercises involved (1) heaviness in the arms and legs, (2) warmth in the extremities, (3) a quiet and regular heartbeat, (4) calm and regular breathing, (5) a warm solar plexus, and (6) a cool forehead.[11] These exercises, which tend to produce normalizing of body functions and healing physiological changes, have since been used for a broad range of diseases, including ulcers, gall bladder attacks, irritated colon, constipation, obesity, angina pectoris, high blood pressure, headaches, thyroid disease, arthritis, and back pain. Asthma patients, for instance, are given the standard exercises with the addition of two phrases: "My throat is cool" and "My chest is warm." Four different reported studies show that between fifty and one hundred percent of the asthma patients are symptom free after doing these exercises regularly.[12]

A patient reported to my office because of chronic itching, redness, and discomfort in the skin. A classical appearance of her skin established the diagnosis of neurodermatitis. I suggested to her that medication applied topically might help reduce the itching and that regular use of a visualization would help to clear the difficulty. She agreed. I instructed her to do the visualization at least once and, preferably, two or three times daily, beginning with a relaxed state, breathing deeply and calmly, closing her eyes, and imagining herself walking up a long, curving golden stairway to a special room above everything else that she could see, where the sun's rays were making the room very warm. I asked her to enter this special room, close the door and find within a very relaxed atmosphere with warmth, a great amount of white light, and a chair in which she could relax and be very comfortable. I asked her then, in her imagination, to place herself in the comfortable chair and then expose the various parts of her skin, beginning with arms and legs to the white light and picture at the same time the inflammatory skin condition gradually fading and the skin returning to normal.

One week later, she left a note with my receptionist which indicated great ecstasy over the exercise which in seven days had reduced the condition almost completely to normal, an improvement for which she was both grateful and enthusiastic. The improvement had occurred so rapidly that she had not bothered to fill the medication prescription.

Visualization can also be quite helpful in terms of weight loss. One of my patients, for example, expressed an interest in losing weight. She weighed about 225 pounds, and we decided after some discussion that she could comfortably choose as her goal to weigh 150 pounds. She knew all about diets and wanted no specific dietary help from me. I suggested that she begin by regularly visualizing herself slim as she stood in front of a mirror, clad in a bathing suit. I then suggested that once she imagine her 150-pound self putting her hands on her waist (in her mind's eye), feeling her slimness, and accompany the visualization with a feeling of being whole, healthy, light, and energetic.

For several months I did not see the patient, and from time to time I wondered whether she was having success or not. A number of months later, she returned to my office and I commented on what I was certain was a considerable loss of weight. She stated that two weeks after she started the regular visualization exercise I recommended—and without changing anything in her diet to her knowledge—she had lost five pounds. She then became so enthusiastic that she made added attempts to restrict her food intake and began to lose weight rapidly. Several weeks later, she suddenly realized that the visualization was interfering with a previous habit which she had enjoyed, namely, that of periodically gorging herself with food. She became very resentful that the visualization was taking away that "privilege" of hers, stopped the exercise, and promptly began to regain almost all the weight she had lost. The battle waged back and forth until utlimately she made the inner decision that she would rather be slim than experience periodic feelings of satisfaction through gorging herself. Resuming the visualization exercise, she again lost consistently and at the time of her last visit, I estimated her weight at 175 pounds.

"A. R." was a fifty-year-old teacher who suffered from asthmatic attacks which seemed to be brought on by exposure to wood dust in his wood shop class, as well as by the tensions of teaching a class of junior high school students.

In a stress workshop, he learned to assume a relaxed position, breathe comfortably and deeply, and visualize his throat, windpipe, bronchial passages, and lung tissue being relaxed, open, and free. By applying this exercise in his daily routine, he found his asthma attacks ceased almost completely. Those attacks which did occur could be warded off by imagining himself breathing with total freedom.

He also practiced visualization to relieve stomach tightness, indigestion, and muscle tension in the neck, controlling or preventing these symptoms quite readily.

Several techniques have been said to be helpful in dealing with pain, permitting reduction of the intake of pain medications or eliminating the need for them completely. An old Zen technique is utilized as follows: when an uncomfortable feeling such as itching, sharp pain, or unbearable pressure is present, the subject repeats rhythmically words which describe the symptom. Thus, if pain is present, the phrase repeated is "paining, paining, paining . . ." Full attention is given to the pain while the phrase is intoned. It may be that this technique works because the symptom is recognized rather than denied.

Another technique which seems to offer much in the field of pain control is acupuncture, although its principles and the reasons for its success are generally poorly understood in terms of Western medicine. It may be that the acupuncturist deals with the bioplasmic field of energy—a subject being studied by parapsychologists and beyond the scope of this book. In any case, it can be stated that acupuncture works quite well in many cases of distress and disease.

I myself have with some success, used a variation of the disidentification exercise of psychosynthesis (see Chapter 20). Much of what we experience as pain appears to be due to our identification with it: the phrases "I am hurt" or "I am hurting" imply such an identification. Some patients derive relief from repeating phrases such as "I have pain, but I am not my pain" or "Part of me is experiencing pain, but yet I am not that pain."

Experiments have been done at the Menninger Clinic by Drs. Elmer and Alyce Green on Jack Schwarz, a naturopath and psychic who demonstrated an unusually high degree of pain control.[13] While forcing a knitting needle through his arm, he showed no physiological responses that would indicate bodily distress. Additionally, no significant physiological changes were evident when burning cigarettes were held against his forearm for as long as twenty-five seconds. During this time, his electroencephalogram recording showed a steady pattern of Alpha activity. The meaning of this is not totally clear, but it may be that the ability to maintain an Alpha rhythm in the brain tends to inhibit incoming pain signals from the body.

I would like at this point to introduce some of the exercises I ask individuals and groups to use to begin visualizing their control over the autonomic nervous system.

Seat yourself comfortably, either cross-legged on a well-padded floor or on a chair with your feet flat on the floor. Keep your spine fairly straight and balance your head squarely on your shoulders. Let your arms fall loosely into your lap and consciously let your shoulders relax and drop; repeat the procedure until they feel heavy and limp. It is helpful at this stage to close your eyes. Now draw two or three deep breaths, using the muscles of the chest, diaphragm, and abdomen. As you exhale, let everything relax—shoulders, cheeks, jaw, all of the small muscles around the eyes and the rest of the face.

Next, let your mind's eye visualize the centers of control of the autonomic nervous system located in the middle lower portion of the brain. Visualize it as you might any control center with a system where incoming messages may be received and outgoing signals may be initiated. Visualize a series of nerves leaving the control center, proceeding downward through the neck, down through the chest and leading to the heart, down along the gullet or esophagus to the stomach and reaching far beyond into the small intestine, branching out until the final fibers reach the middle of the colon. Picture also another group of nerve fibers extending down the spinal cord and sending branches at many levels to the arms and legs, including blood vessels and skin, to the bladder and urinary system, to the lower colon, and to most of the automatically functioning muscles of the body.

Now picture waves of energy flowing down these nerves of the autonomic system—flowing gently, regularly, rhythmically, reaching the heart, stomach, intestines, lungs, skin, blood vessels, and bladder. If any tension exists in any part of your system, reach up in your mind's eye, "touch" one of the rheostats in the hypothalamic control center, and "turn" the appropriate rheostat counter-clockwise to reduce the energy to the minimum level necessary to continue the activity. If the stomach and intestine are overworking, turn down that rheostat to the absolute minimum, letting the energy flow at a level which is just enough to permit regular, smooth, rhythmical muscular activity. If the blood vessels are constricting and causing high blood pressure, reach up and turn down the rheostat, reducing the energy that flows along the autonomic nerves to the blood vessels in the limbs, head, and trunk. If the bowel is overactive, do the same for the nerves that lead to the lower bowel, turning down their energy to just what is required for normal, regular, comfortable activity. If the heart is tending to race, reach upward in your mind's eye and turn the cardiac nerve rheostat counter-clockwise, reducing the energy to just that which is required to keep the heart beating at a slow, regular, comfortable rhythm. If the limbs are cold, adjust the temperature rheostat so that just the right amount of energy goes to the muscles that constrict the blood vessels, and picture the hands and feet as becoming warm. Picture all of your body parts now functioning normally, rhythmically, quietly, regularly. Picture yourself as whole, energetic, enthusiastic, and confident. Know that you have these controls which you can choose to adjust whenever you are willing to do so.

Now, feel yourself remaining alert but becoming more wakeful, drawing two or three deep breaths in rapid succession, returning your consciousness to the place where you are seated. When you are ready, open your eyes.

This is an example of specific programmed visualizations which apply to specific bodily processes or to specific aspects of the functions of the body controlled by parts of the autonomic nervous system. Receptive visualization is more non-specific in character, although equally valuable. The Samuels', in *Seeing With the Mind's Eye,* describe an excellent technique for preparing for receptive visualization.[14]

Lie down in a quiet place at a time when you will not be disturbed. Place your arms at your sides, close your eyes, and let your feet separate slightly at the ankles. Breathe slowly and deeply with both the chest and abdomen. As you breathe out, relax, and say to yourself, "I am becoming quite relaxed." Give yourself permission to feel calm, warm, and comfortable. Imagine your legs and feet becoming very heavy and more and more relaxed. Imagine your thighs, pelvis, abdomen, and shoulders becoming more and more relaxed. Imagine your arms, neck, and head becoming very heavy, relaxing and resting comfortably on the surface on which you are lying. Enjoy the feeling of total body relaxation. You are now in a calm, relaxed state. Permit your emotions to become calm and relaxed. Now, imagine yourself in a building before an elevator door. Allow the door to open and step in. As the door closes, notice that you are on the tenth floor and watch the automatic indicator as the elevator descends to the first floor. The numbers pass slowly—nine—eight—seven—you are more and more deeply relaxed—six—five—more and more deeply relaxed—four—three—still deeper, deeper, and deeper—two—one—.

You are now in an open, deep state of mind. You are alert but in a comfortable, easy way. The elevator door opens and you enter a dimly lit room; on the far wall, you observe a large screen. Seat yourself in a soft, comfortable chair facing the screen. Say to yourself, "I am deeply relaxed, my mind feels clear, alert, and tranquil. I can visualize vividly and easily. I am open and receptive to all images that will be helpful to me. I look at the screen and see images come into view and disappear. I hold onto the images, look closely at them, and, if I have a question about them, I see other images that will help me find the answer. I find answers to a problem and I find images that give me ideas and creative suggestions."

Stay in the soft, comfortable chair as long as you wish. Whenever you want to return to your normal state of consciousness, merely get up from the chair, reenter the elevator, go to the tenth floor, and back to your normal state. When you have opened your eyes, write down some of the images that have come forth, since they will tend to slip away unless recorded.

In this way, many persons create their own solutions, and find the best precise wording for exercises to apply to their own particular state and their own particular problems. It is much like going up to a salad bar in a restaurant and "making your own salad." Unexpected, correct, creative solutions to problems seem to come easily in this kind of receptive state. It would seem that the higher unconscious or the superconscious of which Assagioli speaks is more readily contacted in such a state.

Creative and artistic people have frequently commented on the importance of getting in touch with this internal realm with its altered state of consciousness. Einstein is said to have described discovering the theory of relativity by picturing himself riding on a ray of light. Musical solutions came to the composer Tchaikovsky in so complete and finalized forms that he frequently had to scurry to get them written down. Amy Lowell, the well-known American poet, commented that the creation of a poem seemed as if it came through simply gazing at a piece of paper which hypnotized her into an awareness of the subconscious; the concentration necessary for achieving this was in her case like a sort of trance.[15]

Jerome Bruner, the famed Harvard professor of psychology, suggests a division of predisposing conditions for creativity into mental attitudes and actions.[16] The first necessary element, he suggests, is the attitude of detachment. This is a matter of placing some distance between one's own frame of reference and conventional ideas. Next is commitment by the creation of a deep need to understand the situation being worked on. Following this is the cultivation of passion and decorum. Passion he describes as the ability to let inner impulses express themselves in one's work. Decorum means respect for the forms and materials which express the creator's ideas in concrete aspects. Following this is the freedom to be dominated by the object, that is, the ability to identify with the created idea and temporarily to serve it with energy. Postponement and immediacy have to be balanced to find the ideal time for the creative solution. Finally, he mentions internal drama, meaning the awareness of all the figures personifying different aspects of oneself, each approaching the creative solution to the problem in a different way. The latter are similar to the subpersonalities of psychosynthesis, previously discussed.

I hope that this chapter on visualization—which may be widely applied in physical, mental, and emotional healing, in everyday existence, in interpersonal relationships, creativity, and in the process of growth itself—has demonstrated the potentially great healing power of imagery and the imagination. The words holiness, holistic, and wholeness are very closely related: it is the use of the inner world of the mind and of the self which challenges us to explore with enthusiasm these parts of ourselves as we strive for a greater and healthier unity with our higher selves and with all humankind. If creative solutions are to be found to our individual and collective problems and if progress toward the highest universal values is to be made, surely these will derive from the development of man's vast untapped inner resources.

NOTES

CHAPTER 1   STRESS

[1] Solomon, George F., "Stress and Antibody Response in Rats," *International Archives of Allergy,* 35 (1969):97.

[2] Missildine, Hugh. *Your Inner Child of the Past.* New York:Simon & Schuster, 1963.

[3] Holmes, Thomas H., and Rahe, R. "The Social Readjustment Rating Scale," *Journal of Psychosomatic Research,* 11 (1967):213–218.

[4] Selye, Hans. *Stress Without Distress.* Philadelphia and New York:J. B. Lippincott, 1974, p. 28.

[5] Salk, Jonas. "Biological Basis of Diseases and Behavior," *Perspect. Biol. Med.,* 5 (1962):198.

[6] Mutter, A. Z., and Schleifer, M. J., "The Role of Psychological and Social Factors in the Onset of Somatic Illness in Children," *Psychosomatic Medicine,* 28 (1966):333.

[7] Wolff, Harold G., Wolf, Stewart G., and Goodell, H. *Stress and Disease.* Springfield, Ill.:Charles C. Thomas, 1968, p. 8.

[8] Rushmer, Robert F., and Smith, O. A., "Cardiac Control," *Physiological Review,* 39 (1959):41.

[9] Hebb, D. O. "Drives and the Central Nervous System," *Psychological Review,* 62 (1955):243.

[10] Toffler, Alvin. *Future Shock.* New York:Random House, 1970.

CHAPTER 2   TENSION

[1] Wolff, Harold G., Wolf, Stewart G., and Goodell, H. *Stress and Disease.* Springfield, Ill.:Charles C. Thomas, 1968, p. 4.

[2] Vargiu, James G. *A Model of Creative Behavior.* San Francisco:Psychosynthesis Institute, 1973, p. 11.

[3] MacDougald, Dan. "Emotional Maturity Instruction." Unpublished materials; Box 20076/ Station N., Atlanta, Georgia 30325.

[4] Shands, Harley. "Integration, Discipline and the Concept of Shape," *Annals of the New York Academy of Science,* 164 (1969):578–587, quoting Andre Lwoff, "Interactions Among Virus Cells and Organisms," *Science,* 152 (1966): 1216–1220.

CHAPTER 3   PHYSICAL DISTRESS

[1] Jenkins, C. David, Rosenman, R. H., and Zyzanski, S. J. "Prediction of Coronary Heart Disease by a Test for the Coronary-Prone Behavior Pattern," *New England Journal of Medicine,* 290, 23 (June 6, 1974):1271–1275.

[2] Friedman, Meyer, and Rosenman, Ray H. *Type A Behavior and Your Heart.* New York:Alfred A. Knopf, 1974, p. 16.

[3] Wolff, Harold G., Wolf, Stewart G., and Goodell, H. *Stress and Disease.* Springfield, Ill.:Charles C. Thomas, 1968, p. 78–80.

[4] Flynn, J. T., Kennedy, M. A. C., and Wolf, Stewart G. "Essential Hypertension in One of Identical Twins," *Procedures of the Association for Research in Nervous and Mental Diseases,* 29 (1950):954.

[5] Alexander, F. "Emotional Factors in Essential Hypertension," *Psychosomatic Medicine* (1939):173.

[6] Valdman, Chernorutskii, and Lan-Belonogova. Quoted by Hoffmann, B., in "Blood Pressure and Subarctic Climate in the Soviet Union." (Survey of the Russian Literature and Investigations on Delayed Repatriates.) English translation by E. A. White, Res. Assoc. I.C.R.S., New York, Fordham University. Publ., Prof. Dr. Med., Max Brandt, East Europe History of Berlin Free Univ., Medical Series 16, 1958.

[7] Grace, W. J., and Graham, D. T. "The Specificity of the Relation Between Attitudes and Disease," *Psychosomatic Medicine,* 14 (1952):243.

[8] Dunbar, Flanders. *Psychiatry in the Medical Specialties.* New York:McGraw-Hill, 1959.

[9] Cobb, Sidney, and Rose, R. "Hypertension, Peptic Ulcer and Diabetes in Air Traffic Controllers," *Journal of the American Medical Association,* 224:4 (23 April, 1973):489.

[10] Lacey, John E., and Lacey, B. C. "Verification and Extension of the Principle of Autonomic Response-Sterotypy," *American Journal of Psychology,* 71 (1958):50–73.

[11]Robbins, Lewis, and Hall, J. *How to Practice Prospective Medicine.* Indianapolis, Ind.:Slaymaker Enterprises, 1970.

[12]Friedman, Meyer, and Rosenman, R. H. *Type A Behavior and Your Heart.* New York:Alfred A. Knopf, 1974, p. 44.

[13]Wertlake, P. T., Wilcox, A. A., Haley, M. I., and Petersen, J. E. "Relationship of Mental and Emotional Stress to Serum Cholesterol Levels," *Procedures of the Society for Experimental and Biological Medicine,* 97 (1958):163.

[14]Adsett, C. A., Schottstaedt, W. W., and Wolf, Stewart G. "Changes in Coronary Blood Flow and Other Himodynamic Indicators Induced by Stressful Interviews," *Psychosomatic Medicine,* 24 (1962):331–336.

[15]Friedman, Meyer, and Rosenman, R. H. *Type A Behavior and Your Heart.* New York:Alfred A. Knopf, 1974, p. 59.

[16]Friedman, Meyer, Byers, S. O., Rosenman, R. H., and Neuman, R. "Coronary Prone Individuals, Growth Hormone Responses," *Journal of the American Medical Association,* 217:7 (16 August, 1971):708.

[17] *Washington State Heart Association Journal,* 14–1, Winter, 1975.

[18]Dreyfus, F., and Czaezkes, J. W. "Blood Cholesterol and Uric Acid of Healthy Medical Students Under Stress of an Examination," *Archives of Internal Medicine,* 103 (1959):708.

[19]Hampton, J. W., Mantooth, J., Brandtt, E. N., and Wolf, Stewart G. "Plasma Fibrinogen Pattern Patients With Coronary Atherosclerosis," *Circulation,* 34 (1966):1098.

[20]Randall, W. C. (ed.). *Nervous Control of the Heart.* Baltimore, Md.:Williams and Wilkins, 1965.

[21]Wolf, Stewart G. "Sudden Death and the Oxygen Conserving Reflex," *American Heart Journal,* 71 (1966):840.

[22]Scholander, P. F. "Physiological Adaptation to Diving in Animals and Man," *Harvey Lectures,* 57 (1961–62):93.

[23]McClure, C. M. "Cardiac Arrest Through Volition," *California Medicine,* 90 (1959):440.

[24]Green, Elmer E., Ferguson, D. W., Green, A. M., and Walters, E. D. *Preliminary Report on Voluntary Controls Project: Swami Rama.* June, 1970. Menninger Foundation, Box 829, Topeka, Kansas 66601.

[25]Stevenson, I., and Duncan, C. H. "Alterations in Cardiac Function and Circulatory Efficiency During Periods of Life Stress, as Shown by Changes in the Rate, Rhythm, Electrocardiographic Pattern and Output of the Heart in Those With Cardiovascular Disease," *Procedures of the Association for Research in Nervous and Mental Diseases,* 29 (1950):25.

[26]Hellerstein, H. D. "Workload and Cardiac Function," in: Conference on Heart in Industry, *N. Y. Heart Association*, (1959):25.

[27]Christenson, William N., and Hinkle, L. E., Jr. "Differences in Illness and Prognostic Signs in Two Groups of Young Men," *Journal of the American Medical Association*, 177 (1961):247–253.

[28]Wolf, George A., and Wolff, Harold G. "Study on the Nature of Certain Symptoms Associated with Cardiovascular Disorders," *Psychosomatic Medicine*, 8 (1946):293.

[29]Wolff, Harold G., Wolf, Stewart G., and Goodell, H. *Stress and Disease.* Springfield, Ill.:Charles C. Thomas, 1968, p. 46.

[30]Goodell, Helen, Lewontin, R., and Wolff, Harold G. "Familial Occurrence of Migraine Headache, A Study of Heredity," *Archives of Neurological Psychiatry*, 72 (1954):325–334.

[31]Almy, T. P., Kern, F., Jr., and Abbott, F. K. "Constipation and Diarrhea as Reactions to Life Stress," *Procedures of the Association for Research in Nervous and Mental Diseases*, 29 (1950):724.

[32]Pelletier, Kenneth, and Garfield, C. *Consciousness East and West.* New York: Harper & Row, 1976, p. 129.

[33]Holmes, Thomas H., and Wolff, Harold G. "Life Situations, Emotions, and Backache," *Psychosomatic Medicine*, 14 (1952):18–33.

[34]Chapman, L. F., Ramos, A. O., Goodell, H., and Wolff, Harold G. "Neurokinin: A Polypeptide Formed During Neuronal Activity in Man," *Transactions of the American Neurological Association*, (1960):42.

[35]Selye, Hans. *Stress Without Distress.* Philadelphia and New York: J. B. Lippincott, 1974, p. 47–48.

[36]Oken, Donald. *Stress: Our Friend, Our Foe.* Blue Cross Pamphlet, 1974, p. 35.

[37]Weissmann, Gerald. "Lysosomal Mechanisms of Tissue Injury in Arthritis," *New England Journal of Medicine*, 286:3 (20 January, 1972):141–147.

[38]Aho, K., and Simmons, K. "Studies of the Nature of Rheumatoid Factor; Reaction of the Rheumatoid Factor with Human Specific Precipitates and with Native Human Gammaglobulin," *Arthritis, Rheumatism, Rheumatic Disease*, 6 (1963):676.

[39]Dixon, F. J., Feldman, J., and Vasquez, J. "Experimental Glomerulnephritis," *Journal of Experimental Medicine*, 113 (1961):899.

[40]Fudenberg, H. H. "Are Autoimmune Diseases Immunologic Deficiency States?," *Hospital Practice*, 3 (1968):43.

[41]Kellgren, et al., (eds.), "Symposium on Population Studies in Relation to Chronic Rheumatic Diseases." (Rome, 1961.) Oxford:Blackwell Scientific Publications, 1963.

[42]Moos, R. H. "MMPI Inventory Response Patterns in Patients with Rheumatoid Arthritis," *Journal of Psychosomatic Research,* 8 (1964):17.

[43]Moos, R. H., and Solomon, G. F. "Psychologic Comparisons Between Women with Rheumatoid Arthritis and Their Non-Arthritic Sisters, II. Content Analysis of Interviews," *Psychosomatic Medicine,* 27 (1975):135, 150.

[44]Holmes, Thomas H., Goodell, H., Wolf, Stewart G., Wolff, Harold G. *The Nose: An Experimental Study of Reactions Within the Nose in Human Subjects.* Springfield, Ill.:Charles C. Thomas, 1950.

[45]Holmes, Thomas H., Treuting, T., and Wolff, Harold G. "Life Situations, Emotions, and Nasal Disease: Evidence on Summative Effects Exhibited in Patients With Hay Fever," *Procedures of the Association for Research in Nervous and Mental Diseases,* 29 (1950):545.

[46]Grace, W. J., and Graham, D. T. "The Specificity of the Relation Between Attitudes and Disease," *Psychosomatic Medicine,* 14 (1952):243.

[47]Stein, Marvin, Schiara, R. C., and Lupurello, T. J. "Hypothalamus and Immune Process," *Annals of the New York Academy of Sciences,* 164 (1969): 464–471.

[48]Holmes, Thomas H., Goodell, H., Wolf, Stewart G., and Wolff, Harold G. *The Nose: An Experimental Study of Reactions Within the Nose in Human Subjects.* Springfield, Ill.:Charles C. Thomas, 1950.

[49]Christenson, W. N., Hinkle, L. E., Jr., et al. "Factors Apparently Influencing the Clinical Manifestations of Illness," *Abstracts of the American Review for Respiratory Diseases,* 88 (1963):129.

[50]Kaprowski, Hilary. "Latent or Dormant Viral Infections," *Annals of the New York Academy of Sciences,* 54 (1952):963–976.

[51]Adams, W. F. *Ireland and Irish Emigration to the New World.* New Haven, Conn.:Yale University Press, 1932.

[52]Moorman, L. J. "Tuberculosis on the Navajo Reservation," *American Review of Tuberculosis,* 61 (1950):586.

[53]Day, G. "The Psychosomatic Approach to Pulmonary Tuberculosis," *Lancet,* 1 (May, 1951):1025–1028.

[54]Imboden, J. B., Carter, A., and Leighton, S. C. "Convalescence from Influenza: A Study of the Psychological and Clinical Determinants," *Archives of International Medicine,* 108 (1961):115.

[55]Greenfield, M. S., Russler, R., and Grossley, A. P., Jr. "Ego Strength and Length of Recovery from Infectious Mononucleosis," *Journal of Nervous and Mental Disease,* 128 (1966):125.

[56]Soloman, George F. "Emotions, Stress, the Central Nervous System and Immunity," *Annals of the New York Academy of Sciences,* 164 (1969):335–343.

[57]Dubos, René. "The Germ Theory Revisited," Cornell University Special Lecture Series. March 18, 1953.

[58]Soloman, George F., and Moos, R. H. "Emotions, Immunity and Disease: A Speculative Theoretical Integration," *Archives of General Psychiatry*, 11 (1964):657.

[59]Soloman, George F., Amdraut, A. A., and Kasper, P. "Immunity, Emotions and Stress," *Annals of Clinical Research*, 6 (1974):313–322.

[60]Korneva, E. A. "The Effect of Stimulating Different Mesencephalic Structures on Protective Immune Response Patterns," *Fiziol, Zh. SSSR, Sechenov*, 53 (1967):42.

[61]Korneva, E. A., and Khai, L. M. "Effect of Destruction of Hypothalamic Areas on Immunogenesis," *Fiziol, Zh. SSSR, Sechenov*, 49 (1963):42.

[62]Soloman, George F., Amdraut, A. A., and Kasper, P. "Immunity, Emotions and Stress," *Annals of Clinical Research*, 6 (1974):313–322.

[63]Rasmussen, A. G., and Marsh, J. T., Jr. "Response of Adrenals, Thymus, Spleen and Leucocytes to Shuttle Box and Confinement Stress," *Procedures of the Society for Experimental and Biological Medicine*, 104 (1960):180.

[64]Bennette, Graham. "Psychic and Cellular Aspects of Isolation and Identity Impairment in Cancer. A Dialectic of Alienation," *Annals of the New York Academy of Sciences*, 164 (1969):264–352.

[65]Dixon, F. J., Feldman, J., and Vasquez, J. "Experimental Glomerulonephritis," *Journal of Experimental and Biological Medicine*, 113 (1961):899.

[66]Bogdanoff, M. D., Bogdanoff, N. N., and Wolf, Stewart G. "Studies on Salivary Function in Man; Variations in Secretory Rates as Part of the Adaptive Pattern," *Journal of Psychosomatic Research*, 5 (1961):70–174.

[67]Wolf, Stewart G., and Wolff, Harold G. *Human Gastric Function—An Experimental Study of a Man and His Stomach.* New York:Oxford Press, 1943 and 1947.

[68]Wolf, Stewart G. "Observations on the Occurrence of Nausea Among Combat Soldiers," *Gastroenterology*, 8 (1947):15.

[69]Grace, W. J., and Graham, D. T. "The Specificity of the Relation Between Attitudes and Disease," *Psychosomatic Medicine*, 14 (1952):243.

[70]Almy, T. P., Kern, F., Jr., and Abbott, F. K. "Constipation and Diarrhea as Reactions to Life Stress," *Procedures of the Association for Research in Nervous and Mental Diseases*, 29 (1950):724.

[71]Grace, W. J., Wolf, Stewart G., and Wolff, Harold G. *The Human Colon: An Experimental Study Based on Direct Observation of Four Fistulous Subjects.* New York:Hueber, 1951.

[72]Engel, George L. "Studies of Ulcerative Colitis, III—Nature of the Psychologic Process," *American Journal of Medicine,* 19 (1955):231–256.

[73]Arfwidson, S. "Pathogenesis of Multiple Diverticula of the Sigmoid Colon in Diverticular Disease," *Acta. Chir. Scand.* (Supplement), 342, 1964.

[74]Schottstaedt, W. W., Grace, W. J., and Wolff, Harold G. "Life Situations, Behavior, Attitudes, Emotions and Renal Excretion of Fluid and Electrolytes, III, Diuresis of Fluid and Electrolytes," *Journal of Psychosomatic Research,* 1 (1956):203–211.

[75]Schottstaedt, W. W., Grace, W. J., and Wolff, Harold G. "Life Situations, Behavior Patterns, and Renal Excretion of Fluid and Electrolytes," *Journal of the American Medical Association,* 157 (1955):1485–1488.

[76]McLellan, Allister M., and Goodell, H. "Pain from the Bladder, Ureter and Kidney Pelvis," *Procedures of the Association for Research in Nervous and Mental Diseases,* 23 (1943):252.

[77]Wolff, Harold G., Wolf, Stewart G., and Goodell, H. *Stress and Disease.* Springfield, Ill.:Charles C. Thomas, 1968, p. 89.

[78]Hinkle, L. E., Jr., Conger, G. B., and Wolf, Stewart G. "Studies on Diabetes Mellitus: The Relation of Stressful Life Situations to the Concentration of Ketone Bodies in the Blood of Diabetic and Non-Diabetic Humans," *Journal of Clinical Investigation,* 29 (1950):754.

[79]Hinkle, L. E., Jr., Edwards, C. J., and Wolf, Stewart G. "Occurrence of Diuresis in Humans in Stressful Situations and Its Possible Relation to the Diuresis of Early Starvation," *Journal of Clinical Investigation,* 30 (1951):809.

[80]Hetzel, Basil, Grace, W. J., and Wolff, Harold G. "General Metabolic Changes During Stressful Life Experience," *Journal of Psychosomatic Research,* 1 (1956):186–202.

[81]Greiland, R. "Thyrotozicosis at Ulleval Hospital in the Years 1934–1944 with a Special View to Frequency of the Disease," *Acta. Chir. Scand.,* 125 (1946):108.

[82]Graham, D. T. "The Pathogenesis of Hives: Experimental Study of Life Situations, Emotions and Cutaneous Vascular Reactions," *Procedures of the Association for Research in Nervous and Mental Diseases,* 29 (1950):987.

[83]Graham, D. T., and Wolf, Stewart G. "The Pathogenesis of Urticaria. Experimental Study of Life Situations, Emotions and Cutaneous Vascular Reactions," *Journal of the American Medical Association,* 143 (1950):1396.

[84]Graham, D. T., and Wolf, Stewart G. "The Relation of Eczema to Attitude and to Vascular Reactions of the Human Skin," *Journal of Clinical Medicine,* 42 (1953):238.

[85]Wolff, Harold G., Lorenz, T. H., and Graham, D. T. "Stress, Emotions and Human Sebum: Their Relevance to Acne Vulgaris," *Transactions of the Association of American Physicians,* 64 (1951):435.

[86]Barker, Wayne. "Studies in Epilepsy: Personality Pattern, Situational Stress, and the Symptoms of Narcolepsy," *Psychosomatic Medicine*, 10 (1948): 193.

[87]Kissen, David M. "Relationship Between Lung Cancer, Cigarette Smoking, Inhalation and Personality and Psychological Factors in Lung Cancers," *British Journal of Medical Psychology*, 37 (1964):203–216.

[88]Eysenck, H. O. "The Differentiation Between Normal and Various Neurotic Groups on Maudsley Personality Inventory," *British Journal of Medical Psychology*, 50 (1959):176–177.

[89]Kissen, David M. "Psychosocial Factors, Personality and Lung Cancer in Men Aged 55 to 64," *British Journal of Medical Psychology*, 40 (1967):29–43.

[90]Thomas, Carolyn B., and Duszynski, K. R. "Closeness to Parents and the Family Constellation in a Prospective Study of Five Disease States: Suicide, Mental Illness, Malignant Tumor, Hypertension, and Coronary Heart Disease," *Johns Hopkins Medical Journal*, 134 (1974):251–269.

[91]Bahnson, C. B. "Psychophysiological Complementarity in Malignancies," *Annals of the New York Academy of Sciences*, 164:2 (1969):319–333.

[92]Kidd, J. G. "Does the Host React Against His Own Cancer Cells?," *Cancer Research*, 21 (1961):1170.

[93]Sommers, S. C. "Host Factors in Fatal Human Lung Cancer," *Archives of Pathology*, 65 (1958):104–111.

[94]Prehn, R. T. *Role of Immune Mechanisms, Biology of Chemically and Physically Induced Tumors*. New York:Hueber, 1963.

[95]Southam, C. M., Moore, A. E., and Rhoades, C. P. "Homotransplantation of Human Cell Lines," *Science*, 125 (1957):158.

[96]LeShan, L. L., and Worthington, R. E. "Personality as a Factor in Pathogenesis of Cancer: Review of Literature," *British Journal of Medical Psychology*, 29 (1956):49.

[97]Baker, Elsworth F. *Man in the Trap: The Causes of Blocked Sexual Energy*. New York:Avon Books, p. 239–41.

[98]Klopfer, B. "Psychological Variables in Human Cancer," *Journal of Projective Techniques*, 21 (1957):331–340.

[99]Southam, Chester M. "Discussion: Emotions, Immunology, and Cancer: How Might the Psyche Influence Neoplasia?," *Annals of the New York Academy of Sciences*, 164, (1969):473–475.

[100]Rotkin, I. C., Quenk, M., and Couchman, M. "Psychological Factors in Cervical Cancer," *Archives of General Psychiatry*, 13 (1965):532.

[101]Quinsberry, W. B. "Sociological Factors in Cancer in Hawaii," *Annals of the New York Academy of Sciences*, 84 (1965):795.

[102]Boothe, Gothard P. "General and Organic Object Relationships in Cancer," *Annals of the New York Academy of Sciences,* 164 (1969):568–577.

[103]Simonton, Carl O. "Science and Psi," Copies of lecture given at Stanford and UCLA (October 1972) available through Academy of Parapsychology and Medicine, 314 A Second St., Los Altos, Calif. 94022.

[104]Shealy, Norman. *The Pain Game.* Millbrae, Calif.: Celestial Arts, 1976, p. 3.

[105]Graham, D. T. "The Pathogenesis of Hives: Experimental Study of Life Situations, Emotions and Cutaneous Vascular Reactions," *Procedures of the Association for Research in Nervous and Mental Diseases,* 29 (1950):987.

[106]Wolff, Harold G., Wolf, Stewart G., and Goodell, H. *Stress and Disease.* Springfield, Ill.:Charles C. Thomas, 1968, p. 67–68.

[107]Pelletier, Kenneth, and Garfield, C. *Consciousness East and West.* New York: Harper & Row, 1976, p. 129.

Chapter 4   Emotional Distress

[1]Plutchick, Robert. *The Emotions.* New York:Random House, 1962.

[2]Wolff, Harold G., Wolf, Stewart G., and Goodell, H. *Stress and Disease.* Springfield, Ill.:Charles C. Thomas, 1968, p. 231.

[3]Missildine, Hugh. *Your Inner Child of the Past.* New York:Simon & Schuster, 1963.

[4]Deckert, Gordon. Transactional Analysis Lectures. American Academy of Family Physicians, Los Angeles, October, 1974.

[5]Loomis, Evarts, and Paulson, J. Sig. *Healing For Everyone—Medicine of the Whole Person.* New York:Hawthorn Books, 1975.

[6]James, Muriel, and Jongeward, D. *Born to Win.* Reading, Mass. and Menlo Park, Calif.:Addison-Wesley, 1971, p. 192.

[7]Luria, Alexander R. *The Role of Speech in Regulation of Normal and Abnormal Behavior.* Oxford:Pergamon Press, 1961, p. 95.

[8]Coopersmith, Stanley. *The Antecedents of Self-Esteem.* San Francisco and London:W. H. Freeman and Co., 1967.

[9]Bahnson, C. B. "Psychophysiological Complementarity in Malignancies," *Annals of the New York Academy of Sciences,* 164:2 (1969):319–333.

[10]Greenfield, M. S., Russler, R., and Grossley, A. P., Jr. "Ego Strength and Length of Recovery from Infectious Mononucleosis," *Journal of Nervous and Mental Disease,* 128 (1966):125.

[11]Horney, Karen. *New Ways in Psychoanalysis.* New York:W. W. Norton, 1939.

[12]Perls, Frederick S., Hefferline, R. F., and Goodman, Paul. *Gestalt Therapy.* New York:Dell Publishing, 1951, p. 123.

[13]McClary, A. R., Meyer, E., and Weitzman, D. J. "Observations of the Role of Mechanism of Depression in Some Patients with Disseminated Lupus Erythematosus," *Psychosomatic Medicine,* 17 (1955):311.

CHAPTER 5   MENTAL DISTRESS

[1]Missildine, Hugh. *Your Inner Child of the Past.* New York:Simon & Schuster, 1963, p. 85.

CHAPTER 6   SELF-DESTRUCTIVE HABITS

[1]Robbins, Lewis C., and Hall, J. H. *How To Practice Prospective Medicine.* Indianapolis:Slaymaker Enterprises, 1970.

[2]Remen, Naomi. *The Masculine Principle—The Feminine Principle and Humanistic Medicine.* San Francisco, Calif.:Institute for the Study of Humanistic Medicine, 1975, p. 67.

[3]Loomis, Evarts J., and Paulsen, J. Sig. *Healing for Everyone—Medicine of the Whole Person.* New York:Hawthorn Books, 1975, p. 48.

[4]Steiner, Claude. *Games Alcoholics Play.* New York:Grove Press, 1971, p. 83.

[5]Robbins, Lewis C., and Hall, J. H. *How to Practice Prospective Medicine.* Indianapolis:Slaymaker Enterprises, 1970, p. 45.

[6]Loomis, Evarts, and Paulson, J. Sig. *Healing For Everyone—Medicine of the Whole Person.* New York:Hawthorn Books, 1975.

SECTION II   A FUNCTIONAL MODEL OF MAN

[1]Andrews, Donald. *The Symphony of Life.* Lee's Summit, Mo.:Unity Books, 1966, p. 42.

[2]Young, J. Z. *A Model of the Brain.* London:Oxford University Press, 1964.

[3]Herrick, Charles. *The Evolution of Human Nature.* Austin:University of Texas Press, 1956.

[4]Harris, Thomas. *I'm O.K., You're O.K.* New York:Harper & Row, 1967, p. 30.

[5]Riffenburgh, Robert H. "A Speculative Mathematical Model of the Psycho-physiologic System," *Annals of the New York Academy of Sciences,* 164 (1969): 409–424.

CHAPTER 7   PERCEPTION OF DATA OR STIMULI

[1]Hyden, H. "RNA: A Functional Characteristic of Neuron and Glia in Learning," in M. Brazier (ed.), *RNA and Brain Function in Learning.* Berkeley and Los Angeles:1964.

[2]Penfield, Wilder. *AMA Archives of Neurology and Psychiatry,* 67 (1952): 178–198.

[3]Harris, Thomas. *I'm O.K., You're O.K.* New York:Harper & Row, 1967, p. 9.

[4]Assagioli, Roberto. *Psychosynthesis: A Manual of Principles and Techniques.* New York:Viking Press, 1965, p. 17.

[5]Jung, Carl G. *Modern Man in Search of a Soul.* New York:Harcourt, Brace & World, 1933, p. 90.

[6]Hernandez-Peon, Raul, Scherrer, H., and Jouvet, M. "Modification of Electric Activity in Cochlear Nucleus During 'Attention' in Unanesthetized Cats," *Science,* 123 (1956):331–332.

[7]Galambos, Robert. "Suppression of Auditory Nerve Activity by Stimulation of Efferent Fibers to Cochlea," *Journal of Neurophysiology,* 19 (1956): 424–437.

[8]Galambos, Robert, Picton, T., Hillyard, S., and Schiff, M. "Human Auditory Attention: A Central or Peripheral Process?," *Science,* 173 (23 July, 1971):351–353.

[9]Miller, George. "The Magical Number Seven ± Two; Some Limits on Our Capacity for Processing Information," *The Psychological Review,* 63 (2 March, 1956):81–97.

[10]Pelletier, Kenneth, and Garfield, C. *Consciousness East and West.* New York: Harper & Row, 1976, p. 12.

[11]MacDougald, Dan. "Emotional Maturity Instruction." Unpublished materials; Box 20076/ Station N., Atlanta, Georgia 30325.

[12]Hall, E. T. *The Hidden Dimension.* New York:Doubleday, 1966, p. 125.

[13]Luria, Alexander R. *The Working Brain.* New York:Basic Books, 1973, p. 271.

[14]———, p. 60.

[15]———, p. 259.

CHAPTER 8   ATTITUDES AND GOALS

[1] Shealy, Norman. *The Pain Game.* Millbrae, Calif.:Celestial Arts, 1976, p. 155.

[2] Luria, Alexander R. *The Working Brain.* New York:Basic Books, 1973, p. 57.

[3] Wolff, Harold G., Wolf, Stewart G., and Goodell, H. *Stress and Disease.* Springfield, Illinois:Charles C. Thomas, 1968, p. 128.

[4] Luria, Alexander R. *The Working Brain.* New York:Basic Books, 1973, p. 56.

[5] Rosenthal, Robert, and Jacobson, Lenore F. "Teacher Expectations for the Disadvantaged," *Scientific American,* April, 1968, 19–23.

CHAPTER 9   DATA PROCESSING

[1] Luria, Alexander R. *The Role of Speech in Regulation of Normal and Abnormal Behavior.* Oxford:Pergamon Press, 1961, p. 95.

[2] Luria, Alexander R. *The Working Brain.* New York:Basic Books, 1973, p. 57.

[3] Riffenburgh, Robert H. "A Speculative Mathematical Model of the Psychophysiologic System," *Annals of the New York Academy of Sciences,* 164 (1969): 413.

CHAPTER 10   OUTPUT SYSTEM

[1] Shealy, Norman. *The Pain Game.* Millbrae, Calif.:Celestial Arts, 1976, p. 23.

[2] Maltz, Maxwell. *Psychocybernetics.* New York, Pocket Books, 1966, p. 34.

[3] Korneva, E. A. "The Effect of Stimulating Different Mesencephalic Structures on Protective Immune Response Patterns," *Fiziol, Zh. SSSR, Sechenov,* 53 (1967):42.

[4] Korneva, E. A., and Khai, L. M. "Effect of Destruction of Hypothalamic Areas on Immunogenesis," *Fiziol, Zh. SSSR, Sechenov,* 49 (1963):42.

[5] Pitts, F. N., and McClure, J. N., Jr. "Lactate Metabolism in Anxiety Neurosis," *New England Journal of Medicine,* 277 (1967):1329–1336.

[6] Green, Elmer E., Ferguson, D. W., Green, A. M., and Walters, E. D. *Preliminary Report on Voluntary Controls Project: Swami Rama.* June, 1970. Menninger Foundation, Box 829, Topeka, Kansas 66601.

CHAPTER 11   THE SELF AND THE WILL

[1] Jung, Carl G. *Man and His Symbols.* New York:Doubleday and Co., 1964, p. 161. (M.-L. von Franz, *The Process of Individuation.*)

[2] Maslow, Abraham H. *Motivation and Personality.* New York:Harper & Row, 1954, p. 2.

[3] Assagioli, Roberto. *Psychosynthesis.* New York:Viking Press, 1965, p. 18.

[4] Assagioli, Roberto. *The Act of Will.* New York:Viking Press, 1973, p. 9.

[5] Wolff, Harold G., Wolf, Stewart G., and Goodell, H. *Stress and Disease.* Springfield, Ill.:Charles C. Thomas, 1968, p. 133.

[6] Assagioli, Roberto. *The Act of Will.* New York:Viking Press, 1973, p. 10.

[7] Assagioli, Roberto. *Psychosynthesis.* New York:Viking Press, 1965, p. 22.

[8] Assagioli, Roberto. *Psychosynthesis.* New York:Viking Press, 1965, p. 86.

CHAPTER 12   THE FEEDBACK NATURE OF THE MESSAGE SYSTEM

[1] Luria, Alexander R. *The Role of Speech in Regulation of Normal and Abnormal Behavior.* Oxford:Pergamon Press, 1961, p. 17.

[2] Shands, Harley C. "Integration, Discipline and the Concept of Shape," *Annals of the New York Academy of Sciences,* 164 (1969):578–587.

CHAPTER 15   RELEASE OF TENSION THROUGH ACTIVITIES

[1] *Washington State Heart Association Journal.* 14–1. Winter, 1975: Report on Research by Dr. Peter Wood, Stanford Heart Disease Program.

[2] Morehouse, Lawrence, and Gross, L. *Total Fitness.* New York:Simon & Schuster, 1975, p. 184.

[3] Loomis, Evarts, and Paulson, J. Sig. *Healing For Everyone—Medicine of the Whole Person.* New York:Hawthorn Books, 1975, p. 93.

[4] Boyer, John L., and Kasch, F. W. "Exercise Therapy in Hypertensive Men," *Journal of the American Medical Association,* 211 (March, 1960):1668–1671.

[5] Cardiac and Pulmonary Research Institute, 914 E. Jefferson, Seattle, Wash. 98122.

[6] Olsen, Ken. *The Art of Hanging Loose in an Uptight World.* Phoenix, Ariz: O'Sullivan Woodside, 1974, p. 44.

[7]Lowen, Alexander. *Depression and the Body: The Biological Basis of Faith and Reality.* New York:Coward, McCann & Geoghegan, 1972.

[8]Deckert, Gordon. Transactional Analysis Lectures. American Academy of Family Physicians, Los Angeles, October, 1974.

CHAPTER 16   CONSCIOUS PASSIVE RELAXATION

[1]Barber, Theodore, Stoyva, J., et al. (eds.). *Biofeedback and Self-Control: A Reader on the Regulation of the Bodily Processes and Consciousness.* Chicago: Aldine-Atherton, 1972.

[2]Schultz, J. H., and Luthe, Wolfgang (eds.). *Autogenic Training: A Psychophysiologic Approach in Psychotherapy.* New York:Grune & Stratton, 1959.

[3]Green, Elmer E., Green, Alyce M., and Walters, E. Dale. *Self Regulation of Internal States.* London:Procedures of the International Congress of Cybernetics, 1969.

[4]Assagioli, Roberto. *The Act of Will.* New York:Viking Press, 1973, p. 52.

[5]Pelletier, Kenneth, and Garfield, C. *Consciousness East and West.* New York: Harper & Row, 1976, p. 257.

[6]Benson, Herbert. *The Relaxation Response.* New York:Avon Books, 1975, p. 98.

[7]Benson, Herbert, Shapiro, D., Tursky, B., and Schwartz, G. E. "Decreased Systolic Blood Pressure Through Operant Conditioning Techniques in Patients With Essential Hypertension," in *Biofeedback and Self-Control,* Theodore Barber, J. Stoyva, et al. (eds.). Chicago:Aldine-Atherton, 1972.

[8]Weiss, T., and Engel, B. T. "Operant Conditioning of Heartrate in Patients with Premature Ventricular Contractions," in *Biofeedback and Self-Control,* Theodore Barber, J. Stoyva, et al. (eds.). Chicago:Aldine-Atherton, 1972.

[9]Sargent, Joseph D., Green, E., and Walters, D. "Preliminary Report on the Use of Autogenic Feedback Techniques in the Treatment of Migraine and Tension Headaches," *Psychosomatic Medicine,* 35 (1973):129–135.

[10]Gannon, L., and Sternbach, R. A. "Alpha Enhancement and a Treatment for Pain: A Case Study," *Journal of Behavior Therapy and Experimental Psychiatry,* 2 (1975):209.

[11]Haugen, G. B., Dixon, H. H., and Dickel, H. A. *A Therapy for Anxiety Tension Reactions.* New York: Macmillan, 1963.

[12]Crosby, W. H., and Segal, Julius. "Biofeedback as a Medical Treatment," *Journal of the American Medical Association,* 232 (April 14, 1975):179–180.

[13]Shealy, Norman. *The Pain Game.* Millbrae, Calif.:Celestial Arts, 1976, p. 133.

Chapter 17 Meditation

[1] LaMott, Kenneth. *Escape From Stress.* New York:Berkeley Publishing Corp., 1975, p. 68.

[2] Wapnick, K. "Mysticism and Schizophrenia," *Journal of Transpersonal Psychology* (1969):42–68.

[3] Naranjo, Claudio, and Ornstein, R. E. *On the Psychology of Meditation.* New York:Viking Press, 1971.

[4] Deikman, A. "Bimodal Consciousness," *Archives of General Psychiatry,* 25 (1971):481–489.

[5] Pahnke, W. N., and Richards, W. A. "Implications of L.S.D. and Experimental Mysticism," *Journal of Religion and Health,* 5 (1966):175–208.

[6] Assagioli, Roberto. *The Act of Will.* New York:Viking Press, 1973, p. 218–229.

[7] Benson, Herbert. *The Relaxation Response.* New York:Avon Books, 1975, p. 98–99.

[8] Hess, W. R. *The Functional Organization of Diencephalon.* New York:Grune & Stratton, 1957.

[9] Pelletier, Kenneth, and Garfield, C. *Consciousness East and West.* New York: Harper & Row, 1976, p. 127.

[10] Wallace, R. K. "Physiological Effects of Transcendental Meditation," *Science,* 167 (1970):1751–1754.

[11] Hartman, E. *The Biology of Dreaming.* Springfield, Ill.:Charles C. Thomas, 1967.

[12] Wallace, R. K., and Benson, H. "The Physiology of Meditation," *Scientific American,* 226 (1972):84–90.

[13] Orme-Johnson, B. "Transcendental Meditation and Autonomic Lability," First International Symposium on the Science of Creative Intelligence, Humboldt State College, Arcate, California, August, 1971.

Chapter 18 Fulfilling Recognition Needs

[1] Solomon, George F., Levine, S., and Kraft, J. "Early Experience and Immunity," *Nature,* 220 (1968):821.

[2] James, Muriel, and Jongeward, D. *Born to Win.* Reading, Mass. and Menlo Park, Calif.:Addison-Wesley, 1971, p. 46.

[3]Jarvis, Davis B. Transactional Analysis Lectures. Washington Academy of Family Physicians, Committee on Mental Health, Seattle, Wash., Spring 1975.

[4]Gordon, Thomas. *Parent Effectiveness Training.* New York:Wyden Books, 1970, p. 118.

[5]Berne, Eric. *Games People Play.* New York:Grove Press, 1964.

CHAPTER 20   CULTIVATION OF POSITIVE ATTITUDES

[1]Wolff, Harold G., Wolf, Stewart G., and Goodell, H. *Stress and Disease.* Springfield, Ill.:Charles C. Thomas, 1968, p. 231.

[2]MacDougald, Dan. "Emotional Maturity Instruction." Unpublished materials; Box 20076/ Station N., Atlanta, Georgia 30325.

[3]Assagioli, Roberto. *Psychosynthesis.* New York:Viking Press, 1965, p. 22.

[4]Assagioli, Roberto. *Psychosynthesis.* New York:Viking Press, 1965, p. 74.

[5]Thigpen, Corbett H., and Cleckly, Harvey M. *The Three Faces of Eve.* New York:McGraw-Hill, 1957.

CHAPTER 21   THE SETTING OF GOALS

[1]Assagioli, Roberto, *The Act of Will*, New York: Viking Press, 1973, p. 135.

[2]Wolff, Harold G., Wolf, Stewart G., and Goodell, H. *Stress and Disease.* Springfield, Ill.:Charles C. Thomas, 1968, p. 133.

[3]MacDougald, Dan. "Emotional Maturity Instruction." Unpublished materials; Box 20076/ Station N., Atlanta, Georgia 30325.

[4] *Ibid.*

CHAPTER 22   CREATIVE VISUALIZATION FOR GOAL REINFORCEMENT AND FUNCTIONAL CHANGES

[1]Samuels, Mike, and Samuels, Nancy. *Seeing with the Mind's Eye.* New York: Random House/Bookworks, 1975, p. 145.

[2]Maltz, Maxwell. *Psychocybernetics.* New York:Pocket Books, 1966, p. 13.

[3]Isherwood, Christopher, and Prabhavananda, Swami. *How to Know God: The Yoga Aphorisms of Patanjali.* Hollywood, Calif.:Vendanta Press, 1953, p. 20.

[4]Assagioli, Roberto. *Psychosynthesis.* New York:Viking Press, 1965, p. 17.

[5]Richardson, A. *Mental Imagery.* New York:Springer Publishing Co., 1969, p. 88.

[6]Richardson, A. *Mental Imagery.* New York:Springer Publishing Co., 1969, p. 56.

[7]Maltz, Maxwell. *Psychocybernetics.* New York:Pocket Books, 1966, p. 32.

[8]Maltz, Maxwell. *Psychocybernetics.* New York:Pocket Books, 1966, p. 40.

[9]Bolen, J. "Meditation and Psychotherapy in the Treatment of Cancer," *Physician* (July, 1973):20–21.

[10]Rugg, Harold. *Imagination.* New York:Harper & Row, 1963, p. 309.

[11]Luthe, Wolfgang. *Autogenic Therapy.* Vol. I. New York:Grune & Stratton, 1969.

[12]Luthe, Wolfgang. *Autogenic Therapy.* Vol. II. New York:Grune & Stratton, 1969, p. 96.

[13]Green, Elmer, and Green, Alyce. "Biofeedback and Volition, New Dimensions of Habilitation for the Handicapped," University of Florida Conference, Gainsville, Florida, June, 1974.

[14]Samuels, Mike, and Samuels, Nancy. *Seeing with the Mind's Eye.* New York: Random House/Bookworks, 1975, p. 152.

[15]——, p. 250–251.

[16]Gruber, H. *Contemporary Approaches to Creative Thinking.* New York:Atherton Press, 1962, p. 12.

SELECTED BIBLIOGRAPHY

For additional sources in journals and periodicals, consult Notes.

ANDREWS, DONALD. *The Symphony of Life.* Lee's Summit, Mo.:Unity Books, 1966.

ASSAGIOLI, ROBERTO. *The Act of Will.* New York:Viking Press, 1973.

———. *Psychosynthesis: A Manual of Principles and Techniques.* New York:Viking Press, 1965.

BAKER, ELSWORTH F. *Man in the Trap: The Causes of Blocked Sexual Energy.* New York:Macmillan, 1967.

BARBER, THEODORE, STOYVA, J., et al. (eds.). *Biofeedback and Self-Control: A Reader on the Regulation of the Bodily Processes and Consciousness.* Chicago:Aldine-Atherton, 1972.

BENSON, HERBERT. *The Relaxation Response.* New York:Avon Books, 1975.

BERNE, ERIC. *Games People Play.* New York:Grove Press, 1964.

COOPERSMITH, STANLEY. *The Antecedents of Self-Esteem.* San Francisco and London:W. H. Freeman & Co., 1967.

CURETON, THOMAS. *Physical Fitness and Dynamic Health.* New York:Dial Press, 1965.

FRIEDMAN, MEYER, and ROSENMAN, RAY H. *Type A Behavior and Your Heart.* New York:Alfred A. Knopf, 1974.

GORDON, THOMAS. *Parent Effectiveness Training.* New York:Wyden Books, 1970.

GRACE, W. J., WOLF, STEWART G. and WOLFF, HAROLD G. *The Human Colon: An Experimental Study Based on Direct Observation of Four Fistulous Subjects.* New York:Hueber, 1951.

GRUBER, H. *Contemporary Approaches to Creative Thinking.* New York:Atherton Press, 1962.

HALL, E. T. *The Hidden Dimension.* New York:Doubleday & Co., 1966.

HARRIS, THOMAS. *I'm O.K., You're O.K.* New York:Harper & Row, 1967.

HARTMAN, E. *The Biology of Dreaming.* Springfield, Ill.:Charles C. Thomas, 1967.

HAUGEN, G. B., DIXON, H. H., and DICKEL, H. A. *A Therapy for Anxiety Tension Reactions.* New York:Macmillan Co., 1963.

HERRICK, CHARLES. *The Evolution of Human Nature.* Austin:University of Texas Press, 1956.

HESS, W. R. *The Functional Organization of Diencephalon.* New York:Grune & Stratton, 1957.

HOLMES, THOMAS H., GOODELL, H., WOLF, STEWART G. and WOLFF, HAROLD G. *The Nose: An Experimental Study of Reactions Within the Nose in Human Subjects.* Springfield, Ill.:Charles C. Thomas, 1950.

ISHERWOOD, CHRISTOPHER, and PRABHAVANANDA, SWAMI. *How to Know God: The Yoga Aphorisms of Patanjali.* Hollywood, Calif.:Vendanta Press, 1953.

JAMES, MURIEL, and JONGEWARD, D. *Born to Win.* Reading, Mass. and Menlo Park, Calif.:Addison-Wesley Publishing Co., 1971.

JUNG, CARL G. *Man and His Symbols.* New York:Doubleday & Co., 1964.

LAMOTT, KENNETH. *Escape from Stress.* New York:Berkeley Publishing Corp., 1975.

LOOMIS, EVARTS, and PAULSON, J. SIG. *Healing for Everyone—Medicine of the Whole Person.* New York:Hawthorn Books, 1975.

LOWEN, ALEXANDER. *Depression and the Body: The Biological Basis of Faith and Reality.* New York:Coward, McCann & Geoghegan, 1972.

LURIA, ALEXANDER R. *The Role of Speech in Regulation of Normal and Abnormal Behavior.* Oxford:Pergamon Press, 1961.

———. *The Working Brain.* New York:Basic Books, 1973.

LUTHE, WOLFGANG. *Autogenic Therapy.* 2 vols. New York:Grune & Stratton, 1969.

MALTZ, MAXWELL. *Psychocybernetics.* New York:Pocket Books, 1966.

MASLOW, ABRAHAM. *The Farther Reaches of Human Nature.* New York:Viking Press, 1971.

———. *Motivation and Personality.* New York:Harper & Row, 1954.

MISSILDINE, HUGH. *Your Inner Child of the Past.* New York:Simon & Schuster, 1963.

MOREHOUSE, LAWRENCE, and GROSS, L. *Total Fitness.* New York:Simon & Schuster, 1975.

NARANJO, CLAUDIO, and ORNSTEIN, R. E. *On the Psychology of Meditation.* New York:Viking Press, 1971.

OLSEN, KEN. *The Art of Hanging Loose in an Uptight World.* Phoenix, Ariz.:O'Sullivan Woodside, 1974.

PELLETIER, KENNETH, and GARFIELD, C. *Consciousness East and West.* New York:Harper & Row, 1976.

PERLS, FREDERICK S., HEFFERLINE, R. F., and GOODMAN, PAUL. *Gestalt Therapy.* New York:Dell Publishing Co., 1951.

PLUTCHICK, ROBERT. *The Emotions.* New York:Random House, 1962.

PREHN, R. T. *Role of Immune Mechanisms, Biology of Chemically and Physically Induced Tumors.* New York:Hueber, 1963.

RANDALL, W. C. (ed.). *Nervous Control of the Heart.* Baltimore, Md.:Williams and Wilkins, 1965.

REICH, WILHELM. *The Cancer Biopathy.* New York:Orgone Institute Press, 1948.

RICHARDSON, A. *Mental Imagery.* New York:Springer Publishing Co., 1969.

ROBBINS, LEWIS, and HALL, J. *How to Practice Prospective Medicine.* Indianapolis, Ind.:Slaymaker Enterprises, 1970.

RUGG, HAROLD. *Imagination.* New York:Harper & Row, 1963.

SAMUELS, MIKE and NANCY. *Seeing with the Mind's Eye.* New York:Random House/Bookworks, 1975.

SCHULTZ, J. H., and LUTHE, WOLFGANG (eds.). *Autogenic Training: A Psychophysiologic Approach in Psychotherapy.* New York:Grune & Stratton, 1959.

SELYE, HANS. *Stress Without Distress.* Philadelphia and New York:J. B. Lippincott, 1974.

SHEALY, NORMAN. *The Pain Game.* Millbrae, Calif.:Celestial Arts, 1976.

STEINER, CLAUDE. *Games Alcoholics Play.* New York: Grove Press, 1971.

TOFFLER, ALVIN. *Future Shock.* New York:Random House, 1970.

VARGIU, JAMES G. *A Model of Creative Behavior.* San Francisco:Psychosynthesis Institute, 1973.

WOLF, STEWART G., and WOLFF, HAROLD G. *Human Gastric Function—An Experimental Study of a Man and His Stomach.* New York:Oxford University Press, 1943 and 1947.

WOLFF, HAROLD G., WOLF, STEWART, and GOODELL, H. *Stress and Disease.* Springfield, Ill.:Charles C. Thomas, 1968.

YOUNG, J. Z. *A Model of the Brain.* London:Oxford University Press, 1964.

INDEX

Acceptance of truth, 196
Accident prone, 31
Accidents, 79
Accommodation to drugs, 139
Accountants, 43
Acupuncture, 213
Acetylcholine, 72
Acne, 73
Activities, release of tension
    through, 143–154
Adaptability, 31, 133
Adaptation, 28, 30–31
Adrenal, 46, 78
  cortex, 56, 62, 69, 124
  medulla, 124
Adrenalin, 124–125
Adrenocorticotropic hormone
    (ACTH), 56
Agape, 190
Aggression, 125
Aha experience, 30–31
Alarm-rat reaction, 56
Alcohol, 98
Aldosterone, 69

Alimentary tract, 63
Allergic disorders, 58–59
Alpha brain waves, 114, 165, 213
Altered states of consciousness, 170
Amenorrhea, 71
Amino acids, 97
Amphetamines, 101
Analgesics, 137
Anger, 21, 81, 87–88, 150–151, 196
  in migraine, 49
Angina pectoris, 33, 147
Anorexia, 66
Anterior pituitary, 56, 62–63
Antiarrhythmic drugs, 137
Antibiotics, 137
Antibodies, 55, 62, 175
  anticolon, 68
  incompetent, 57
  islet cell, 70
Antidepressants, 137
Antidiuretic hormone, 69
Antigen-antibody complex, 56–57,
    62–63, 68
Antiinflammatory drugs, 137

Antiinflammatory effects, 55–56
Anxiety, 22, 29, 31, 37, 52–53, 60,
    64, 86–87, 125, 137, 151–152,
    167
  fatigue, 83
  in obsessive-compulsive persons,
    92
  "to choke", 86
Appendicitis, 53
Appetite, 88
Apprehension, 53
Arteriole, 38
Arteriosclerosis, 34
Arthritis (see Rheumatoid)
Asbestos, 75
Assagioli, Roberto, 109, 128–129,
    131, 171, 197, 199–200, 208
Asthma, 59, 99, 193
Atria, 46
Atrial flutter, 127
Attitudes, 28, 114–119, 129, 158,
    189–199, 203
  definition, 114
  in diabetes, 69
  in hay fever, 58
  in hives, 72
  holding on, 67
  negative, 114, 189
  positive, 114
  readiness, 53
  wariness, 40
Auto seat belts, 102
Autoantibody, 56, 63
Autogenic training, 168, 172, 210
Autoimmune reaction, 57, 62
Autonomic nervous system (ANS),
    44, 63, 67, 84, 126–127, 213
  feedback, 127
  parasympathetic, 45
  sympathetic, 45
  voluntary control of, 127
Awareness, 28, 118, 128, 170

Backache, 53, 88, 167
  profile of, 53
Bahnson, C. B., 76–77, 89
Barker, Wayne, 74

Behavior, 118, 200–201
Benson, Herbert, 172–173
Bernard, Claude, 21
Berne, Eric, 180
Beta brain waves, 165, 167
Biofeedback, 165–168
  definition, 165
  principles, 166
  use in disease, 167
Blood pressure, 17, 37–42
  See also Hypertension
Body, 31
Body therapies, 151
Boothe, G., 78–79
Boredom, 31
Bradykinin, 54
Brain, 30, 45, 56
Breast, 78, 124
Breathing, costal, 163
  diaphragmatic, 163
  techniques in, 152, 163–164
Bronchitis, 99
Bruner, Jerome, 217
Bulk, 98
Bursitis, 57

Cancer, 62, 74–79, 210
  breast, 78
  cervix, 78
  environmental causes, 75
  lack of closeness, 76
  latent cells, 77
  liver, 75
  mourning and, 77
  profile, 75–77
  prostate, 78
  resistance, 77
  self esteem, 89
  stomach, 78
Canker sores, 63
Carbohydrates, 98
Cardiac arrest, 47
Cardiorespiratory training, rules of,
    146
Catalysts, 82
Catatoxic hormones, 55

Cervix, cancer of, 78
Challenge, 26
Charlie horse, 53, 155
Cholesterol, 33–34, 42–44
  control of, 43
  dietary, 34
  and heredity, 35
Cirrhosis, 101
Clean-plate syndrome, 97
Clotting of blood, 44, 78
Coenzymes, 82
Cold sores, 60, 63
Colon, 63, 66–68
Complement, 57
Concentration, 169
Conditioning, 28, 96, 118
Conflict, 31, 201
Conformity, 68
Conscientiousness, 68
Consciousness, 128
Constipation, 67, 88
Copper, 82
Coronary artery disease (CAD),
  33–37, 44
Cortisone, 56, 124–125
Cough, chronic, 100
Creativity, 149, 172, 216
Crutches, 139
Crying, 88, 152
Cultural pressures and perception,
  28
Cure, 139

Data perception, 107–113
  emotions, 107
  external, 107
  internal, 107
  memory, 108
Day, G., 61
Deaths from heart disease, 45
Deckert, Gordon, 152
Deikman, A., 170
Deja vu, 108
Delta brain waves, 165
Demands, 21, 29, 191, 194
  for adaptation, 24, 26

canceling, 193
Depression, 88–89, 91, 137
  excess tension, 89
  and fatigue, 83
  formula for, 182
  and influenza, 61
  manifestations, 88
  and tuberculosis, 61
Dermatological diseases, 71–74
Dermatomyositis, 57
Desoxyribonucleic acid (DNA), 75,
  95, 108
Diabetes, 34–36, 42, 70, 139
  acidosis, 70
  coma, 70
Diaphragm, 163
Diarrhea, 66–67, 185
Diencephalon, 123
Diet, 98
Discounting, 177
Disease, 20–21, 35, 136
Disidentify, 131, 197
Distress, 14, 31–32, 136
Diverticulosis, 68, 98
Divorce, 142
Dreaming, 173
Dreyfus, F., 44
Drugs, 137–140
Dubos, René, 61
Dunbar, Flanders, 41
Duncan, C. H., 48
Duodenal ulcer (see Ulcer)
Duszynski, K. R., 76

Eczema, 59, 72
Edema, 69
Ego states, 83
Einstein, Albert, 216
Electroencephalograph, 165
Electrolyte regulation, 125
Electromyograph, 167
Emotions, 21, 31, 38, 123, 131,
  150–153
  anger, 21
  and cancer, 75
  definition, 85–86

fear, 21
  hormones, 125
  and infection, 60
  list, 123
  loss, sense of, 21
  and mind, 123
  muscular activity, 51
  and pain, 81
  and resistance, 62
  sadness, 21
  suppression of, 38
Empathy, accurate, 195
Encephalography, 165
Endocrine system, 40–41, 70–71,
    124–126
Energy, 30, 82
  tedious activities, 83
Engel, B. T., 167
Ennui, 31
Environment, 141–142
  versus heredity, 39–40
Enzymes, 82
Epilepsy, 74, 139
Epinephrine, 124
Estrogen, 78, 124
Excusing, 21
Exercise, physical, 102, 143–148
Exercises, relaxation, 156–168
  visualization, 213–216
Exhaustion, 82
  sleeplessness, 84
Exocrine glands, 126
Extrasystoles, 47

Fatigue, 82–84, 167
Fats, polyunsaturated, 98
Fear, 21–22, 31, 70, 83, 86–87, 152
Feedback, 115, 125, 132–133, 190,
    196
Fever blisters, 60
Fibrinogen, plasma, 44
Fibrositis, 54, 58
Fight or flight, 19, 37, 125, 172
Fitness test, 145
Fluid retention, 69, 88
Flynn, J. T., 39

Forgetting, 21
Forgiveness, 192
Friedman, Meyer, 35, 42–43
Frontal lobe, 121
Frustration, 53, 60
Functional disturbances, 155
Functional model of man, 104, 132
  points of entry, 133

Galambos, Robert, 110
Gannon, L., 167
Garfield, Charles, 170, 172
Gastric reactions, 64
Gastrin, 65
Gastrocolic reflex, 66
Gastrointestinal disturbances, 63–68
Genetic makeup and perception, 28
Genitourinary disturbances, 69–70
Glandular disturbances, 32
Glaucoma, 167
Globus syndrome, 63
Glucagon, 43, 124
Glucocorticoids, 55
Glucose, 70
Goals, 28, 114–119, 129, 200–205
  positive, 202
  unconscious, 129
Goodell, Helen, 50, 58
Grace, W. J., 40, 54, 66
Graham, D. T., 40, 54, 66, 71–72,
    81
Green, Alyce, 213
Green, Elmer, 47, 127, 166, 213
Growth, 31, 32
Growth hormone, 43, 62
Guilt, 53, 60, 83, 89–90
  eating, 97

Habits, self destructive, 83, 94–102
Habituation, 117
  to drugs, 139
Hallucinate, 26
Hallucinogens, 101
"Harold", 97
Harris, Thomas, 104
Hartman, E., 173

Hatred, 87–88
  poisonous nature, 87
Haugen, G. B., 167
Hay fever, 58–59
Headache, 13, 31, 196
  biofeedback and, 167
  cluster, 49
  depression and, 88
  migraine, 48–50
  muscle contraction (tension), 52
Health Hazard Appraisal Study, 42
Heart, 38
  attack, 33, 41, 74, 99
  rate, 45
  rhythm disturbances, 44–48
    and activity, 48
    and biofeedback, 167
    and death, 45
    functional, 46, 48
Heat prostration, 19
Helplessness, 75, 89
Hemolytic anemia, 57
Heredity, 118
  in migraine, 50
  versus environment, 39–40
Hernandez-Peon, R., 109
Herpes simplex, 60
High blood pressure, 25, 37–42
  and exercise, 147
  See also Hypertension
Higher self, 131
Hilton, Conrad, 209
Hives, 71
  profile of, 72
Hobbies, 150
Holiness, 217
Holistic, 217
Holmes, Thomas H., 22–25, 53, 58
Homeostasis, 32
Hormones, 40–41, 69, 124–125
  antidiuretic, 69
  catatoxic, 55
  syntoxic, 56
Hostility, 36–37, 70, 87, 189
  gastric reactions, 64
  migraine, 50

Human growth hormone, 124–125
Humiliation, 53
Humor, 154
Hunger, 26, 95
Hydrocortisone, 62
Hypertension, 35–42, 167
  exercise pattern, 38
  high resistance pattern, 38
Hyperthyroidism, 70
Hyperventilation, 59, 167
Hypothalamus, 38, 45–46, 63, 65,
    78, 84, 123–137, 168, 172
  and antibodies, 62, 73
Hypothermia, 19
Hypothyroidism, 35

I-messages, 178
Identification, 131
Illness, 24
Immune reaction, 55
Immunity, 89, 124
  cellular, 62, 77
  chemical, 62
Immunological disturbances, 61–63
Inadequacy, 89
Indecision, 68
Indians, 34, 61, 78
Infections, 20, 62, 137
Infectious mononucleosis, 61, 89
Inflammatory response, 49, 54–58
Influenza, 61
Input, 32, 132
Insomnia, 88, 154, 167
Instincts, 19, 95
Insulin, 124
Internal speech, 120, 206
Intestines, 63
Iron, 82
Irritable bowel syndrome, 67–68,
    98
Islet cells, 124
Itch, 17

Jacobsen, Lenore, 118
Jenkins activity survey, 35–36
Jenner, Edward, 20

Journal keeping, 153
Jung, Carl, 109, 128

Kallikrein system, 49, 54–55, 57
Kennedy, M. A. C., 39
Kidd, J. G., 77
Kidneys, 46
Kinin, 57
Kissen, David, 76
Klopfer, B., 77
Koans, 171
Koch, Robert, 20

Lactic acid, 52–53, 84, 125
Latter Day Saints, 99
Learning, 31, 196, 207
Leningrad, 40
LeShan, L. L., 77
Lethargy, 82–84
Lewontin, R., 50
Limbus, 112, 120, 123
Lipoproteins, 42–43
Loomis, Evarts, 102, 145
Loss, sense of, 21–22, 152
Lotus position, 173
Love, 189
    definition, 190
Lowell, Amy, 217
Lowen, Alexander, 151
Lupus erythematosis, 57, 90
Luria, Alexander, 113, 120, 133
Luthe, Wolfgang, 166
Lysosomes, 57

McClure, C. M., 47
MacDougald, Dan, 205
Magnesium, 82
Maltz, Maxwell, 207–209
Manganese, 82
Manic depressive disease, 91
Marasmus, 175
Maslow, Abraham, 128
Mast cells, 57
Master gland, 124
Medication
    as crutches, 139

problems of, 137–138
use of, 137–140
Meditation, 169–174
    concentration, 169
    definition, 169
    habituation, 173
    physiologic changes in, 172
    stages, 170
    starting, 173
    themes for, 171
    transcendental, 169
    types, 171
Memory, decreased, 93
Menstrual cycle, 71, 125
Metabolism, 125
Methodist Hospital Study, 99
Microbe, 21
Migraine, 48–50
    profile of, 49
Miller, George, 111
Mind, 31
    sets, 190
Mineral activators, 82
Mineralocorticoids, 55
Minerals, trace, 82
Minimizing, 21
Minnesota Multiphasic Personality
        Inventory (MMPI), 57
Missildine, Hugh, 87
Moniliasis, 20
Mononucleosis, 89
Morality, 68
Morehouse, Lawrence, 144
Mormons, 99
Multiple sclerosis, 74
Muscle
    atrophy, 144
    contraction
        and backache, 31
        board-like, 53
        and headache, 31
        rotation of, 51
    middle pharyngeal constrictor,
        64
    smooth, 127
    voluntary, 123

Muscular disturbances, 32, 50–54
Myasthenia gravis, 57, 74
Myocardial infarction, 33
    See also Heart attacks
Myositis, 54, 58

Narcolepsy, 74
Narcotics, 101
Nausea, 66, 88
Neatness, 68
Needs, 28
    frustration of, 22
Nerve
    cardiac, 44
    oligo-cochlear bundle, 110
Nervous, 18, 87
    system, 30
        inhibitory, 110–111
Neurodermatitis, 13, 72–73
Neurokinin, 49, 54–55
Neurological diseases, 74
Neuroses, 91
Numbers game, 37

Obesity, 97
Observer, 130
Obsessive-compulsive tendency, 68, 92
Occipital lobe, 121
Olson, Ken, 154
Oracle message, 178
Organization, point of, 130
Orienting reflex, 113
Osler, William, 61
Output system, 122–127, 132
Ovaries, 124
Overcoercion, 21
Overindulgence, 21
Overintellectualization, 68
Oversubmissiveness, 88
Ovulation, 125
Oxygen, 44

Pahnke, W. N., 171
Pain, 52, 69, 79–81, 213
    accidents, 79

drugs, 137
    secondary gain, 80
    spasm cycle, 53
    threshhold, 80–81
Pancreas, 124
Panic, 22, 86–87, 152
Parasympathetic nervous system, 45
Parietal lobe, 121
Passivity, 75
Pasteur, Louis, 20–21
Paulson, J. Sig, 145
Pelletier, Ken, 170, 172
Penfield, Wilder, 93, 108–109
Pepsin, 65
Perfectionism, 29–30, 92
Perls, Fritz, 90
Personality, 128
Phobias, 167
Physical exercise, 102, 143–148
    advantages, 143
    and cholesterol, 144
    well being, 146
Physical inactivity, 35
Pigment of skin, 124
Pineal, 124
Pituitary, 46, 124, 126
    anterior, 56
    ovarian axis, 71
    posterior, 69
Plasmin, 57
Plutchick, Robert, 86
Pneumonia, 20, 99
Poliomyelitis, 20
Pollen, 58
Pollutants, 19
Polyunsaturates, 98
Positive regard, 191
Pregnenolone 16-alpha-carbonitrile, 55
Primal therapy, 151
Profiles
    asthma - hay fever, 58
    backache, 53
    cancer, 75–76
    constipation, 67
    coronary artery disease, 36

herpes simplex, 60
hives, 72
hypertension, 40
irritable bowel syndrome, 66
migraine, 49
painful urination, 70
rheumatoid arthritis, 57
ulcer, 65
ulcerative colitis, 68
urinary retention, 70
Progesterone, 78, 124
Proinflammatory steroids, 55
Prolactin, 124
Prostate, 78
Protein, 82
  animal versus vegetable, 98
Psychodrama, 151
Psychoses, 91, 93, 173
Psychosynthesis, 131
Puberty, 124
Pulse, basic training, 145
Puritan heritage, 191

Rahe, Richard, 24, 25
Raynaud's phenomenon, 50, 167
Recognition, 92, 175–182
Recruiting, 123
Reflex
  gastrocolic, 66
  orienting, 113
Regard
  negative, 190
  positive, 191
  unconditional positive, 190
Reich, Wilhelm, 77, 151
Reinforcement, 133
Rejection, 21
Relaxation, 84, 155–169
  definition, 155
  education in, 159
  habit, 156
  physiological effects, 166–167
  response, 172
Repetition, 205
Repressing, 21

Resentment, 49, 53, 64, 70, 87–88,
  90, 151
Resistance, 21, 62
  of bacteria, 139
  lack of, 138
Respiratory disorders, 58–60
Responses
  goal oriented, 116
  unconscious, 94
Responsibility, 194
Restlessness, 88, 100
Reticular system, 112
Rheumatic fever, 57
Rheumatoid arthritis, 54, 56, 63,
  137
  profile, 57
Rheumatoid factor, 56–57, 63
Rhythm disturbances of heart,
  44–48
Richards, W. A., 171
Riffenburgh, Robert, 105
Rosenman, Ray H., 35, 42–43
Rosenthal, Robert, 118
Runners, long distance, 44
Rushmer, Robert, 25

Sadness, 21, 83, 152
Saliva, 63
Salk, Jonas, 24
Samuels, Mike and Nancy, 208, 215
Sargent, J. D., 167
Schizophrenia, 91
Schultz, J. H., 166, 210
Schwartz, Jack, 213
Scleroderma, 57
Sebum, 73
Sedatives, 101
Self, 128–131
  actualizing, 128
  defined, 128
  higher, 131
Self awareness, 199
Self effacement, 75
Self esteem, 37, 61, 89, 190
Self image, 207
Self worth, 89

Selye, Hans, 22, 26, 31, 55–56
Servo-mechanism, 207
Seventh Day Adventists, 99
Sex drive, 125
Shame, 60
Sharing, in anxiety, 151
Shealy, Norman, 167
Side effects of drugs, 138
Simonton, Carl, 79, 210
Sinus difficulty, 99
Smallpox, 20
Smoking, 35, 42, 99–100
Social disorganization and illness, 25
Somatotropin, 125
Sommers, S. C., 77
Speech
  in anxiety, 152
  internal, 120, 206
Steiner, Claude, 101
Sternbach, R. A., 167
Stevenson, I., 48
Stimulation, 26
Stimuli, 27, 107
Stomach, 78
Stress, 13, 17–28, 30, 32, 35, 43, 47, 60, 71, 74, 142, 167
  asthma, 59
  and cancer, 75
  categories, 27
  definition, 18
  and eczema, 72
  immunology, 62
  inflammatory response, 56
  interview, 58
  meditation, 173
  and pain, 167
  Raynaud's phenomenon, 50
  salivation, 63
  tuberculosis, 60
Stressor, 26
Striated muscles, 123
Stokes, 41–44, 74, 99
Strokes of recognition, 175–182
  definition, 176
  negative, 176

  positive, 176
  rules, 176–180
Substituting, 21
Sugars, 35, 98
  blood, 95
Suicide, 88
Superconscious, 208
Surgeon General's 1964 Cancer Report, 78, 99
Swami Rama, 127
Sympathetic nervous system, 45
Synergism, 20
Synovitis, 54
Syntoxic hormones, 56

Tchaikovsky, Petr Ilich, 216
Teeth grinding, 54
Temporal lobe, 121
Tendonitis, 58
Tension, 13–14, 26, 28–32, 74, 101, 112, 142, 149, 201
  acne, 73
  amenorrhea, 71
  cancer, 75
  depression, 89
  edema, 69
  energy of, 31
  excess, 31, 83–84, 93, 96, 150, 154
  headache, 52
  manageable limits, 28, 31, 91, 111
  migraine, 50
  and pain, 80
  positive value, 202
Testicles, 124
Testosterone, 124–125
Thalamus, 112
Theta brain waves, 165
Thomas, Carolyn, 76
Three neuron arc, 51
Thrush, 20
Thymico-lymphatic system, 55–56, 61
Thymus, 55, 61, 124

Thyroid, 43, 46, 124
  hyperfunction, 70
  stimulating hormone, 126
Thyroxin, 43, 124–126
Tobacco, 99
"Tom," 64–66
Tranquilizers, 137
Transactional analysis, 83, 88
Transcendental meditation, 169
Transmitter chemicals, 122
Triglycerides, 98
Truth, 196
Tuberculosis, 60–61
Twins and hypertension, 39
Type A, 35–37
Type B, 35–37
Typhus, 20

Ulcer, 13, 40, 65–66, 99, 141
  duodenal, 65
  gastric, 56
  peptic, 65
  profile, 65
Ulceration, bladder, 70
Ulcerative colitis, 68
Unconditional positive regard, 190
Unconscious, 208
  higher, 208
Urinary retention, 70
Urination, 69

Vargiu, James, 30
Vasomotor rhinitis, 58
Ventricles, 46

Viral disease, 60
Visualizing, 203, 211
  exercises, 213
  positive, 208
  receptive, 215
Vitamins, 82
  A, 99
  B and C, 99
  D, 20, 99
Voluntary muscles, 123
Volunteer, 150

Wallace, R. K., 172–173
Wapnick, K., 170
Water regulation, 125
Weiss, T., 167
Wholeness, 217
Will, 128–131, 201
  function of, 130
  stages, 200
  versus habitual behavior, 129
Wolf, G. A., 60
Wolf, Stewart G., 39, 58, 72
Wolff, Harold G., 25–26, 49–50, 53,
    58, 60, 64–65, 87, 129, 189
Work, as exercise, 148
Worthington, R. E., 77
Writing, 153–154
  in insomnia, 154

You-message, 178

Zinc, 82